White-Collar
BUSINESS CRIME

White-Collar
BUSINESS CRIME

HEIDI LAUTJÄRVI

EDITA • HELSINKI

Cover: Anu Korpijärvi
Layout: M-L Koskenranta
Cover image: Billion Photos / Shutterstock.com.

Publisher: Edita Publishing Ltd
www.edita.fi

ISBN 978-951-37-8940-4

Give us feedback on the book: toimitus.laki@edita.fi

Printed by: Books on Demand

"There have been tyrants ... and for a time they can seem invincible, but in the end they always fall. Think of it. Always.[1]"

FOREWORD

In this book, you will find the real-life accounts of people who, for one reason or another, found themselves guilty of committing white-collar crimes. Some thought they were doing nothing wrong, but were still convicted, while others intentionally broke the law, but thought they would get away with it. Many buried their secrets deep and successfully avoided detection for a considerable number of years; however, in the end, they were exposed and held to account.

This book is about white-collar crime and the numerous grey areas companies and their employees find themselves in when they stray from the legal and ethical path. Here you will read about power, money and prestige, about crime, immorality, unethical behaviour, old boys' networks and company secrets – all the things that push successful and wealthy people over the line.

For companies and those who act on their behalf, the business world is a minefield, full of traps that are all too easy to fall into. These dangers are thoroughly explored, and the book discusses where and how such risks emerge and where crimes may occur. For those who commit white-collar crimes, they very often see the world in which they operate in shades of grey. This is a problem when it comes to determining which behaviour is legal and ethical and which isn't. This is also true for those who interpret the law. The courts are required to intervene to the best of their ability and monitor the ever-changing legal landscape to ensure their decisions strike the correct balance between a successful economy but also properly regulated corporate activity that is both legal and ethical.

White-collar criminals are found engaging in an extremely wide range of activities, from stock frauds and bribery to workplace health and safety violations. This book digs deep into a grubby world of greed-fuelled immorality, tax evasion, counterfeiting, bribery, abuses of power and so much more. Many of the most sensational cases have taken place in the United States, and these are extensively documented here.

1 Quote by Mahatma Gandhi.

In each section of the book, there are numerous case examples of how people have chosen to go the wrong way. The most interesting point is that many of them say not so much about why. Therefore, I will explain the dark side of the human mind theoretically —the forces that drive ordinary people to commit crimes also detailing the white-collar workers' responsibility and role in organizations—is looked at in detail. Starting with the definitions of business crime and white-collar crime, the book goes on to give multiple examples of improper conduct and criminal activity, especially focusing on bribery.

The temptation experienced by some businesspeople to enrich themselves or perhaps improve business conditions for the company they work for by taking advantage of their position is often enormous – perhaps irresistible – and can, unfortunately, lead too many to break both the law and their ethical responsibilities. I wrote this book so people would learn from the mistakes of others, and avoid making their own. I am fascinated by and interested in the psychological issues related to why white-collar crimes take place repeatedly, such as in banks, and why mere opportunity is enough to make a thief. The underlying narrative of double standards in international law as well as the amount of different moral dimensions cannot be ignored either. Without clear legal frameworks, professional ethics and the moral guidance of a healthy corporate culture, many organisations and the people who work for them can soon find themselves labelled as white-collar criminals.

ACKNOWLEDGEMENTS

I have been very lucky and remain thankful to have had help from Juha Koponen. He and his office have helped me considerably in finishing this book. I would especially like to thank Borenius Attorneys at Law Ltd New York and the Helsinki offices. Sincere thanks to Monika Dziewa and Kenneth Kraszewski for the section dealing with competition law, and also the tax team for their comments on that particular area of law.

In addition, I would like to thank professors Matti S. Kurkela and Matti Rudanko for their continued support. First, for the Finnish business crime book (*Business Crime – Minefield of Leaders,* Edita Publishing Ltd, 2018), and now for this English international version. I have had many conversations and meetings with both professors, and my interest in white-collar crime has grown over time. In fact, it grew so much that found myself really enjoying the white-collar business crime stories I was reading. My discussions years ago with professors Kurkela and Rudanko helped me realise there was a need for a book on case-specific white-collar business crime. Professor Kurkela pointed out the international need regarding business crime, much of which I had not considered before our discussions. Therefore, I will always remain grateful to him.

I would also like to express my gratitude to all the CEOs, managers, lawyers and directors worldwide who have commented on this book. I have been so lucky to be around these amazing, motivating and inspirational leaders. I have been very fortunate to have also worked with several extraordinary international colleagues and people worldwide. Their encouraging example of how to do things right inspired me to write this book. Since many of you did not wish to be mentioned by name, I only name those who gave their permission—but the rest of you know who you are. Kaisa Mäkelä, CEO, my sincere thanks for commenting on the section on psychology. Your energy and talent helped me understand more deeply the roots of the human mind. Rami Korhonen, CEO, thank you for commenting on the book generally. Your talent for spotting inconsistencies gave me more understanding. Jerry Härkönen, IP lawyer, shared ideas which were inspirational and absolutely needed to give clarity to the section on IPR. Warm thanks go to Linda Piirto, Commercial Counsellor at the Finnish Ministry Foreign Affairs, for commenting on the sections on human rights and CSR. Your comments and modifications were exactly what this book needed. Thanks also go to the qualified language professionals and friends who proofread this book and without whom it would not have been completed.

I also want to express my sincere gratitude to US lawyer Roxanna Chacon for your numerous insightful comments on every chapter in this book. You helped me put my thoughts together.

I would like to offer my sincere thanks to Doctor of Technology Heikki Piirainen for commenting on the text—your contribution was just perfect. You went into details and uncovered issues that needed further reading and more consideration. You really pushed me to the limits of my endurance.

I am extremely grateful to Delingua Language Services and Daniel Merry, English Language Specialist, whose amazing comments were absolutely needed in order to get the book ready. You helped me consider issues more deeply and push this book forward. Your thoughtful advice is much appreciated, and you taught me a lot. I would like to thank the whole team at Edita Publishing Ltd and Nordic Morning Group for helping me write the international version of my book. Your work has been just amazing, and I cannot thank you enough.

Finally, my thanks go to my employer and to my family. I changed jobs in 2019, just when this book project started, and my new employer has supported me in every way possible, for which I could not be more grateful. I do not think I could have found a better workplace, one that has given me the time I needed to write this book. A supportive workplace, a supportive family and an amazing publisher are crucial for writing a book like this.[2]

2 The originality of this book has been verified with Plagiarisma, Plagiarism Checker and Scribbr.

ABBREVIATIONS

AFA	Agence Française Anticorruption
AI	Artificial Intelligence
ASEAN	Association of Southeast Asian Nations
AUD	Australian Dollar
BEPS	Base Erosion and Profit Shifting
Billion	Thousand million, 1,000,000,000. European term: milliard. American term: billion. American term is used in this book.
CDO	Collateralized Debt Obligation (investment product)
CEO	Chief Executive Officer
CFO	Chief Financial Officer
CFR	Council on Foreign Relations
CFTC	US Commodity Futures Trading Commission (US)
CG	Corporate Governance
CIA	Central Intelligence Agency
CJIP	La convention judiciaire d'intérêt public
CLO	Chief Legal Officer
CMA	Competition and Markets Authority
CMS	Centers for Medicare & Medicaid Services
CNBC	Consumer News and Business Channel
CNN	Cable News Network
Co.	Company
CoCom	Coordinating Committee for Multilateral Export Controls
CPS	Crown Prosecution Service
CSR	Corporate Social Responsibility
CTC	Counter-Terrorism Committee
DD	Due Diligence
DECA	Development of Espionage and Counterintelligence Awareness
DGSE	Direction Générale de la Sécurité Extérieure (FR)
DOJ	Department of Justice (US)
DOS	Department of State (US)

DPA	Deferred Prosecution Agreement
DST	Direction de la Surveillance du territoire (FR)
EC	European Commission
ECJ	European Court of Justice
EEC	European Economic Community
EFSA	European Union Food Safety Authority
EOIR	Exchange of Tax Information on Request
ESG	Environmental, Social and Corporate Governance
EU	European Union
FATF	Financial Action Task Force (on Money Laundering)
FBI	Federal Bureau of Investigation
FCA	Financial Conduct Authority
FCPA	Foreign Corrupt Practices Act (US)
FIFA	Fédération Internationale de Football Association
FSA	Financial Services Agency
FTA	Forum on Tax Administration
FTC	Federal Trade Commission
G7	Group of Seven (Canada, France, Germany, Italy, Japan, the United Kingdom and the United States)
GDPR	General Data Protection Regulation 2016/679
GRI	Global Reporting Initiative
IAAF	International Association of Athletics Federations
IAS	International Accounting Standards
ICC	International Chamber of Commerce
ICN	International Competition Network
ICT	Information and Communications Technology
IFRS	International Financial Reporting Standards
IMF	International Monetary Fund
ILO	International Labour Organization
IoT	Internet of Things
IPO	Initial Public Offering
IPR	Intellectual Property Rights
ISAR	International Standards of Accounting and Reporting

ISO	International Organization for Standardization
LLC	Limited Liability Company
M	Million
MFI	Micro Finance Institution
NASDAQ	National Association of Securities Dealers Automated Quotations
NCP	National Contact Point
NGO	Non-Governmental Organization
NSA	National Security Agency
OCCRP	Organized Crime and Corruption Reporting Project
OECD	Organisation for Economic Co-operation and Development
OFAC	Office of Foreign Assets Control
OFT	Office of Fair Trading
OPEC	Organization of the Petroleum Exporting Countries
PCAOB	Public Company Accounting Oversight Board
PCB	Polychlorinated Biphenyls
PNF	Parquet National Financier (France)
POIG	Palm Oil Innovation Group
PRI	Principles for Responsible Investment
RICO	Racketeer Influenced and Corrupt Organizations
SAS	Société par actions simplifiée
SEC	US Securities and Exchange Commission
SFO	Serious Fraud Office
SOX	Sarbanes-Oxley Act
S.p.A	Società per Azioni
SWIFT	Society for Worldwide Interbank Financial Telecommunication
TBML	Trade Based Money Laundering
TI	Transparency International
Trillion	1,000,000,000,000
TRIPS	Agreement on Trade-Related Aspects of Intellectual Property Rights
U.C.C.	Uniform Commercial Code
UK	United Kingdom
UN	United Nations
UNCAC	United Nations Convention against Corruption

UNGPML	UN Global Programme against Money Laundering
UNICEF	United Nations Children's Fund
US	United States of America
USC	United States Code
WHO	World Health Organization
WTO	World Trade Organization

CONTENTS

PART I

A Complex World of Business Crime

"My father used to always say to me that, you know, if a guy goes out to steal a loaf of bread to feed his family, they'll give him 10 years, but a guy can do white-collar crime and steal the money of thousands and he'll get probation and a slap on the wrist."[1]

When it comes to understanding the extent of white-collar crime in today's business world, consider the following: of the top 50 executives in the United States—that is, those who are the leaders, the best of the best—many of them have been convicted and either sent to prison and/or fined for committing white-collar crimes. How is this possible? How can we comprehend that these role models in the business world are crooks? These hard-working and intelligent business leaders have made the near-incomprehensible choice to risk it all. And yet, as sad as it seems, many are prepared to cross the line. For some researchers who have attempted to answer this question, the phenomenon is explained by executives momentarily losing sight of their moral and legal responsibilities. However, the impact of an intuition or gut feeling in a given

1 James George Janos also known as Jesse Ventura, former wrestler, American politician and US Navy SEAL veteran.

moment does not by itself explain the crimes that take place in executive suites, that is, the path to perpetrating business crimes is usually a long one and not a spontaneous act.[2] We are entering a complex world!

In order to understand what pushes law-abiding businesspeople over the edge, we need to take into account a wide variety of factors, including economic, environmental, legal, genetic, neurological and psychological, and we will do so with numerous examples from around the business world. There are some discussion and examples of genetic, neurological and psychological factors but the hard core is in economic, environmental and legal factors. By focusing on these factors, we see that these rogue executives don't see the consequences of their actions in the same way as others. For example, Soltes, who interviewed a number of top executives in jail, found that they had a very different mindset from the average employee: they were extremely ambitious, narcissistic, with low levels of self-control and a lack of empathy, all of which combine and lead to an absence of guilt or remorse. One executive he spoke to even stated that while the wrongdoing their case was illegal it was not unethical. This is a key observation: these corporate crooks draw a clear distinction between what is legal and what is ethical. For some, this distinction has even cost them their life: Eli Black, Chairman of United Brands, jumped from the 44th floor of a building in New York after it was revealed that in 1974, he had paid $1.25 million to the president of Honduras to secure a reduction in banana export tax. The shame he felt was too great a burden to carry.[3] In such cases, crime may pay in the short term, but the cost to the perpetrator may ultimately be too great.

Business crime and white-collar crime

Before diving into the main subject of this book, white-collar business crime, we need to understand that business crime refers to negative behaviour committed by a company. The FBI uses the term corporate crime. In this book, white-collar business crime consists of 1) business crime and 2) white-collar crime. The image below illustrates how these are linked to each other.

2 Soltes, 2016, 24–33.
3 Soltes, 2016, 24–33.

Image 1. White-collar business crime consists of two elements: business crime and white-collar crime. A business crime is committed by a company, a white-collar crime refers to the crimes of individuals.

Before diving into white-collar business crimes to the micro economic level, let's look at some macroeconomic factors that explain the complexity of the world. And at some level macroeconomic factors also give more understanding how complexity gives more "chances" for white-collar business crimes.

Five key megatrends that shape global consumer behaviour

As we have seen so far in this chapter, the world, especially the environment in which companies do business, is rapidly changing, and new and different megatrends are emerging. This complex international environment has become a dangerous minefield for business leaders. On the one hand, companies rightly fear negative publicity and the losses this may involve. On the other hand, business leaders are also addicted to profit. As Mark Manson in *The 3 Paradoxes of Life* (2019), has pointed out, if you have enough money, the need for money doesn't go away, it in fact grows and this creates anxiety. Also, with the increased complexity of the business environment comes the opportunity for improper conduct and even criminal activity.[4] Opportunity makes a thief.

White-collar business crimes do not exist in a vacuum but play out in a complex world or economic, political, social, environmental, technological and moral factors that heavily impact on consumer behaviour, which in turn shapes

4 Manson, 2019.

and directs corporate activity. The five most important key megatrends that shape consumer behaviour globally are: 1) shifting economic power, 2) changes in population, 3) environmental shifts and pressures, 4) changes in technology and 5) changes in values.[5]

The first two megatrends, especially global economic growth and shifts in the global economy (advanced economy stagnation) suggest that the Chinese economy will be 1.8 times larger than the US economy by 2030. In addition, if we look at the fact that by 2030 already three quarters of the world's population is expected to be connected to the internet, this clearly predicts changes in consumer expectations and pressure on companies. On the other hand, it also provides more opportunities for improper conduct or even criminal activity. This also creates opportunities for companies and inspires new digital business models.[6]

Regarding the other three megatrends, the global population, lifestyles and purchasing decisions will be very different in the next twenty years due to urbanisation, migration and ageing. Also, it has been seen that a global pandemic such as COVID-19 can severely impact purchasing decisions. Rapid urbanisation and industrialisation have already led to huge pollution and waste problems. When the population increases, the consumption of energy, food and water also increases.[7]

Ethical consumers buy environmentally responsible products. They also target ethical investments, which means that they invest primarily in companies whose values are close to their own and secondly in those which make a profit. Changing consumer values means that consumers want speed and convenience when it comes to their purchases. They value the experience over material goods. This shift is already happening and, by 2030, it is expected that consumers in

5 Euromonitor, 2019. Some people even consider ESG information before making, for example, investment decisions. E(conomical), S(ocial), and G(overnance) are megatrends that are here to stay in decision-making processes. In 2019, the Independent Research in Responsible Investment (IRRI) Survey ranked MSCI ESG Research as the best ESG number provider. The research received 954 responses from 44 countries. It is worth keeping in mind, though, that ESG cannot be the only driver when evaluating companies, and in most cases it is likely that companies might not even reveal their ESG numbers. More information Albuquerque – Wallin, 2019.

6 In 2020, there were millions of people who were not part of the digital economy due to the lack of bank accounts. This, in turn, might mean that the Internet of Things (IoT) will be the next crucial evolutionary leap in economic competitiveness and will take machine-to-machine communications totally to the next level. Without IoT, the full usage of AI (artificial intelligence), for example, will never happen. IoT means that technology is spread globally so that everybody can enter into agreements and transfer value without intermediaries. It pays no attention to location or time. This, in turn, means that new generation services will no longer be dependent on, for example, Amazon, Google or Apple platforms. However, IoT needs a nation-wide strategy to succeed. Germany, for example, has already started to construct a national blockchain infrastructure. It goes without saying that all of this creates conditions for criminals as well. PWC, 2017. Nasdaq, 2019. Moné, 2019.

7 In 2022, we are talking about degrowth.

developed countries will spend $3.8 billion on services and only $5.3 million on durable goods.[8]

Importantly, in this context, companies also need to adapt and change the way their people work, i.e. a company's code of conduct becomes an essential tool in promoting proper corporate behaviour and combatting crime. Transparency in business activities is a commonly held value; however, when abused in practice it becomes a cloak for improper conduct and criminal activity. Transparency is such a key virtue that if it were properly observed, we would not be reading headlines such as the following:[9]

"European lenders take Libor scandal hit"
"Horse meat in Tesco burgers"
"Volkswagen in meltdown after faked diesel tests"
"High-flying Alibaba executive demoted over personal scandal"
"Japan trade minister Sugawara resigns over money scandal"

Ethical corporate behaviour

In *The 3 Paradoxes of Life* (2019), Mark Manson writes: "The anxiety of needing to make money does not go away once we are successful—it instead morphs into an anxiety of not losing the money." He states three issues you should concentrate on instead of money: 1) control, 2) choice and conformity that leads to growth, 3) discipline and acceptance. Although Manson is talking specifically about relationships, his analysis is a perfect metaphor for considering the directors in a company: healthy companies need a healthy relationship with fine tolerances.[10] This, in turn, leads us to ethical corporate behaviour—the principles that guide everyday business: norms, values, ethical and especially unethical practices. In other words, it is about how companies really take care of ethical principles, and how they handle moral dilemmas that arise in the corporate environment in which they operate. Ethics and ethical considerations are everywhere: inside companies, among individuals and in legal systems.[11]

8 The study horizon is between 2018–2030. Ethical and responsible investments are slightly different. Responsible investments are based more on ESG matters, while ethical investments underlie the values of the companies. Euromonitor, 2019.

9 Ahlberg – Romberg, 2019, 5.

10 Manson, 2019.

11 Moriarty, 2017. Ferrell, 2016. The use of the term "business ethics" increased dramatically during the 1980s and 1990s. Many major corporations have started to emphasise their commitment to non-economic values: ethics codes, social responsibility measures and charts. Ethics cannot be controlled governmentally, but details and areas of behaviour can be implicitly regulated. Formal ethics regimes were established because large corporations had only limited relationships and sensitivity to the communities in which they operated. Jones – Parker et al., 2005, 17.

1. Bad Apples Among the Good – Defining Business Crime

A company is a business entity with its own legal personality that is separate from the individuals managing its activities. In the worst cases, business crime can lead to the dissolution of a corporate entity, i.e. the dissolution of a company is the equivalent of the death penalty for a person. Under this procedure a company is forced to dissolve or cease to exist due to criminal business activities. Companies do exist as separate corporate entities, but it is the actions of its officers that are imputed to it.

Not all questionable behaviour is considered criminal, and not all jurisdictions regard the same actions in the same way. For example, insider trading, which is generally regarded as improper, could be considered as acceptable in some countries.[12]

Business crime is often referred to when speaking about white-collar crime, organised crime and state-corporate crime. White-collar professionals are those people who act on behalf of a company. Normally, the interests of white-collar professionals are the same as those of their employer. It is worth bearing in mind that there are also organisations which are established for the sole purpose of crime, such as a company that is set up specifically to launder criminal proceeds. In 2000, De Brie estimated that this type of business crime (gross criminal product) accounts for as much as 20% of world trade.[13] Today, two decades later, it is even more. Also, the relationship between a state and a company might make it possible for an individual or individuals to commit crimes.[14]

How then can this sort of behaviour be regulated? In the United States, it is regulated by civil and criminal law. Companies can commit the same offences as persons. It becomes criminal when the behaviour is proscribed in law as a crime. Simpson argues that we should think more in terms of which behaviour causes mostly loss and damage.[15] There is always a link between states and companies or the business sector. It means that the business sector supplies stability and that the state regulates individuals and companies.[16] Corporate profitability needs well-managed corporate operations.[17]

12 Heal – Serafeim, 2019. Please see Hall, 2019.

13 de Brie, 2000.

14 *Wikipedia*, 2020: Casare Beccaria. Mr. Beccaria (1738–1794) is thought to have pioneered the study of crime and criminology and is therefore called the father of the classical school of criminology.

15 Simpson, 2002.

16 See Snider, 1993. Snider – Pearce, 1995. Pearce – Tombs, 1992. Schulte – Bockholt, 2001. Reed – Yeager, 1996, 357–382. Before Sutherland developed the theory of white-collar crime in 1949, business crime was not recognised officially at all. He was the first person to study this type of crime inside organisations. Schlegel – Weisburd, 1992.

17 Kicenski, 2002.

> The decision in *US v. Southern Pacific Railroad* in 1886 is probably the most cited in courts worldwide and therefore crucial. In the decision, a **corporation was defined as a legal person.**[18] The constitution affords protection to all "legal persons" within its jurisdictions, i.e. to natural as well as artificial legal entities. The 14th amendment in the Constitution of the United States writes that "no State shall make or enforce any law which shall abridge the privileges or immunities of citizens of the United States; nor shall any State deprive any person of life, liberty, or property, without due process of law; nor deny to any person within its jurisdiction the equal protection of the laws". In English law, a similar decision in found in *Salomon v. A Salomon & Co Ltd*[19]. In Australia, China and New Zealand, the definition of a legal person rests on *Salomon v. A Salomon*. The impact of decisions such as these is that, among other things, a company can own assets and have debts independent of its employees. It has its own legal liability.[20]

Not all legal systems recognise corporate criminal liability. It is currently recognised in the United States, Spain and France. Corporate criminal liability exists also in Austria, Denmark, Italy and the Netherlands. In Poland, the discussion on corporate criminal liability is ongoing. German law does not recognise it, but German corporations are subject to fines for administrative violations called *Ordnungswidrigkeiten*.[21]

The discussion concerning business crime is a particularly sensitive political question in some parts of the world, such as the UK.[22] "The laws in the different jurisdictions provide various scales for the amount of the fine, varying from the type of crime committed, daily rates, size of business, percentage of sales (up to 10%) and a reduction due to the imposition of a compliance structure or the internal investigation efforts of the company. If the responsibility of the company is low due to compliance and cooperative investigation of the case, the prosecution may be concluded against certain charges or with a reduced fine or even without any charges or fine at all."[23] Typically, companies must have efficient compliance and legal controls in order to avoid liability.

---

18 *The United States Supreme Court, Santa Clara County v. Southern Pacific Railroad.*

19 *Salomon v. A Salomon & Co Ltd.*

20 Anderson, 2008. Radcliffe, 2009.

21 *Jones Day*, 2020.

22 This is because of the fatal accidents that happened on the rail network and at sea. The term used to refer more than anything to corporate manslaughter. Moreover, it is used to refer to some technological hazards "posed by business enterprises". See Wells, 2001.

23 Alliuris, 2019.

Business crime is a mix of social, behavioural and environmental issues.[24] This type of crime involves individuals, groups, companies and organisations within an organisational context. It has a lot to do with personality as well as processes and social and environmental factors at both the micro and macro levels. Corporate culture itself—that is, a company's set of shared attitudes, values, goals and practices—may even lead to deviant acts and a grey zone.[25] As Herb Kelleher, Chairman of the Board of Southwest Airlines, has put it: "Culture is what happens when no one is looking."[26]

An attempt to understand business crime has been set in motion by investigating cultures such as organised crime, cults, gangs and deviant corporations. In such investigations, deviance was present within a framework of toxic leadership, leveraging reputation through publicity to attract new members, misinformation and violence. This mix of psychological forces, combined with an employer's need to survive in business life, gives crime a heavy gravitational pull. What all these cultures have in common is that influencers use group dynamics, organisational culture, inter-organisational forces, pressures and constraints. Influencers also use personal, psychological or other internal forces exercising influence over an individual's behaviour.[27]

Investigators found that economic cycles result in strain[28]. This was seen as a precipitating factor in **organi-cultural deviance.**[29] Deviance stems from social pressure and economic forces, which might engage in business crime. Regardless of the background and position of an employee, most strive for monetary success.[30]

24 Later in Part II on white-collar business crime there is more information about Edwin Sutherland (1949), who referred to corporate crime as white-collar crime. In Sutherland's view "corporate crime is done by an individual as an isolated end unto itself". This means that an individual's basic needs play an important role. However, that is not all. Business crime is a mix of law, psychology, neuroscience and philosophy, as Soltes, 2016, 8, explains it. For more, see: Sutherland, 1949. Husted, 2008. Gendron – Husted, 2010.

25 Husted, 2008.

26 Milligan, 2016.

27 Gendron – Husted, 2011, II.

28 The term **economic cycle** means fluctuation of the economy between growth and recession. For example, GDP and interest rates can determine the current economic cycle stage.

29 Gendron – Husted, 2012. The term **organi-cultural deviance** is also referred to as **deviant corporate culture**. Both explain how the processes of individual and group socialization work. They also explain how deviant corporate cultures have a link to Abraham Maslow's (1954) hierarchy of needs. See: Gendron – Husted, 2011, I. Maslow, 1954.

30 During different cycles, companies need different kinds of leaders as well. First, when a company is established, there is a need for a visionary and entrepreneurial personality. These types of leaders are also needed in times of recession. This makes sense since visionary leaders can motivate, innovate and develop new products or services. When the first obstacles arise in economic downturns and the company reaches a certain level of maturity, companies usually want leaders with a more bureaucratic approach. These leaders set standards and operations for the company's success. At the peak of the business life cycle, the leader type changes again to a person who promises the same as previous leaders but with higher rates of return. However, therein lies the problem: these leaders who tend to display this pseudo-transformational feature are more prone to deviant practices to maintain the illusion of doing better and greater than the previous leaders. See more: Gendron – Husted, 2012. Merton, 1938, 132, 672–682. Cernkovich – Giordano – Rudolph, 2000.

The Federal Bureau of Investigation (FBI) has named and ranked business crime among its highest enforcement priorities. One reason for this is that not only does it lead to "significant financial losses for investors" but "has the potential to cause immeasurable damage to, for example, the US economy and investor confidence".[31]

31 The FBI coordinates these issues with the US Securities and Exchange Commission (SEC), Commodity Futures Trading Commission (CFTC), Financial Industry Regulatory Authority, Internal Revenue Service, Department of Labor, Federal Energy Regulatory Commission, the US Postal Inspection Service, and other regulatory and/or law enforcement agencies. See more in *FBI*, 2020: White Collar Crime. *Investopedia*, 2020: White Collar Crime.

PART II

White-Collar Crimes and Other Crimes

As we saw in Part I, white-collar business crime is a complex question that requires some understanding of the broader megatrends that influence the business environment as well as the dramatic consequences that can follow from the behaviour of rogue executives, either personally or for the companies they are employed by. The core question remains: why do people in positions of great responsibility commit business crimes? The short answer was stated precisely in a magazine published by Aalto University in Finland: the decision maker is temporarily incapable of seeing the ethical dimension of a decision at stake.[32] Let's take a much closer look at what this means. Most people who commit business crimes might think that their crimes are not harmful to anybody near them. In fact, harm to strangers is easier to accept than harm to people close to you.[33]

Before we look more into this issue, it is necessary to first distinguish white-collar crime from all the other varieties of crime that are committed within the corporate context. As we are here only concerned with white-collar crime, it is important to be clear about what it is and also what it is not. It means that we have gone from the short explanation of why people commit business crimes to providing a definition of the different types of crimes, designated according to the colour of collar.

The image below represents the different designations of workers and the associated crimes they might commit:

32 Palazzo, 2019.

33 Soltes, 2016, 7.

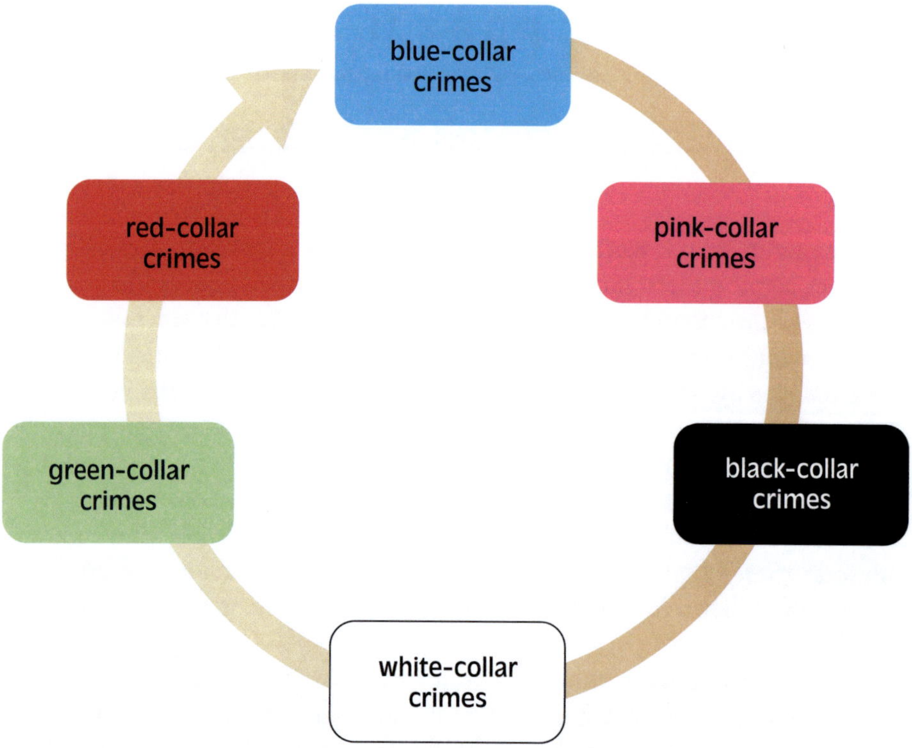

Image 2. The different designations of workers and the associated crimes they might commit. These all relate to individual crimes.

White-collar crime in almost every instance is non-violent. In most cases, it is committed in order to receive a financial or monetary gain or benefit. According to the FBI, "crimes are characterized by deceit, concealment, or violation of trust". The motivation for such crimes is normally to obtain or avoid losing money, property, or services, or to secure a personal or business advantage.[34]

Edwin Sutherland provided what is today regarded as the formal definition of white-collar crime: "a crime committed by a person of respectability and high social status in the course of their occupation."[35] In addition to Sutherland's definition, white-collar crime is also described by O'Grady and includes:

(i) misrepresentation in financial statements of corporations
(ii) manipulation in the stock market
(iii) commercial bribery

34 *Investopedia*, 2020: White Collar Crime.

35 *FBI*, 2020: White Collar Crime.

(iv) bribery of public officials, directly or indirectly
(v) misrepresentation in advertisements and salesmanship
(vi) embezzlement and misappropriation of funds
(vii) misapplication of funds in receiverships and bankruptcies".[36]

Supervising ethical behaviour is not easy for business organisations. Actually, it is one of the most pervasive and complex problems in any organisation.[37] This can be seen as a must-win battle. When leaders decide something, they must get the support of the whole personnel. The support of the personnel cannot risk the ethical stance. If the personnel start to lead the director's decision-making process at the risk of ethics, leaders lose clear direction and goals, transparency, rectitude, focus, simplicity and right timing.[38]

But what makes people do bad things and fall into ethical blindness?

"It is always the same story: top down created corporate cultures that are broken. Cultures that steer people to do wrong things. It has nothing to do with everybody involved being criminals – it is about leaders not thinking carefully about their style of leadership," says Professor Guido Palazzo of the University of Lausanne.[39]

It goes without saying that greedy personalities often possess the traits necessary to lead them into unethical decision-making processes. Still, even a person with the best values can become ethically blind under great pressure. People easily become blind within a powerful environment. Take, for example the case of Wells Fargo, where over 5,000 company salespersons were caught acting fraudulently because the environment in which they operated was led by fear. In this case, it was not bad people doing bad things—it was good people with good intentions deciding to act wrongly. People did not really understand the big picture themselves, as they thought they were only doing what managers wanted them to do. Huge scandals of this nature typically involve big companies simply because it is in such environments that no one really has time for ethics. Ethics are certainly mentioned, such as on the company website, but in practice the reality is quite different.[40]

Gendron and Husted found many aspects that are likely to increase white-collar crime. One of these is group dynamics, which is very similar to how gangs, cults and organised criminal organisations operate. The leaders of such organisations also use pressure with which they influence individual behaviour and cognition. Deviant organisations believe that through social dynamics they

36 O'Grady, 2011.
37 Stead – Worrell – Stead, 1990, 233–242.
38 Alahuhta, 2016, 22.
39 Palazzo, 2019.
40 Palazzo, 2019.

can lure in and capture individuals. When an individual starts to demonstrate a need to belong to the organisation, the process starts. When the individual becomes dependent on the organisation and through social pressure and some pressure from an influencer, the individual starts to see their actions in a completely different light and can begin to justify their actions.[41]

When deviance occurs, it involves aspects of manipulation and twisting the truth, while still maintaining the individual's basic needs for self-actualisation. This is often called **psychological violence**. This type of violence might merge with coercive power or monetary threats. What is essential is that organisations maintain a firm grip on these individuals. Moreover, the individuals become psychologically unwilling to leave.[42]

Harvard Business School identified five warning signals of when a company is edging dangerously close to a scandal: 1) total blindness towards occurrences around the leader; 2) incentives become toxic in nature (before this, fear seems to rise) and, moreover, a sense of urgency is always present which, in turn, lowers the threshold for critical questions; 3) the company's headquarters seem to be isolated from the company's other areas, groups or teams, and the headquarters lose their visibility to other areas, and it becomes easy for any leader with an authoritarian mindset to start leading the group badly; 4) decisions are made in isolation; and 5) teams start to compete against each other, and success becomes the norm which defines the individual's wellbeing. In addition, this type of team starts to use its own vocabulary, in-group jokes and euphemisms.[43]

In 2019, intensive debate in the US centred on the contention that white-collar crimes are treated more leniently in the US than anywhere

41 Gendron – Husted, 2011, I.

42 Gendron – Husted, 2011, II. One factor that explains white-collar crimes is defense mechanisms. Defense mechanism is "an unconscious or automatic mental activity a person engages in to balance subjectivity and reality. In psychoanalytic theory, they refer to a constellation of mental processes developed to protect the integrity of the ego system (mind). As such, defenses protect against threatening impulses and desires (internally generated) as well as against potential threats from the external environment." Gerson, 2020. Freud's defense mechanisms and John Bolwby's attachment theory explain the crimes at some level. A director could use a defensive mechanism that twists the conception of the world, and this might lead to a wrong assessment in critical thinking. For example, a white-collar worker could analyse a situation purely based on the facts, without any emotions involved. It means that unpleasant issues are put aside. This is Freud's basic defense mechanism. A white-collar worker could even blame others for something they did not do, in order to protect themself. This is called the unadaptive defense mechanism. The most serious of all are psychotic defense mechanisms, which means that the truth is distorted. One of these mechanisms is denial. In this case, the white-collar worker might deny the existence of some issues or a person. This might happen if they fear something. The other is distorting the truth: the white-collar worker might imagine issues that are not true while another might punish a subordinate because they were angry at the superior in the first place.

43 Taylor, 2017.

else in the world. The discussion escalated when Amy Klobuchar, Democratic Senator for Minnesota and presidential candidate, tweeted: "Crimes committed in an office building should be treated as seriously as crimes committed on a street corner." Democratic Congresswoman Alexandria Ocasio-Cortez tweeted that "justice isn't blind, it's bought".

What led to this exchange? US District Court Judge T. S. Ellis sentenced Paul Manafort to 47 months in prison for fraud. The judge's behaviour and charges against him of fraud were estimated to have cost millions of dollars, leading many to question why the sentence was so shockingly low.

In the US, bank fraud is punishable by up to 30 years in prison and a maximum fine of $1 million. Another example of leniency in a case of white-collar crime concerns the French banker and rogue trader Jerome Kerviel, who was found guilty of one of the biggest banking frauds ever. He lost $4.9 billion through unauthorised transactions. In 2010, he was sentenced to only three years in prison.

Martin Walsh tweeted on 8 March 2019 as follows: "Paul Manafort hides $55m in secret offshore accts to avoid paying $6m tax, defrauds 3 banks of $25m, lies, shows no remorse, sentence recommended 19-24, gets only 47 months. Chrystal Manson accidentally votes in the 2016 US election shows remorse, gets 5 yrs jail". This tweet illustrates the core problem in the US: people found guilty of other crimes are either sentenced to the maximum the law permits or at least harshly in comparison to white collar economic crimes. According to a study in 2017, "[judges] frequently sentence well below the fraud guideline".[44]

44 Bennett – Levinson – Hioki, 2017. Pierpoint, 2019.

2. Examples of White-Collar Business Crime

Many reported cases of corporate fraud involve **accounting schemes**. These schemes aim to deceive certain people, such as investors and auditors, by giving untrue information about a corporate entity's financial affairs. For example, this might occur by manipulating a company's financial information and share price to suggest the company is doing better financially than it actually is. In addition to the previous chapter, the following are some examples of more recent cases involving accounting scandals.

> In 2019, Swedish net operator Ericsson agreed to pay over $1 billion to settle accusations of corruption. According to US prosecutors, Ericsson had used corruption and questionable accounting to secure a better market position in China, Indonesia, Vietnam, Kuwait and Djibouti in the period 2000–2016. Ericsson admitted its internal control was not adequate and it had a lack of respect for ethical codes.[45]
>
> ***
>
> In 2015, the CEO of Japanese electronics conglomerate Toshiba Corporation resigned due to an accounting scandal. The scandal concerned $1.2 billion in overstated operating profits. The actions took place over the seven previous years under three different CEOs. Before the resignation of CEO Hsiao Tanaka, evidence showed that the company had inappropriate accounting practices and misconduct, weak corporate governance, poor internal controls and weak risk management.[46]
>
> ***
>
> In 2003, HealthSouth, one of the largest health care service providers in the US, became aware of certain accounting problems. Executives had falsified earnings reports years before SEC announced exaggerated revenues by $1.4 billion. CEO Richard Scrushy had instructed employees to inflate revenues and overstate the company's net income. This fraud came to light when CFO William Owens heard Scrushy discussing it and got it on tape. Owens had a dual role—he was also working with the FBI but Scrushy did not know this. Scrushy was convicted of bribery and later was able to arrange a political contribution of $500.000, which gave him a seat on a hospital's regulatory board.[47]
>
> ***

45 *Deutsche Welle*, 7 December 2019.

46 Addady, 2015. Schmidt, 2016. Bhattacharyya, 2015.

47 Freudenheim, 2004.

In 2002, telecommunications giant WorldCom followed Tyco International with an accounting scandal. The company had recorded operating expenses of $3.8 billion (e.g. papers and pencils) as investments for many years. This meant exaggerated profits although the company had already become unprofitable. When the company crashed, the greatest losers were employees and investors.[48]

***

The year 2002 was memorable in many ways, but also for Tyco International when its unapproved loans and fraudulent stock sales were exposed. Tyco's CEO Dennis Kozlowski was named by *BusinessWeek* as one of the Top 25 corporate managers in the world. "Along with CFO Mark Swartz and CLO Mark Belnick, Kozlowski received $170 million in low-to-no interest loans without shareholder approval. Kozlowski and Belnick arranged to sell 7.5 million shares of unauthorised Tyco stock for a reported $450 million. These funds were smuggled out of the company, usually disguised as executive bonuses or benefits. Kozlowski used the funds to pay for his lavish lifestyle, which included multiple properties, an infamous $6,000 shower curtain, and a $2 million birthday party for his wife." Needless to say, when the scandal came to light, the company's share price was zero. The executives received sentences of 25 years in jail.[49]

***

In 2001, the seventh largest company in the US, energy-trading company Enron, collapsed due to complicated accounting practices. The company had used shell companies, which were revealed later when

48 Beltran, 2002. MCI Inc., previously known as WorldCom or MCI WorldCom, was a telecommunications company, the second largest long-distance telephone company after AT&T. It had operations in about 65 countries. The company mismanaged its accounts for many years. What was fatal to the company was its rapid growth when it acquired other telecommunication companies. MCI Inc. ended in bankruptcy in 2002, but it preceded a large accounting scandal where CEO Bernard Ebbers was convicted along with several other executives. Ebbers made his fortune when the company's stock price rose. It all went well until 2000 when a large downturn struck the whole telecommunications industry. That stopped WorldCom's growth, which in turn affected the merger with Sprint. The stock price was also falling and the pressure grew around Ebbers. The fraudulent activity to hide declining earnings started in 1999 modestly and by 2002 it was already at a risky level. Totally misleading financial information was given to keep the stock price high. This very imaginative accounting was showing a profit although it should have been a loss. When the fraudulent activity was finally exposed, it revealed "nearly $4 billion in misdemeanors". The debts were so great that WorldCom went bankrupt in 2002. In January 2006, the company was acquired by Verizon Communications and was later integrated into Verizon Business. *See WorldCom, Inc. 2004 and 2005. Tran, 2002. MCI Inc – SC 13D/A – LCC International Inc, 2003. CNN,* 2003. *Fox News*, 2015.

49 Herold, 2020.

> hundreds of millions of dollars in debt was found on the company's books. The company had fooled investors, accountants and analysts and faked its real financial status. Enron's chief auditor, David Duncan a partner at Arthur Andersen, ordered thousands of documents to be shredded. This meant not only the end for Enron but also for Arthur Andersen.[50]
>
> ***
>
> In 1997, Canadian mining company Bre-X Minerals Ltd. perpetrated what is probably one of the largest financial frauds in the industry's history. The company had a property in Indonesia, which was considered to be the world's richest gold mine, with 200 million ounces of gold. With this information in 1995, the stock price went up as high as CAD$286.50 with split adjusting. This turned ordinary shareholders into millionaires overnight, with a company market capitalisation of a staggering CAD$6 billion. In late 1997, the claims made about the gold mine were shown to be fraudulent.[51]

If an employee enriches themself to the financial detriment of investors or other parties, it is also considered to be corporate fraud, known as **self-dealing**. The most egregious form of self-dealing is **insider trading**. This means that confidential, unpublished information is used for the benefit of the information holder. Another example could be fraud committed using mutual hedge funds with late-day trading or similar features.

In **money laundering,** cash is "earned from dirty or illicit activities" and transferred "clean" back to bank accounts so that the original crime is hidden. Money laundering will be examined in more detail in Part IV; however, here, let us take the virtual currency bitcoin as an example.

> Virtual currency company OneCoin fell into chaos in 2020 due to the collapse of a huge pyramid scheme. OneCoin's leader Konstantin Ignatov, the brother of the founder, was the subject of an investigation concerning criminal actions over a period of many years. In 2019, he confirmed the investigation was real. He confessed to his crimes and made a smooth exit from the OneCoin leadership team. Over a period of decades of the company's operations, some countries had invested tens of millions of euros in the company. According to the BBC, the company gained over $15 billion during its existence.[52]

---

50 *Arthur Andersen LLP v. United States.* To be precise, Arthur Andersen did not go to bankrupt but gave up the license to operate on its own initiative in 2002. Consulting continued on its own and is known today as Accenture.

51 Fernando, 2020.

52 Virtual currency is digital money. Governments or central banks have no involvement. The most common virtual currency is Bitcoin, and its value is based on supply and demand. Virtual currency is created by complex algorithms. *BBC*, 6 January 2020.

3. Definition of Blue-Collar Crime

There is no formal legal classification for **blue-collar crime** in law since the term is only descriptive in nature. Blue-collar[53] crime can be described as a crime committed by a person or individual who is most likely from a lower social class. Normally, instead of working in an office, the blue-collar worker works in, for example, a factory. Blue-collar crimes contrast fundamentally with white-collar crimes since blue-collar workers have no access or opportunity to commit high-level crimes such as securities fraud, embezzlement or similar. Simply put, they lack the status and power within the organisation in which they work to commit such crimes. Blue-collar crimes are typically smaller in nature, and their immediate beneficial gain goes normally directly to the individual or group involved, as would be the case in theft, burglary or assault. It is not only low-income earners in working life but also the unemployed who might commit such crimes. However, it is also worth pointing out that white-collar workers might commit blue-collar crimes, like thefts and burglary and therefore this topic is discussed here shortly.[54] Having said this, the social status of the perpetrator is not simple. This means that not always white-collar would mean high social status and blue-collar would mean low social status. Social class is a sociological question and goes beyond the matter of a contract of employment.

In blue-collar crimes, there is little or no relation between unemployment factors, underclass and crime. It is important to consider different factors together: personality, family, school, peers and work.[55] In other words, it might be significant to take into account, for example, the duration of unemployment and whether the individual seeks blame of any kind, or whether the individual feels hopeless, compares themself to other groups, their previous experience of employment and future prospects. These are the factors that might cause crime.[56]

Crime rates are higher during periods of unemployment than during employment, especially in the case of property crimes. This might also require the availability of "criminal opportunities in the environment" combined with social standing in the class system. There has been a lot of debate about this issue and there is no definitive answer to how conditions eventually lead to crimes.[57] However, we can probably agree on the following: "a moral education

53 The term relates to America in the 1910s and 1920s, when people working manually wore blue-coloured shirts because stains did not stand out too much on dark blue material. Many workers also needed to wear uniforms, and they happened to be blue. Manual workers (e.g. janitors, construction workers, millwrights or production labourers) were part of a lower social class. Therefore, "blue-collar" began to be a term for people on low incomes. Wickman, 2012.

54 Williams, 2020. Roberts, 2020.

55 *NCJRS.*

56 Box 1987, 96–97.

57 *NCJRS.*

cannot be effective in an economically unjust society." An unjust society here could be underpinned by the following factors: potential punishment versus the chance of being caught, law enforcement efforts, education level opportunities and incentives compared to a country's standard of living.[58]

The role of the media is also quite important. For example, when the media starts running stories that certain areas are dangerous or crimes occur more frequently in certain areas, it becomes something of self-fulfilling prophecy for those areas.[59] One study on the power of media was conducted among Australia's aboriginal population. Researchers found clear geographical and demographic similarities regarding the likelihood of crimes. Factors such as how you raise your children or how developed the community you live in is have a far greater impact on blue-collar crime than issues of employment or unemployment or how high your income may be.[60]

58 Durkheim, 1895. Paulsen, 2002.

59 Durkheim, 1895. Paulsen, 2002.

60 McCausland – Vivian, 2010.

4. Other Types of Business Crime

In addition to white-collar and blue-collar crimes, several other types of crime fall within the context of business, each with their own colour code, and although they are not the primary focus of this discussion are mentioned for the sake of completeness.

Black-collar crimes are crimes most likely committed by the leaders or members of religious organisation. The connecting factor for crimes of this type is that the crimes are backed up by the members of the organisation. A Pennsylvanian grand jury investigating black-collar crimes revealed that, especially in certain areas, such crimes are more frequent than might be expected.[61]

> In the United States, Ted Haggard, a pastor known for his homophobic views, was arrested after he hired a male prostitute from whom he also bought methamphetamine.[62]
>
> ***
>
> Italian Cardinal Angelo Becciu committed a lot of financial misdeeds. In fact, so many that the case against him was referred to as the biggest Vatican trial ever, including a disastrous attempt to purchase the Harrods warehouse in London. Millions of dollars in donations were lost. The trial started in 2021 and is expected to last many years.[63]

Crimes against the environment are referred to as **green-collar crimes.** It is important to note that these are acts which are stated in law as illegal. There are many more moral issues when it comes to green-collar crimes, but these acts of moral wrongdoing are not subject to legal sanctions. Green-collar crimes are examined further in the section on Environmental Business Crime.

The term **red-collar crime** refers to white-collar crimes where the perpetrators of those crimes turn violent. Violence is typically used to avoid detection of fraud. These types of crime are normally related to financial gains already received and the fear of the perpetrator being exposed. When the crime is exposed, the white-collar criminal might resort to extreme violence and even end up killing someone. This is called fraud-detection homicide.[64]

> Linda Williams, who used to be an accountant for a law firm in Florida, attempted to kill her supervisor with a knife twice during the same day

61 YouTube, 2020 II.

62 Serrano, 2006. Harris, 2006.

63 Sherwood, 2021.

64 Rosten – Bowler, 2018. Brody – Kiehl, 2010, 351–364. Kramer, 2018.

in 2020. She had been questioned about irregularities and caught in a fraudulent scheme concerning accounts for which she was responsible. The case is still ongoing, and the supervisor survived the attack.[65]

Pink-collar business crimes relate employees are typically women who, through their work, have access to financial records. For these women, it is easy to steal from their workplace as they tend to occupy positions in bookkeeping and clerical professions. However, the emphasis here is on the position and not so much gender. Crimes in this category are typically non-violent.[66]

One example of a pink-collar crime concerns the founder and CEO of Theranos, Elizabeth Holmes, and a scheme in 2018 to commit fraud amounting to $700 million. Holmes might be seen as the female version of Bernie Madoff now charged with conspiracy and wire fraud.[67]

***

The former owner of Southlake Texas "Millennium Mobster" Nancy Jackson Carroll stole a client's funds. She was sentenced to 10 years in prison in 2018.[68]

***

The queen of pink-collar crimes is surely Rita Crundwell. Crundwell worked for the City of Dixon, Illinois, US, as controller and treasurer. Over a period of many years she systematically committed the largest municipal fraud in US history. With the almost $54 million of municipal money she embezzled, she funded her own horse breeding operation. In 2013, she was sentenced to serve nineteen and a half years in prison, of which she only served eight and a half.[69]

65 Paxton, 2020, 78.
66 Paxton, 2020.
67 Paxton, 2020, 40.
68 Paxton, 2020, 40.
69 Paxton, 2020, 40.

5. Why to risk it all?

The question remains: why are so many successful and powerful people ready to risk it all and step over the line? In the five years from 2002–2006, US federal prosecutors secured convictions against 214 CEOs, 50 CFOs and 128 vice presidents. And it is not only in the United States that cases are brought against business executives—the problem is global. In Oman in 2013, the CEO of an oil company was sentenced to 23 years in prison for bribery. In the same year in South Korea, the wealthiest executive in the country, Chey Tae-won, was found guilty of embezzlement and sentenced to four years in prison. In Brazil in 2018, the world's seventh richest person, Eike Parista, was sentenced to 30 years in prison.[70] The list goes on. Over recent decades, many scholars, neuroscientists, journalists and academic writers have tried to understand this phenomenon, developing models, from benefit-cost calculations and psychology, to get to the bottom of the problem. When does a shade of grey eventually turn black? Below is an image from Soltes (2016, 83) explaining why good people do bad things. Three conditions need to prevail:

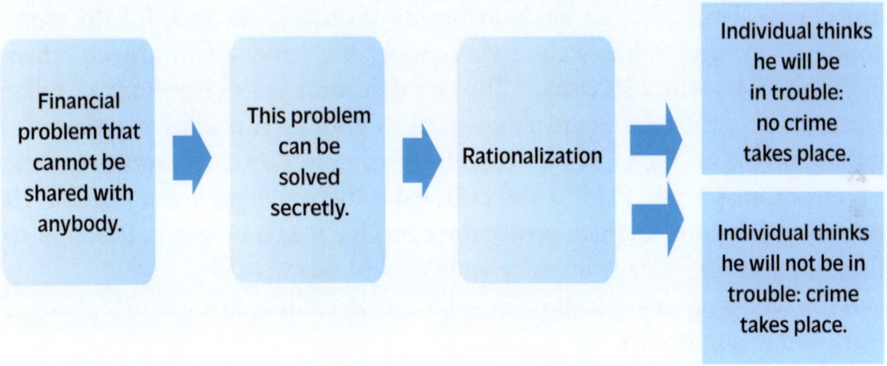

Image 3. Illustration of why white-collar workers end up committing crimes. If a financial problem can be solved secretly, the human mind rationalises the likelihood of getting caught as small. (Original source: Soltes, 2016)

Among the executives who have committed and been caught for their white-collar crimes, replacing their butlers and luxury hotels for an unfurnished room for one that locks from the outside, a few individuals probably stand out more than others:

70 Soltes, 2016.

> Ivan Boesky was known as the man who nearly brought the whole of Wall Street down in 1986. Boesky was fined $100 million and sentenced to three and a half years in prison after pleading guilty.[71]
>
> ***
>
> Bernard Ebbers destroyed WorldCom in 2000 and died in 2020 just a few months after his release from jail. He had been sentenced to 25 years in prison in 2005 but was released after 13 years due to declining health.[72]
>
> ***
>
> Michael Milken, also known as the "Junk Bond King", was sentenced to serve 10 years in prison and ordered to pay $600 million in fines in 1989. Milken earned his nickname because he traded in high-yield bonds. By cooperating with officials, good behaviour and testifying against former colleagues, his prison sentence was reduced to two years. Milken is listed among the world's top 1,000 wealthiest people.[73]

The debate about whether the punishment of these individuals fits the crime continues to rage. While some have received life sentences in prison, others might serve less than 30 years.[74] The fact that there are so many white-collar criminals whose sentences are almost next to nothing continues to enrage the public and the media. In 2014, Bernie Ecclestone, former chief executive of the Formula One Group, paid to end criminal bribery charges and a possible 10 years in jail, leaving German prosecutors and the media in shock. Reaction to Ecclestone paying his way out of trouble was considerable.[75]

The following examples provide some understanding that not everything is black and white though.

> Tom Petters was convicted in a Ponzi scheme in 2010. The business mogul was sentenced to serve 50 years in prison for losing over $3.8 billion of investors' money. Prosecutors had sought a sentence of 335 years in prison.[76]

---

71 Gonzalez Ribeiro, 2021.

72 Gonzalez Ribeiro, 2021.

73 Gonzalez Ribeiro, 2021.

74 More about Mr. Ivan Boesky on *Youtube*, 2019 I. Sen, 2020.

75 Soltes, 2016, 43.

76 *The New York Times*, 8 April 2010.

Chalana McFarland made a fortune with real estate flipping deals. This is a typical real estate white-collar crime. Being a real estate attorney, McFarland used inflated property loans and real estate flipping deals that created for lenders a $20 million bubble in defaulted loans in 2015. Against her, the court heard charges of fraud, identity theft, mortgage fraud and money laundering, among others. The court found her guilty as charged and she was sentenced to serve 30 years and ordered to pay $12 million in restitution for her crimes. In this respect, given that McFarland could have been given a life sentence, her 30 years in prison seems quite moderate. Still, this was considered a harsh sentence handed down for this offence. McFarland was transferred first to home confinement in 2020 due to COVID-19 and released 9 June 2020 serving 15 years of her sentence.[77]

***

The National Heritage Life Insurance Company was forced to end its business operations due to an insurance fraud perpetrated by Sholam Weiss in 1996. The punishment Weiss received in Florida in 2000 was one of the longest in insurance fraud history: he was sentenced to 845 years in prison for money laundering, wire fraud and racketeering. In its reasoning, the court explained the severity of Weiss' punishment due to the number of investors he had defrauded: 25,000. Weiss was not present when the sentence was handed down as he had fled the country with millions of dollars. The resulting year-long FBI manhunt eventually tracked him to Austria in 2002, from where he was extradited to the US and prison. US President Donald Trump commuted his sentence in 2021.[78]

***

In 2010, BAE Systems PLC was ordered to pay $400 million in criminal fines. Acting Deputy Attorney General Gary G. Grindler stated: "Today, BAE Systems pleaded guilty to knowingly and wilfully making false statements to US government agencies. The actions of BAE Systems impeded US efforts to ensure international trade is free of corruption and to maintain control over sensitive US technology." He continued that "BAE Systems will pay a $400 million fine for its criminal conduct – one of the largest criminal fines ever levied in the United States against a company for business-related violations. The remediation measures BAE Systems have undertaken, in conjunction

77 Inman, 2005.
78 *CNBC*, 2010.

> with its agreement to retain an independent compliance monitor, are evidence supporting BAE Systems' stated commitment to ensure that it operates in a transparent, honest and responsible manner going forward. The Department of Justice will continue to hold accountable companies that impair the operations of the US government by lying about their conduct and operations."[79]

***

Vicarious liability was discussed in 1946 in the case *Pinkerton v. United States.* The United States Supreme Court decided that co-conspirators are responsible for each other's acts. This is known as The Pinkerton Doctrine.[80]

> In 2007, airline company British Airways (BA) faced a price fixing scandal in a dual action by the UK and US competition authorities. The company pleaded guilty and was fined £270 million for fixing fuel surcharges on BA's long-haul flights. The Office of Fair Trading (OFT) fined BA £121.5 million, which is the biggest penalty the OFT has imposed on a company for infringement of competition law. The acting associate Attorney General William W. Mercer said: "When British Airways, Korean Air and their co-conspirators got together and agreed to raise prices for passenger and air cargo fares, American consumers and businesses ended up picking up the tab for their illegal conduct."[81]

---

79 *The US Department of Justice,* 2010.

80 Strader, 2017, 66.

81 Walsh, 2007. Wilson, 2008.

Part II Conclusions on Defining White-Collar Crime and Other Crimes

In Part II, we have seen that white-collar business crime is not simply one-sided: it presents a complex picture where there are more losers than winners when a crime is exposed. Moreover, it is costly and humiliating for a company's reputation and image. Although excellent risk-handling processes exist, a failure to meet corporate governance standards and basic business ethics persists. Where there is a corrupt company culture, overly distributed organisation models and bad management, crimes can flourish. In countless examples, a common factor has been aggressive sales targets with high bonuses. Such ambitious targets rapidly evolve into increasingly impossible results, and individuals run even faster to meet these targets with all the means at their disposal. The image below demonstrates the complexity of such crimes and provides a visual summary of Part II:

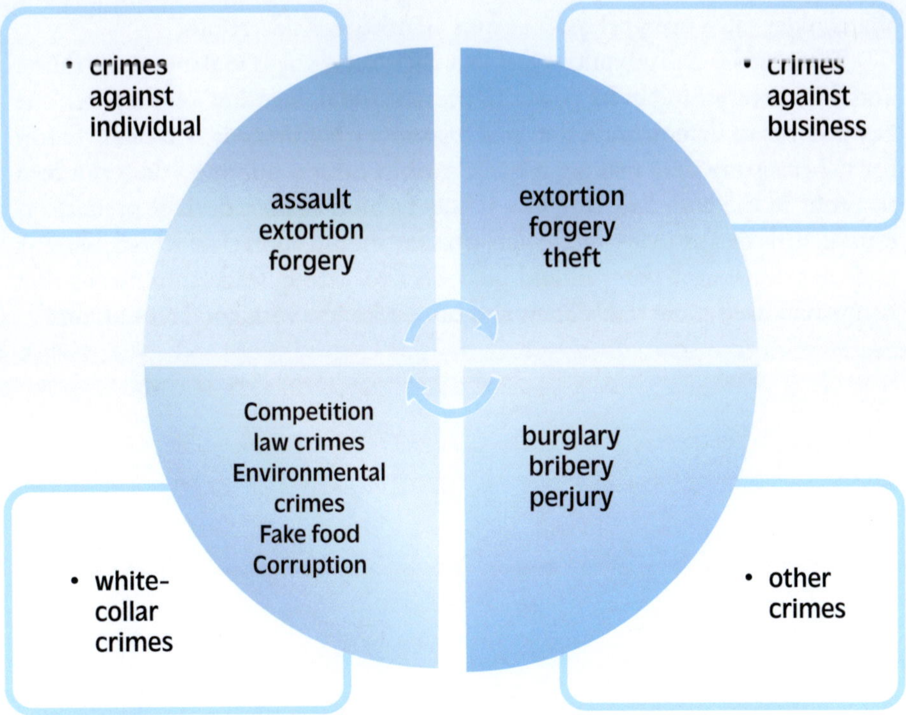

Image 4. The image illustrates only a small number of possible crimes that fall into the category of white-collar business crimes. The image shows the complexity of business crimes and crimes committed by a person and/or a business.

White-collar business crime has significantly diminished shareholder value, such as in companies like Telia Company, Siemens AG, Volkswagen AG and Odebrecht S.A. (today known as Novonor). The drain on the time and energy required to settle these fraudulent acts is enormous. It impacts on personnel and productivity: volatility among personnel increases and commitment decreases. Those employees who are most impacted by these crimes typically have nothing to do with the scandals themselves. [82]

Increased legal regulation might not be the solution to minimising or even ending white-collar business crimes. The fact is that white-collar business crimes are on the rise and it cannot be ignored that the media do love a good crime story. In the legal process, you need to have proof that a white-collar worker did something wrong, did it intentionally and had information that should not be in their possession. This is very difficult to prove and, as a result, many white-collar workers avoid conviction. However, this is not the fault of poor legal drafting but rather bad management practices and a twisted organisational culture in which numerical targets must be met at any cost. The signs that something is wrong are often visible long before a scandal goes public. All too often, it is too late to stop the train, and the risk only gets bigger. The target all companies set for themselves of beating their competitors and increasing shareholder value takes precedence over all other considerations.

When white-collar workers feel that their company is looking to the future and doing everything in its power to prevent fraud, it makes a difference. The key point is to demonstrate that making money legitimately is actually better for the company than making it questionably. Ethical blindness does not lead to profit in the end. Reacting in a timely fashion against deviant practices is crucial. This means that white-collar workers should appreciate whistleblowers and that decision-making should be collective. Strong leadership means that companies need more transparent and honest leaders with good reputations.[83]

82 When the bribery scandal hit Siemens, the company had to pay more than $1.6 billion in fines in 2008. Lichtblau – Dougherty, 2008. Papachristou, 2019. Hotten, 2015. Gallas, 2019.

83 Palazzo, 2019.

PART III

Rules and Principles of International Law

"Companies not yet exposed for wrongdoing fear reading about themselves in the headlines and try to learn from the mistakes of others."[84]

Now we will move on to consider a number of important concepts and terms related to the subject of white-collar business crime, and also explain what those crimes are in detail. As you will see, executives must be aware of all these issues or they run the risk of getting into very serious trouble. Companies today face a multitude of threats and dangers, especially from the outside. Additionally, new generations of customers and stakeholders evaluate companies by new standards, placing entirely new demands on how companies behave in the business world, from soft values and concerns over the environment to respect for privacy and data. In short, a thorough understanding of the international regulatory backdrop is essential for companies and business leaders.

84 Ahlberg – Romberg, 2019, 5.

External threats to companies

Business crime is a minefield for leaders, especially when a company has not prepared itself for the possibility of crime. Through data system break-ins or hacking, criminals can gain access to the confidential information regarding millions of users. Companies have been forced to pay damages to customers that in some cases has amounted to millions of dollars.[85]

> In 2021, concern over data theft was dramatically proved to be right. According to CNBC, the world's biggest crypto currency theft (almost $610 million) hit the Poly Network platform, which combines different block chains together.[86]

Knowledge of business crime and effective law is a good start, but it is not enough. The law is constantly playing catch as business environments constantly change. The new normal for companies is to fight against the unknown. This places leaders and managers in a crucial position regarding their ability to learn and maintain a forward position. You never know what tomorrow may bring—but you can be prepared[87].

Millennials are changing the business landscape

Millennials—that is, the generation born between 1981–1996—represent the biggest age group in the US alone, and in 2020 consisted of approximately 72 million people. For this generation, smart coffee machines, smart homes, remote work and smart watches are all givens. From companies, millennials expect quick answers to their questions. If quick responses are not forthcoming, millennials do not hesitate to start conversations in social media—and, as we all know, once communications are in the social media arena, they are no longer in the hands of the company in question. Millennials change companies, not vice versa. Not only do they use social media, but they also rely on other, soft values in their decision-making processes. Millennials value companies that are seen to be acting positively for the environment and which are responsive. Core economic drivers, such as making money, are a lesser consideration for them.[88]

---

85 Over 70% of Americans think that compared to manufacturing defects cyber-attack or hacking is a more severe factor. This was revealed in the *Harris Poll* 2016, which emphasised concerns about information security. A survey conducted in 2020 by Baltrusaitis tells the same story..

86 Javers, 2021.

87 IoT, cloud services, mobility and social media increase the risks that need to be considered by corporations. With technology, the leaders of a company get more accurate data, but it also means that leaders should be able to process the information and draw conclusions for decision-making processes. Mach, 2020.

88 McGrath, 2015.

Against this background, many companies have started to lean more on the OECD's guiding principles and other international guiding principles, shifting the focus away from profit towards ethical and responsible choices in the long run. Failing to act responsively or ethically might lead to less than optimal outcomes, directly or indirectly.[89]

The significance of data

Analysing consumers and their purchasing behaviour has become an enormous trend. The original intention was simply to get more information about consumers and keep the most popular products on the shelves. Among others, Facebook started to count creditworthiness in relation to what kinds of friends users have. In addition, the Chicago Police started to conduct home investigations on the basis of the likelihood and probability of committing crimes.[90] This probability calculation failed, and the police received a lot of negative feedback as a result. Analysing consumers led to the very important issue of the **General Data Protection Regulation** (GDPR). GDPR is regarded as containing the world's toughest data protection laws. In terms of sanctions on companies, depending on which is the highest, fines can amount to as much as €20 million or 4% of annual worldwide turnover.

In the **Privacy Shield**, which came before the General Data Protection Regulation, the US and Europe agreed the regulation of transatlantic exchanges of personal data for commercial purposes between the EU and the US. This meant that e.g., Facebook needed to get its security regulations in order.[91] Privacy Shield. Facebook case started in 2014 with a student named Max Schrems. He won a court case against Facebook after Facebook had collected a huge amount of information about EU citizens, justifying their actions with the Safe Harbor program to the US.[92]

89 Lautjärvi, 2018, 19–22. See more on the OECD guidelines in the following chapters.

90 Faggella, 2019. Burdick-Will, 2016, 133–158.

91 This led again to negotiations in the media when Donald Trump was elected as President of the United States. Trump provided for a regulation that private rules would only apply to US citizens. In turn, this resulted in many discussions. One tweet was especially notable, written by European Parliament member Jan Philipp Albrecht: "If this is true @EU Commission has to immediately suspend #privacy-Shield & sanction the US for breaking EU-US umbrella agreement [...]".

92 *Wikipedia*: Max Schrems.

In 2020, Privacy Shield was ruled invalid (also known as Schrems II) by the European Court of Justice. This meant that in order to meet the GDPR rules there would have to be other reasons for data transfer.[93]

> The European Union has fined Google three times (2019, 2020 and 2021) amounting to €8 billion for breaching data protection. In the US, Facebook was fined a record $5 billion for breaching data. Amazon is leading the GDPR fines list ($877 million). France hit Amazon with GDPR fines in 2020 for cookie consent failure. In 2019, Google was fined €50 million in France, British Airways was fined over €200 million in the UK, and Marriott over €100 million for breaching GDPR rules. In 2021, WhatsApp was hit with a massive GDPR fine of €225 million. The court case is expected to last many years.[94]

***

> In 2019, food delivery giant Delivery Hero was fined €195,000 for breaching GDPR rules in Germany. The company sent ads against clients' wishes.[95]

In 2019, the US lawmakers passed the **Cloud Act** (Clarifying Lawful Overseas Use of Data Act). The intention was to update the older Stored Communications Act so that officials could better prevent terrorism and criminalisation. The new legislation prohibits officials from using data stored in the cloud for whatever means, and from giving them the freedom to use data stored in the cloud unless there are serious suspicions of a crime. In such cases, a judge will need to request this information and the information must relate to a suspected crime. The request must also be accurate and clear in nature.

When comparing the US to the EU, the problem is that the US citizens do not have privacy protection as a basic right in the same way as EU citizens have. Also, the understanding of the content of the law is different in the US and the EU. For example, in the EU, Member States protect their citizens, whereas in the US, citizens reject state interference in their daily lives.[96]

---

93 After the Court of Justice of the European Union had regulated data transfers and invalidated the Privacy Shield, Google informed all customers that it will be moving to Standard Contractual Clauses (SCCs) for transfers of online advertising and measurement of personal data out of the Europe Economic Area, Switzerland and the UK. European Court of Justice, 2020. As a result, the UK, for example, updated its guidance on international transfers. The European Data Protection Board published on 24 July 2020 frequently asked questions on the topic for companies and countries.

94 Tessian, 2021.

95 *Easy GDPR*, 2019.

96 See Maria Wasastjerna's doctoral thesis from 2019 for more details.

6. Company Vicarious Liability and Corporate Liability

In the European context, there is no mention of the voluntary responsibilities of companies because there is already **regulation of accountability**. The European Parliament has, on several occasions, called on the European Commission to establish regulation, particularly with regard to due diligence in relation to human rights.[97]

> One example of excellent accountability is Lars Rebien Sørensen, CEO of the Danish pharmaceutical company Novo Nordisk. He has been named the world's best performing CEO (by *Harvard Business Review*) twice (2015 and 2016) due to the company's adherence to high accountability. One example of good accountability is that the company has made attention to diabetes treatment.[98]

In Europe, there has been growing frustration concerning corporate accountability, especially in relation to long supply chains. Consumers are becoming increasingly aware of what they buy and eat. As a result, national regulations have been adopted in different European countries, such as the 2017 due diligence regulation in France. In 2017, the Netherlands' parliament adopted a law on child labour prevention.[99] These examples demonstrate that in several European countries there already exists national due diligence regulation of companies.[100]

Social responsibility relates closely to corporate liability. **Social responsibility**[101] is not a new issue and there is a long history of different policy guidelines and principles regarding the voluntary and responsible conduct of

97 Note that the European Commission presented a legislative proposal on due diligence in 2021.

98 Ignatius - McGinn, 2015. See also: UN Guiding Principles on Business and Human Rights, ILO's Declaration of Principles Concerning Multinational Enterprises and Social Policy. OECD's Guidelines for Multinational Enterprises and UNICEF's guidelines on the prevention of child labour are worth reading.

99 This means that the law has been accepted but not yet enforced. The Netherlands decided in October 2020 that if the regulations regarding due diligence in the EU do not go forward as planned, the country will continue with this regulation. Later in December 2022, Council of the European Union adopted position on due diligence rules for large companies. This due diligence directive applies to large EU companies and to non-EU companies active in the EU.

100 European Commission (CSR). The regulations for the UK, France and the Netherlands can be found in the reference list.

101 CSR is discussed, for example, in the UN Guiding Principles on Business and Human Rights as well as in the OECD's Guidelines for Multinational Enterprises. See also GRI Sustainability Reporting Standards and ISO standards.

businesses. Many international standards have been created to monitor and measure accountability. For example, the Social Accountability International SA 8000 standard contains regulations on working hours, wages, health and safety.

> In 2019, the top five companies when it came to corporate social responsibility reputation were Rolex, Lego, Disney, Adidas and Microsoft. Rolex's position might not be a surprise since the company has supported individuals for over 40 years working on scientific and technological innovations. The company has also done excellent work with different ecosystems and endangered species. It aims to preserve culture in developing countries and has increased the quality of life in these countries. Also, the second and third runners up have done significant work for the wellbeing of children all around the world.[102]

In 1976, the OECD provided companies with guidance, and the International Labour Organization (ILO) did the same one year later in 1977. If the companies infringe the recommended approaches, the problem lies in the fact that such **soft law standards**[103] often do not have any legal or administrative consequences. It may cause them financial consequences, as many investors follow the final statements of the OECD National Contact Points and act according to them.

In addition to this, a few countries link OECD guidelines and economic diplomacy. For example, in the Netherlands, participants on export promotional trips must commit to complying with the instructions. In Canada, export credits and admission for export promotion trips may be refused if a company is found to have infringed OECD guidelines. If business management is looking at accountability from a purely legal point of view, it easily forgets the power of public dissatisfaction. This can have a significant economic impact on the reputation of a company, on investor attraction and on its attractiveness to potential workers.

In addition, companies should also remember other agreements that may contain references to accountability standards—in this case, violating standards may become a legal issue. Liability issues are difficult. A company might be held responsible for secondary damages as well, such as in a situation where

102 Gonçalves, 2019.

103 Soft law means that the standards are not legally binding, and hard law means they are. Soft law includes, for example, guidelines, declarations and action programmes published by public authorities. For example, the UN Declaration on the Rights of Indigenous Peoples adopted by the UN General Assembly.

service has failed in its task. Questions of liability for product performance and warranties are complex and therefore not discussed in this book.[104]

> In 2020, German web service provider Trivago N.V. was found to have breached Australian Consumer Law. The company misled consumers regarding prices. The service did not show the cheapest prices but rather listed those hotels which actually paid Trivago more. Consumers were led to believe that the prices were low, although they could find cheaper hotel nights elsewhere. Trivago was ordered to pay estimated damages of roughly $10 million ($7MAUD) and failed to appeal a federal court ruling.[105]

A new trend is to transfer company production back to Europe from Asia. This is due to digitalisation, where the physical location of machinery is no longer very significant. Also, rapid production changes in Asian countries have caused a lot of information security problems, mostly as a result of easy copyright or IPR theft and a lack of necessary laws. Another problem with accountability is that the reports produced by companies are often incomplete, and issues that put the company in an unfavourable light are left out of them. According to a recent study by the University of Leeds, many reports contain inaccurate figures and even outright misinformation. As corporate responsibility reports are not required to meet any specific standards, each company is allowed to prepare a report of its own choosing.[106]

Under the US Sarbanes–Oxley Act, CEOs and CFOs must personally certify that financial reports are accurate and compliant with applicable laws. In cases of wilful misconduct, there are criminal penalties that include fines of up to $5,000,000 and a prison sentence of up to 20 years.[107]

In the UK, under section 172 of the Companies Act, there is a "duty to promote the success of the company" that determines that a board member

104 The Ministry of Economic Affairs and Employment in Finland published a judicial analysis on the Corporate Social Responsibility Act in September 2020. The analysis outlines the nature of the due diligence obligations and especially in what circumstances it would be possible to impose a duty of due diligence on companies in Finland. The link to the analysis can be found in English in the reference list.

105 *ACCC*, 2020. Bungard, 2020.

106 Jowit, 2011.

107 Sarbanes–Oxley Act 2002. The Sarbanes–Oxley Act (SOX) or Public Company Accounting Reform and Investor Protection Act 2002. The FBI uses financial forensics, in which it combines criminal and financial auditing skills to identify criminal financial activity. The economic and physical harm caused by corporations is enormous. It is also a threat to the welfare of the community. Consultancy Europe, 2019. Carberry – Engelen – Van Essen, 2018.

must act in **good faith**. The US Sarbanes–Oxley Act[108] promotes reformed business practices, such as enhancing corporate responsibility, financial disclosures and combatting fraud. The Sarbanes-Oxley Act (SOX) (see more on page 86) sets out requirements which affect corporate governance in the US. SOX also influences similar laws in many other countries. The main points of SOX are: 1) The Public Company Accounting Oversight Board (PCAOB) is established to "regulate the auditing profession, which had been self-regulated prior to the law. Auditors are responsible for reviewing the financial statements of corporations and issuing an opinion as to their reliability." 2) "The CEO and CFO attest to the financial statements." Without this and before this, CFOs were able to claim in court that they had not reviewed the information. 3) "Board audit committees have members that are independent and disclose whether or not at least one is a financial expert, or reasons why no such expert is on the audit committee." 4) "External audit firms cannot provide certain types of consulting services and must rotate their lead partner every five years. Further, an audit firm cannot audit a company if those in specified senior management roles have worked for the auditor in the past year. Prior to the law, there was the real or perceived conflict of interest between providing an independent opinion on the accuracy and reliability of financial statements when the same firm was also providing lucrative consulting services."[109]

The Sarbanes–Oxley Act also ordered that the audit committee of the board of directors should choose for the company a person who is familiar with financial reporting and related details. This person is called the financial expert.[110] The act also ensures the toughest criminal and civil penalties if the provisions of that law are violated. The law was preceded by accounting scandals in several large American companies, such as WorldCom and Tyco International.

108 The UK Companies Act does not have any specific rules for choosing directors of boards or their tasks. These are referred to in the articles of association. There are two types of board members: those who are full-time employed executive directors and those who are non-executive directors. According to the Companies Model Articles Regulations 2008 No. 3229 and the Companies Act Section 20, the UK has model articles for different corporate forms. The Companies Act does not specifically list any duties for a managing director or chief executive officer. If the CEO is not a member of the board, the CEO's tasks are based on delegation or as per the agreement. The Companies Act, Section 250. See Davies-Worthington 2012, 390.

109 SOX 2002. Different countries have different authorities that investigate these types of crimes. For example, the US entities that investigate white-collar crimes are the FBI, the Securities and Exchange Commission (SEC), the National Association of Securities Dealers (NASD) and state authorities. Chen, 2020, I. Kagan, 2020.

110 Afterman, 2016.

6.1. Compliance

Compliance means that a person does what they are expected or required to do. In terms of the law, compliance is expected of each and every one of us who is part of working life. The effective fight against abuse of compliance rules requires that an organisation has established clear rules, operating instructions, policies and reporting systems. It also requires that the company has documented the rules of business ethics in different situations.

Compliance programmes are a company's internal approaches to ensuring the appropriateness of the company's business, both in terms of legislation and ethical practices. Compliance rules are not normally regulated in a country's own regulations. Compliance as such is based rather on recommendations, such as corporate governance.[111] Compliance programmes are about the risks, responsibilities and best practices in a company, that is, how the company operates in different markets in countries, considering the company's values and national laws and regulations.[112]

> In 2020, consumer healthcare company Johnson & Johnson (J&J) was found guilty of unethical business practices. The company added asbestos to baby powder. According to the Missouri Court of Appeals, the product caused many cases of ovarian cancer. Damages amounted to $2.1 billion. J&J stated immediately after the court ruling that it would take the case to the Supreme Court on appeal. The company stopped selling its baby powder in the US and Canada but continued to sell it in other countries. [113]
>
> ***
>
> In 2020, German-based chemical giant Bayer, the new owner of the Monsanto Company, settled many lawsuits regarding products Roundup, PCBs (organic chlorine compound) and Dicamba (used in weed killer). Monsanto is best known for the Agent Orange plant poison used in the Vietnam War. Agent Orange has been investigated over the years for causing deaths and serious injuries. Later, Monsanto ended up producing gene modified soya, which attracted a lot of controversy in

111 OECD Corporate Governance Principles.

112 Important aspects of a compliance programme are often, for example, compliance with competition law, anti-corruption and anti-corruption measures, and the prevention and detection of abuse. *Fondia* (2020) states: "A compliance program is usually based on a careful risk analysis by the company's management of adverse events that could result in fin ancial losses (such as penalties, loss of revenue, lost business, investor flight, etc.) or negative publicity." Companies have also started to appoint a Chief Compliance Officer, such as Facebook, which named Henry Moniz as its first Chief Compliance Officer in 2019.

113 Loftus, 2020.

> Europe. During Monsanto's time, the company was involved in many court cases concerning health and environmental claims mostly, and was under investigation in many countries, such as India, the US, the UK, Argentina, Brazil and China.[114]

Companies should act transparently and ethically because, for example, important decisions taken by leaders can have a large-scale impact. Therefore, different compliance units and managerial responsibilities in the internal audit are set up to ensure the proper functioning of the whole organisation. Units are responsible for the development of business practices, the code of conduct and the evaluation of development work. It explains how employees should act in the company and in business activities with stakeholders. Each company has a different code of conduct, often based on management risk analysis. Risk analysis considers the adverse situations that may result in, for example, the loss of income or fines. An unfavourable situation can arise through negative publicity.[115]

> Clothing and footwear company Sears (officially Sears, Roebuck and Company) was in the middle of a pricing scandal in the 1990s. The pricing concerned a tire service, with the scandal growing wider as the company had secretly violated federal law—and not just over one or two years but over decades. After 22 months of FBI investigations, the company pleaded guilty to one count of fraud. The company paid $60 million to the US government. The Sears case was referred to as "the most serious ethical breach in history". The *Newsweek* citation explains how it started: "It all began with what's known around the federal bankruptcy court in Boston as the letter that cost Sears a half-billion dollars. Scrawling on a yellow legal pad in November 1996, a disabled security guard named Francis Latanowich begged to reopen his bankruptcy case. Although Judge Carol Kenner had wiped out his debts, Latanowich had agreed to repay Sears the $1,161 he owed for a TV, a car battery and other goods. But the monthly payment, he wrote, 'is keeping food off the table for my kids'. Sears, it turned out, had mailed Latanowich an offer. In return for $28 a month from his account, it wouldn't repossess the goods he'd bought with a Sears charge card before he went bankrupt. Urging debtors to sign such deals,

114 Chappell, 2020. *Reuters*, 2018.

115 Aaltonen et al., 2004, 63–65, emphasise a sensible and genuine understanding of the company. A responsible manager acts ethically, even if the situation does not benefit the company. The authors state that there are also irresponsible leaders who think about loopholes and act questionably. Aaltonen et al. list the most important situations in working life where the manager should be especially careful. These can also be considered in terms of information security: recruitment, redundancies, retirements, differences and diversity, and working conditions.

> called reaffirmations, is legal, and roughly a third of bankruptcies do so. However, many judges view them as sucker deals that prevent people from making a fresh start. And every signed reaffirmation must be filed with the court so a judge can review whether the debtor can handle the new payment. Sears hadn't filed this one. Kenner wanted to know why." That was the moment when it all came to light.[116]

A company should not copy its compliance programme directly from other companies. The programme should always be based on the analyses made by the management of the company: its risks, estimates and way of acting. As a guideline, compliance programmes should consider, for example, competition law and the impact on industry, and how corruption or other abuses are prevented and detected. Regarding human rights, companies should assess the risks to people, not just the risks to the company itself.[117] Major companies have developed a range of reporting methods that allow employees to report maladministration within the company. One of these is the whistleblowing directive.[118]

> In 2018, a big information leak hit the headlines in Australia. Thousands of strictly confidential Australian government documents were found in an Australian flea market. As part of a big government campaign to clear out furniture, some cabinets were sold without keys. Someone bought the cabinets at a very low price and, after some months, opened the locked cabinets with a drill and found the documents inside. The documents contained national security information, insider information as well as documents concerning other nations, such as Middle East military plans. As all the documents contained a confidential or strictly confidential stamp, the buyer contacted officials. The case was referred to "The Cabinet Files". [119]

***

116 Gellene, 1992. Mikolajczyk, 1995. McCormick, 1999. Baltimore Sun, 1999.

117 See the UN Guiding Principles Interpretative Guide: "A business enterprise's human rights risks are any risks that its operations may lead to one or more adverse human rights impacts. They therefore relate to its potential human rights impact. In traditional risk assessment, risk factors in both the consequences of an event (its severity) and its probability. In the context of human rights risk, severity is the predominant factor. Probability may be relevant in helping prioritize the order in which potential impacts are addressed in some circumstances [...]. Importantly, an enterprise's human rights risks are the risks that its operations pose to human rights. This is separate from any risks that involvement in human rights impact may pose to the enterprise, although the two are increasingly related."

118 EU member states are required to enforce the directive by 17 December 2021. It involves all companies which employ over 50 people. Enforcing the directive in companies needs to be done by 17 December 2023.

119 McGhee, 2018.

> In 2020, a German auctioneer sold old laptops. The clean-up of the laptops' hard drives had gone wrong. The buyer, luckily a security company called G Data CyberDefense, found a perfect and detailed manual for a German missile system Leflasys Ozelot (Das Leichte Flugabwehrsystem Ozelot). A similar short-range missile system is also used in other countries, such as Finland.[120]

In the above examples, what could have been done to prevent the mistakes made? One good method is an internal audit. Another method is internal control. The first method means there is a check at a certain time, whereas the second means there are ongoing checks to take care of a company's effectiveness and operational efficiency.

Internal control and **internal audit** differ insofar as internal control is precisely the company's internal means of action aimed at making the result legal. Internal audit, on the other hand, is an objective task carried out by a separate inspection organisation, which is motivated by guidelines, rules and standards for operating methods. An internal audit is also often a separate unit for companies. National guidelines, such as the corporate governance code and the Sarbanes–Oxley Act mentioned earlier, are part of this control.[121]

An internal audit helps companies achieve their goals. The role of internal control is to ensure that the business is well-governed. It ensures that the company is meeting the goals set by the management and that it is in line with that guidance. Internal control also guides what needs to be done and develops business practices. It aims to achieve the adequate security of objectives. It cannot ensure that the objectives are fulfilled. Also, internal control is not immune to abuse and inefficiency. It cannot prevent error estimates or incorrect decisions taken by management. Moreover, external factors, such as a recession, and unknown threats like viruses, strikes and natural disasters, can invariably affect the effectiveness of internal control.[122] Internal auditing can work, for example, through internal accounting for financial management and reporting. In addition, various other control measures may be carried out in companies.[123]

> One.Tel Group, whose slogan was "You'll tell your friends about One. Tel", was an Australian telecommunications company. The company had very well-known backers, such as the Murdoch and Parker families.[124] With a focus on creating a youth-oriented image for its products (phones and internet services), the company actually grew and became the fourth largest company in Australia. Soon after its rise, it collapsed

120 Walsh, 2020.

121 Graham, 2015, 4–5, 9. Manoukian, 2016.

122 Ahokas, 2012.

123 Suomela, 2010, 160. *PCAOB*, 2020.

124 Cratchley, 2009.

> in 2001 due to insolvency, due to failings in the company's corporate governance. The company had weak internal control and internal audit processes, communications and financial data, to mention just a few. A total of 1,400 employees were laid off.[125]

In the best instances, internal control prevents and exposes errors and abuses. It delivers a reliable picture of a company's financial condition and sends a message to the market that the company has complied with laws and regulations.[126] The main internal control is the company's internal policy development work, its **code of conduct, corporate conduct.**

> In early 2000, an assistant working for Coca-Cola was accused of using confidential information for monetary gain. In the witness report, the assistant was angry at her employer because she felt she was badly treated in the workplace. As a result, the assistant attempted to sell business secrets to Coca-Cola's largest competitor PepsiCo. According to the evidence presented in the United States in 2007, the assistant had copied confidential information over time. She hoped to receive $1.5 million with her colleagues by selling trade secrets. The compliance programme at PepsiCo worked as planned in these types of situations, and the company contacted Coca-Cola's leadership team to tell them what was happening. The assistant received an eight-year prison sentence. Two other defendants in the case also received sentences of five and two years.[127]

Since the enactment of the Sarbanes–Oxley Act in the United States in 2002, auditors have been obligated to audit company financial reporting and provide a statement. The audit contains, among other things, what the company's internal financial control includes and how it is organised practically so that the company's figures in the financial statements are strictly reliable. The object of the Sarbanes–Oxley Act is to ensure that all the companies have their internal control systematised and structured. This structural requirement may substantially increase the work of the companies' financial departments, as well as the workload of the auditors.

This tightening of internal control in the US met with a cold reception in some companies due to the increased amount of work it involved. To give one example, a group of Finnish companies operating in the United States left

125 Cratchley, 2009. *BBC*, 2001. *BBC*, 2001, II. *BBC*, 2002.

126 Alma, 2016.

127 Clark, 2006. CNN, 2007. See also the final decision after complaints: United States Court of Appeals, Eleventh Circuit. *United States of America, Plaintiff-Appellee, v. Joya WILLIAMS, Defendant-Appellant. United States of America, Plaintiff-Appellee, v. Ibrahim Dimson, a.k.a. Dirk, Defendant-Appellan*t.

the country and the stock exchange when the law came into force. Although the law was welcomed by some companies, unfortunately, it has not prevented compliance problems and company misdeeds since its adoption.[128]

6.2. Moral Hazard

Moral hazard[129] is a situation in which a company knowingly increases its own risk-taking in the market. The company calculates that in these cases some other party will always pay a part of the costs, that is, the consequences of the risks. For example, moral hazard for banks may arise in a case where agreements are verbal and not written. Similarly, when a company's board of directors assesses its own activities, it can be critically questioned whether everything is accurate or whether an external assessment of the board of directors' activities should be carried out.[130]

> In 2009, General Motors (GM) was the subject of a dispute concerning demands from unions for salary increases. The trade unions knew that the employer would not agree to reasonable salary raises because the raises would result in the bankruptcy of GM. If the company had agreed to the raises, this would have, in turn, resulted in the state intervening and ultimately saving the company from bankruptcy. The trade unions therefore brought in the state to help GM in any case, irrespective of how such a "risk-neutral" undertaking might impact the market. GM was rescued several times, but in the end it went bankrupt.[131]

Moral hazard also explains various types of banking crises. If a bank is perceived as being too big to crash, it often takes too many risks in its business. Indeed, it is even sensible for a bank to take on more risk because risk-based business operations might yield greater profits. The problem with a banking crisis is that taxpayers are often the ones who ultimately pay the costs. In order to avoid moral hazard and to maintain fair competition, a company (e.g. a bank) that has grown too big should be split up. Erkki Liikanen, former Governor of the Bank of Finland, has said that every country should have a balanced economic system that is "transparent and credible" to ensure that credit rates do not rise too quickly.[132]

In early 2000, there were a great many economic failures in the United States (similar to the dot-com bubble in 2000–2002) due to the negligence

128 Wagner & Dittmar, 2006.

129 *Cambridge Dictionary,* 2020: Moral hazard is "a situation in which people or organizations do not suffer from the results of their bad decisions, so may increase the risks they take".

130 *Economic Times*, 2020.

131 Keller, 2019.

132 *Economic* Times, 2020. Hellmann - Murdock - Stiglitz, 2000.

or failure of companies to comply with regulations. This sparked a large-scale debate on corporate governance, i.e. the management code.[133] In 2010, the United States enacted the Dodd–Frank Act[134], which prohibits the use of tax funds in banking crises, and the accompanying Volcker Rule[135] prohibiting derivative gambling. This was under threat of being scrapped following an initiative being championed by former US President Donald Trump.[136] In Europe, the draft regulatory proposals of the Basel III Committee were published in 2010 to limit the use of banks' own funds and liquidity.[137] The corporate governance debate started on a large scale from the Sarbanes–Oxley Act[138]. As explained earlier in this book, the act is a federal law that contains provisions on the management of publicly traded companies, among others. It had its beginnings in the United States but has quickly spread to Europe.[139]

The attitudes of various countries towards the banking crises in the 21st century have been muted. For example, the measures taken by Iceland and Ireland stand in opposition to each other. Iceland did not provide any funds to banks but allowed them to manage their indebtedness in accordance with the rules of the free market economy. This did not escalate into a huge world banking crash, whereas the financial bubble of Irish banks caused difficulties throughout Europe. Banks had granted too many loans in Ireland and borrowers were not able to repay them. Finally, the Irish state helped banks cope with tax funds. The moral hazard in these activities was not only a problem for Iceland or Ireland but it almost broke the Euro currency. Different financial institutions had no idea how much the banks in any given country had taken on risk. The 10 largest banks in the world, for example, doubled their size over a five-year period from 2002 to 2007.[140]

---

133 Corporate governance tries to explain all those processes, rules, principles and manners the company has. Taking all of these together, it is possible to develop powerful and effective management and control systems for the company. See more about corporate governance in the next chapter.

134 The definition of the Dodd–Frank Act according to Rosencrance, 2019 is as follows: "The Dodd–Frank Act (fully known as the Dodd–Frank Wall Street Reform and Consumer Protection Act) is a United States federal law that places regulation of the financial industry in the hands of the government. The legislation, which was enacted in July 2010, created financial regulatory processes to limit risk by enforcing transparency and accountability."

135 The definition of the Volcker Rule according to Cole, 2012: "The Volcker Rule is a section of the Dodd–Frank Wall Street Reform and Consumer Protection Act that restricts US banks from making speculative, high-risk investments that do not benefit customers. The rule was initiated by former Federal Reserve Chairman Paul Volcker in response to the financial crisis in the latter part of the past decade.".

136 Smith, 2017.

137 *Bank for International Settlements,* 2011.

138 *Sarbanes–Oxley Act of* 2002, Conference Report.

139 Suomela, 2010, 7.

140 Milne, 2009.

7. Corporate Governance

Corporate governance (CG) is "a system of law and sound approaches by which corporations are directed and controlled focusing on the internal and external corporate structures with the intention of monitoring the actions of management and directors and, thereby, mitigating agency risks which may stem from the misdeeds of corporate officers".[141]

The UK Corporate Governance Code provides a good description of the aim of CG: "The purpose of corporate governance is to facilitate effective, entrepreneurial and prudent management that can deliver the long-term success of the company."

Corporate governance has evolved from the bankruptcies of a few corporate giants, such as Enron and WorldCom. Also, the business crime scandals involving companies like Adelphia Communications, Tyco, Global Crossing and AOL have played their part in its development. Corporate governance took on political overtones in many countries after the financial crisis in 2008.[142]

> The CEO and one of the founders of Adelphia Communications, John Rigas, was dismissed in 2002 after it was revealed that he had stolen $3.1 billion from the company. He never recorded the money in the company's books. Adelphia Communications, which was one of the largest cable companies in the US at the time, did not survive. Rigas was sentenced to 15 years in prison. Prior to his conviction, he had been honoured several times by universities. In 2015, Rigas' lawyers argued for his release from prison as he was terminally ill. Six years later, in 2021, Rigas passed away.[143]

***

> Boeing CEO Harry Stonecipher rewarded managers for their speed and cost-cutting measures. One of the factors not rewarded was safety. After years of bad choices by management, the Boeing 737 Max was grounded after crashes in which many passengers lost their lives.[144]

Corporate governance involves a few challenges. First of all, there is no official definition of the concept. Second, the regulation of corporate governance is both codified and uncodified, i.e. it can be found in a country's own laws, CG

141 Sifuna, 2012.
142 Kaplan, 2012.
143 United States v. Rigas. John Rigas Website.
144 Robinson, 2019.

rules, soft law, self-regulation and in other management and control systems. The lack of coherence in the rules means good governance is vulnerable.

Corporate governance balances the different goals of stakeholders and upper management, and good CG even prevents conflicts of interests and increases transparency inside corporations ("equitable treatment of shareholders"[145]). CG is a list of procedures, objectives and rules for a decision-making process. It is a crucial part of an organisation's work because there is always the possibility for a conflict of interests between upper management and stakeholders or among stakeholders.[146] Companies are controlled and operated through an advanced set of mechanisms, processes and relations in the corporate governance system. Good CG should align all social, regulatory and market environments in which the company is involved. Also, monitoring actions, policies, practices and decisions made should be aligned.[147]

Corporate governance exists mostly for listed companies, which means not all of its rules and procedures are binding. A company can use its own discretion. If it decides not to act according to CG, the company needs to justify this decision.[148] Experience shows that there just cannot be enough good governance. The Enron scandal (see page 125) started because its accounting was too "creative" and everything that its finance people suggested for bookkeeping was accepted by Arthur Andersen, the auditing giant.[149]

7.1. Different Corporate Governance Models around the World

Europe and **Japan** both use a multi-stakeholder approach regarding the decision-making processes in companies. This means that the interests of workers, managers, suppliers, customers and communities are all recognised and considered when making decisions. A distinction can be drawn between market-oriented and network-oriented models of corporate governance.[150] In some European countries, such as **Austria, Germany** and **the Netherlands**, there is a two-tiered system governing the board of directors, in which an executive board is responsible for daily operations and a supervisory board,

145 OECD, 2004. Cadbury, 1992.

146 These are called principal-agent problems and principal-principal problems or multiple principal problems.

147 Lin, 2012. Goergen, 2012. OECD Principles of Corporate Governance, 2004. Tricker, 2009.

148 This is the comply or explain principle. This is not needed if the company publishes a CSR report according to the international guidelines, such as using the UN Global Compact, OECD Guidelines for Multinational Enterprises, ISO 26000. If comply and explain is used, this report should be included in annual reports. See: Directive 2014/95/EU of the European Parliament and of the Council on 22 October 2014 amending Directive 2013/34/EU regarding disclosure of non-financial and diversity information by certain large undertakings and groups.

149 Thomas, 2002. More about the topic: Brown – Dugan, 2002.

150 Douma – Schreuder, 2013.

with non-executive members chosen from among shareholders and employees, decides on matters such as who are the members of the executive board and their compensation, and they also review big business decisions. In Germany, for example, workers have seats on the board of directors, and while these seats act as stakeholders they are still considered "separate from seats accruing to shareholder equity". This is found in the German Codetermination Act of 1976[151].

The governance code of the world's fastest growing economy, China, is from 2002. The Chinese model is not perfect, but it is continuously evolving. The 2020 implementation concerned, among others, the Securities Dispute Representative Litigation Mechanism. Also, a lot of effort has been made in **Saudi Arabia.** In late 2006, the country's Capital Market Authority (CMA) published an Arabic corporate governance code.[152] Ever since the code was published, Saudi Arabia has made "considerable progress", showing good faith towards appropriate good governance methods.[153]

In **India,** one the world's rising economies, the corporate governance code issued by The Securities and Exchange Board was defined in 2021 as follows: "acceptance by management of the inalienable rights of shareholders as the true owners of the corporation and of their own role as trustees on behalf of the shareholders. It is about commitment to values, about ethical business conduct and about making a distinction between personal & corporate funds in the management of a company."[154] Particularly in India, it is crucial that the interests of investors as well as the responsibility of management are not jeopardised. If this is not the case, shareholders' wealth and foreign investments are threatened. This happened once already in the Satyam scandal[155], so the country wants to prevent this happening again. The scandal, referred to as India's Enron, decreased shareholder wealth and investments by billions.[156]

Shareholder interest is at the centre of the **Anglo-American** (US, Canada and UK) CG model. This model is also called "the unitary system" because it relies on a "single-tiered board of directors dominated by non-executive directors". These non-executive directors are elected by shareholders. It is common that the boards do consist of at least some company executives. Non-executive directors are typically outnumbered by executive directors. They

151 For very detailed board structures around the world, see: Alliuris, 2018. Tricker, 2009. Hopt, 1997. A full comparison of the countries can be found in the reference list._

152 Al-Hussain, 2009.

153 Robertson – Diyab – Al-Kahtani, 2013. Al-Hussain – Johnson, 2009, 111–117.

154 *Securities and Exchange Board of India*, 2003. Rahim – Kuruppu, 2016. Ngwu – Osuji – Stephen, 2017.

155 Hindustan Times, 9 April 2015. The Satyam scandal concerned the manipulation of accounts in Satyam Group. This happened in many ways, mostly involving the Chairman Satyam Raju, who later resigned.

156 Sial, 2018.

hold key posts, such as in the audit and compensation committee. The UK and the US differ in this respect: in the UK, the CEO does not also serve as the chairman of the board, whereas this dual role is normal in the US, although it is nevertheless declining.[157] Companies listed in the United States may use a whistleblower system through which improper procedures can be anonymously reported to a company's audit committee.[158]

In the **United States**, "corporations are directly governed by state laws" which have adopted the Model Business Corporation Act[159]. The Delaware General Corporation Law is considered to be the dominant state law for publicly traded corporations. The Delaware General Corporation Law has become the most important jurisdiction in the US. This is because over half of the publicly traded corporations are operating in the state. Individual rules for corporations are based upon the corporate charter and bylaws.[160]

The Foreign Corrupt Practices Act (FCPA), enforced by the US Department of Justice and the Securities and Exchange Commission (SEC), states that bribing government officials is illegal. It also states that corporations need to maintain certain accounting controls. Bribery has led to substantial civil and criminal penalties.[161] In the UK, for instance, the Bribery Act of 2010[162] states that it is illegal to bribe government and private citizens. It is also illegal to use the facilitation of payments to help someone to do tasks more efficiently.

It has been common practice in the US that companies with combined roles appoint a lead director whose role is to improve the independence of the board from the management. This role has not been used so much in the UK or in Germany since the roles are split in almost every company. Which model works the best? The jury is out on this question; however, tellingly, evidence from poorly performing firms is that companies with split roles tend to change their CEO quicker than those where the roles of CEO and chair are combined.[163]

If a company's employee representatives are elected to the board of directors, this may cause problems. This has happened in Sweden, for example, where local unions are very strong and negotiations are mostly local. Whereas in other parts of Europe, the law regulates the same issues directly. Union power over Swedish companies might even be too great. Such a position on a board

157 Mallin, 2011. Bowen, 2008. Sun, 2019.

158 The Dodd–Frank Act, Section 922, even rewards whistleblowers on certain grounds.

159 The Model Business Corporation Act 2002 is a model set of laws used by 24 states in the US. It was prepared by the Committee on Corporate Laws of the Section of Business Law of the ABA. See Bebchuk, 2004.

160 *Delaware*, 2020. Delaware has been chosen by corporations because Delaware has statutes up to date among other benefits.

161 *The FCPA Guide*, 2015.

162 The Bribery Act 2010 covers the criminal law on bribery in the UK.

163 Smith, 2013. Tribbett, 2012.

could lead to tensions if the representatives of the employees are confidently advocating workers' affairs on behalf of the company.[164]

What is the future of corporate governance globally? In 2017, Oxford University outlined a new founder centrism theory of corporate governance. It predicts a narrow "separation between ownership and control". The theory focuses on concentrated equity ownership and concludes that the traditional checklist of best practices is inapplicable. This can be seen, for example, in the following cases: founder-run companies, such as Google and Facebook, are using organisational structure for long-term value creation. However, in founder-centric companies, such as IBM, Apple, Goldman Sachs, the idea is to combine founder and non-founder senior leadership to adopt the owner's mindset.[165]

7.2. OECD Guidelines and Other Important Principles and Guidelines

The most influential guidelines on corporate governance are from the OECD.[166] The OECD Guidelines on Corporate Governance of State-Owned Enterprises[167] are complementary to the OECD Principles of Corporate Governance, and they are intended to provide help in the governance of state-owned enterprises. In 2018, the OECD's Due Diligence Guidance for Responsible Business Conduct was accepted.

The importance of the OECD guidelines is reflected in the fact that countries often refer to them when they are drafting their own local codes or guidelines. The following are the main elements of the OECD guidelines:

- Board members should be informed and act ethically and in good faith, with due diligence168 and care, in the best interests of the company and its shareholders.
- Review and guide corporate strategy, objective setting, major plans of action, risk policy, capital plans and annual budgets.
- Oversee major acquisitions and divestitures.

164 Tiihonen, 2007, 32.

165 Rojas, 2017. The future of CG in the European Union means that in 2021 the European Commission will present a legislative proposal on sustainable corporate governance. See the link in the references for more information.

166 First published as the OECD Principles in 1999, revised in 2004, and revised again and endorsed by the G20 in 2015. See the OECD Principles of Corporate Governance, 2004.

167 OECD Guidelines on Corporate Governance of State-Owned Enterprises.

168 *Merriam Webster Dictionary*, 2020: Due diligence is "the care that a reasonable person exercises to avoid harm to other persons or their property".

- Select, compensate, monitor and replace key executives and oversee succession planning.
- Align key executive and board remuneration (pay) with the longer-term interests of the company and its shareholders.
- Ensure a formal and transparent process for the nomination and election of board members.
- Ensure the integrity of the company's accounting and financial reporting systems, including independent auditing.
- Ensure that appropriate systems of internal control are established.
- Oversee the process of disclosure and communications.
- Where board committees are established, their mandate, composition and working procedures should be well-defined and disclosed.[169]

The OECD guidelines have been so influential that other international organisations, associations and over 20 nationwide corporate governance codes have used them as the template to form guidance on good practices in CG disclosure.[170] This is an internationally agreed benchmark that consists of five categories: 1) auditing, 2) board and management structure and processes, 3) corporate responsibility and compliance, 4) financial transparency and information disclosure and 5) ownership structure and exercise of control rights. The benchmark has over fifty distinct disclosure items.[171]

As stated already, these codes and guidelines are mostly voluntary. This issue was largely debated in the Disney case[172] in 2005:

> The Disney decision made visible the extent to which companies manage their governance responsibilities, i.e. do they try to supersede the legal threshold or create governance guidelines which meet the best practice level? If companies have guidelines of their own, these companies may try to influence other companies to use the same guidelines. The Disney case emphasised that the meaning of corporate governance can change over time. In this case, Disney's own board members breached their fiduciary duties, but the court did not hold the board member liable.[173]

---

169 *OECD Principles of Corporate Governance*, 2004. More on due diligence in the section Company Vicarious Liability and Corporate Liability

170 This means that the OECD guidelines/principles, which are for state-owned businesses have been adopted at some level by private businesses too. Especially in cases where private business engages in a project along with public sector. United Nations Intergovernmental Working Group of Experts on International Standards of Accounting and Reporting (ISAR) produced Guidance on Good Practices in Corporate Governance Disclosure.

171 International Standards of Accounting and Reporting, Corporate Governance Disclosure.

172 See: *The Walt Disney Co. Derivative Litigation.*

173 Kuckreja, 2005.

7.3. Examples of Corporate Governance Failures

Many corporate scandals have led to the reform of corporate governance regulations. In the US, the previously mentioned Enron and MCI Inc. (known as WorldCom) collapses led to the enactment of the Sarbanes–Oxley Act in 2002. Also, federal law intends to improve corporate governance in the US. In Australia, the HIH[174] and One.Tel scandals in 2001 led to the reform of CLERP 9[175], and the failure of Parmalat in 2003 led to regulatory reforms in Italy.[176]

> In 2002, the banking giant Citigroup was hit with a $240 million fine for asking its own officials to forge mortgage bonds. The Bank of America was also caught in 2016. It was fined $1 billion for its activities. Banking giant Deutsche Bank was fined $200 million in 2012 for reselling "mortgages to insolvent debtors" with the rating "first class". None of the banks formally admitted their abuses, but they avoided legal proceedings by paying fines. The market was also buzzing when banking giants Goldman Sachs and Morgan Stanley were rumoured to have purchased oil derivatives in advance in 2012. At the same time, the banks' forecast was that oil would rise to $200 a barrel. Oil prices rose, with the banks making a killing.[177]
>
> ***
>
> In Italy, food company Parmalat S.p.A., a multinational and leading global producer of long-life milk, collapsed in 2003. The company had over 16,000 employees and approximately 5,000 dairy farms in Italy. It is known for having caused the biggest bankruptcy of all time in Europe and having a shortfall in the company's accounts worth €14 billion ($20 billion, £13 billion). Later, Lactalis, a French dairy product company, bought Parmalat in 2011. Parmalat is still operating globally on many

174 Australia's second largest insurance company HIH Insurance (HIH) faced provisional liquidation in 2001. The demise of HIH was the largest corporate collapse in the history of Australia. Liquidators estimated that HIH's losses amounted to A$5.3 billion. The management of HIH were convicted and imprisoned on various fraud-related charges. *Monash University*, 2003. *Australian Broadcasting Corporation*, 2006. Carson, 2010. *Daily Telegraph*, 2010.

175 Corporate Law Economic Reform Program (Audit Reform & Corporate Disclosure) Act 2004, known as CLERP 9, modified the Corporations Act 2001 (Commonwealth) in Australia. The reforms tried to improve investors' confidence, especially in listed corporations and their financial reports.

176 Lee – Shailer, 2008, 123–134.

177 Mattera, 2017. Piskora, 2002. Arnold, 2016. Duronio, 2012. Lambert, 2017. Wyatt, 2011. McCoy – Johnson, 2014.

continents and continues to specialise in dairy products. Today, it has almost 140 production centres, and the company is listed in Italy.[178]

***

The spectacular rise and fall of coworking start-up company WeWork, in less than one year, was dramatic. In 2015, WeWork was the most valuable start-up of all time. It used an investing strategy known as Blitzscaling, through which it is possible to enjoy quick wins and profits—with a lot of debt. Little by little, as profit exceeds debt, the business becomes profitable. WeWork is an example of a failed IPO and the crucial investor Softbank's risky investment. The start-up company had a $47 billion valuation which put it at the highest evaluation in rankings for young start-ups in Silicon Valley. The company, which was a darling of the venture capital world, needed an $8 billion infusion to avoid running out of money. When its charismatic founder Adam Neumann resigned from his position as CEO and Chairman of the Board, he still walked away from WeWork a billionaire. Softbank took over WeWork in 2019. It remains to be seen whether the company will survive.[179]

178 *The Guardian, 2003.* BBC, 18 December 2008. Comlay - Stempel, 2009. *Radiocor*, 2019. Gumbel, 2004. In *Guth v. Loft* duty of care and duty of loyalty were discussed as follows (at 510): "Conflicting interest transactions occur when a director, who has a conflicting interest with respect to a transaction, knows that she or a related person is (1) a party to the transaction; (2) has a beneficial financial interest in, or closely linked to, the transaction that the interest would reasonably be expected to influence the director's judgment if she were to vote on the transaction; or (3) is a director, general partner, agent, or employee of another entity with whom the corporation is transacting business and the transaction is of such importance to the corporation that it would in the normal course of business be brought before the board".

179 *YouTube*, 2019, II.

8. Derivative Action: The Liability of Management Towards Shareholders

According to traditional business law, a company is owned by its shareholders. Shareholders do not typically take part in the daily operations of the company. They appoint directors, who in turn appoint officers or executives to take care of the company's daily operations.[180]

A **shareholder derivative action** refers to a lawsuit which is brought by a shareholder on behalf of a company against a third party. The third party can be, for example, a company insider, such as an executive officer or director. This type of lawsuit is exceptional because generally under traditional business law, it is management who are normally responsible for bringing actions and defending the company against a suit. Shareholder derivative actions permit shareholders to initiate a suit or bring an action against parties who are causing harm to the company.[181]

When shareholders bring an action against a company, this also means that the company's management has failed to do so, i.e. the directors were not willing to file the action. Shareholders might first ask the company to proceed but, if there is no success in the petition, shareholders can bring an action on behalf of the company. This means that the shareholders are acting on behalf of the company and individuals do not stand to gain any benefit when the case is successful. "Appraisal arbitrage" has become one form of shareholder litigation. "Popular among hedge funds seeking to take advantage of favourable case law on valuation, such arbitrageurs buy shares in the target company of a transaction about to close and file suit claiming that the fair value of the company is higher than the ultimate price paid by the acquirer in the acquisition. The financial incentive is cashing in on a higher court-determined price plus default interest at 5% above the Federal Reserve discount rate, compounded quarterly".[182]

> In 2003, it was revealed that the CEO and Chairman of HealthSouth Corporation, Richard Scrushy, had borrowed $25 million from the company, which he used to buy 4,362,297 HealthSouth shares. This was according to the executive equity loan plan which the company's shareholders had approved earlier. This was also possible under the Sarbanes-Oxley Act at that time before amendments were made. According to this plan "HealthSouth could make loans to executive officers in order to help them purchase HealthSouth common stock". Scrushy was later fired due to other problems that arose from financial

180 *Wikimili*, 2019.

181 Erickson, 2008. *Wikipedia*: Derivative Suit.

182 Gerstein, et al., 2015.

misrepresentation. These led to a criminal case against Scrushy and others. In 2002, HealthSouth issued a press release in which the company announced changes in its CMS reimbursement policy. This caused stock prices to plunge. Shareholders launched a derivative action because they felt the company gave shares too generously to Scrushy. Shareholders strongly felt that Scrushy caused the stock price to fall with the accounting scandal and his enrichment was therefore unjust.[183]

In the court case, former HealthSouth executive, CFO Aaron Beam said: "It was so much fun being rich, buying those ties and flying all over the world in our private jets. [...] I should have stood up to Richard and said no. But I stand here before you today telling you that I was a coward. I was intimidated by Richard. I didn't want to be the one to cause his net worth to go down by several hundred million dollars. I knew he had a gun in his briefcase. And, of course, a part of me did not want the party to end. So that night, Bill Owens and I cooked the books."[184]

For a while, HealthSouth's accounting scandal was assumed to be larger than Enron and WorldCom. The gap in reporting and actual financial data was millions of dollars annually. Almost 126,000 fraudulent entries were made. The risk that the top executives took did not pay off. One executive, Weston Smith, who actually blew the whistle when it got out-of-hand was told by Scrushy: "Leading a Fortune 500 company is kind of like leading the Mafia. You don't just walk away." In the end, after many trials, Scrushy was convicted for bribery and mail fraud and sentenced to 82 months in jail, 500 hours of community service, a $150,000 fine and $267,000 in restitution.[185]

8.1. Business Judgment Rule

A **business judgment rule** shows evidence that directors have exercised their fiduciary duty, i.e. their duty to act in good faith and show loyalty and due care for the company when reaching a challenging decision.[186] The business judgment rule summarises moral legitimacy and a company's going concern principle. "In making business decisions not involving direct self-interest or self-dealing, corporate directors act on an informed basis, in good faith, and in the

183 *CourtListener* 2003.

184 *CFO*, 2017.

185 *HealthSouth Corp. Shareholders Litigation. US v. Scrushy. CourtListener*, 2003.

186 See decision: *Cede & Co. v. Technicolor, Inc* from 1993.

honest belief that their actions are in the corporation's best interest."[187] Failing to do so, the Disney decision gave guidance that a plaintiff "is not entitled to any remedy unless the transaction constitutes waste... [that is,] the exchange was so one-sided that no business person of ordinary, sound judgment could conclude that the corporation had received adequate consideration".[188]

The court might not even review the business decisions of directors who performed their duties according to the business judgment rule. The business judgment rule includes a presumption that it releases members of a board of directors from liability for those types of decisions that will result in harm to the company. If a board of directors has taken into account all the information available, they will suffer no legal action just because the decision turns out to be a bad one. The Delaware Supreme Court said: "[a court] will not substitute its own notions of what is or is not sound business judgment" if "the directors of a corporation acted on an informed basis, in good faith and in the honest belief that the action taken was in the best interests of the company."[189]

As part of a director's duty of care, directors cannot "waste corporate assets by overpaying for property or employment services". The business judgment rule is very difficult to surpass. Courts will interfere with directors if it is clear that the directors are guilty of fraud or misappropriation of corporate funds or similar.[190] *Dodge v. Ford Motor Co.*, being one of the earliest cases from 1919, ruled that "courts of equity will not interfere in the management of the directors unless it is clearly made to appear that they are guilty of fraud or misappropriation of the corporate funds, or refuse to declare a dividend when the corporation has a surplus of net profits which it can, without detriment to its business, divide among its stockholders, and when a refusal to do so would amount to such an abuse of discretion as would constitute a fraud, or breach of that good faith which they are bound to exercise towards the stockholders."[191]

The decision in *Grobow v. Perot* (1988) offers guidance on the actions of business directors. These actions include acting in good faith and in the best interests of the company, acting on an informed basis, not being wasteful, or involving self-interest. The last refers to the duty of loyalty.[192]

The merger of Waste Management and Wheelabrator Technologies (WTI) led to a lawsuit in 1995. The shareholders claimed that WTI's

187 *Black's Law Dictionary*, 2001.

188 *The Walt Disney Co. Derivative Litigation*, 2006. B*ristol & West Building Society v. Mothew* (1998) handled fiduciary duty and loyalty.

189 *Sinclair Oil Corp. v. Levien*, 1971. See also: *Kaplan v. Centex Corp.*, 1971 and Robinson v. *Pittsburgh Oil Refinery Corp.*, 1926.

190 See *Aronson v. Lewis*, 1984, *Puma v. Marriott*, 1971.

191 *Dodge v. Ford Motor Co.*, 1919.

192 *Grobow v. Perot* 539 A.2d 180, Delaware 1988.

board of directors did not meet their fiduciary duty. Shareholders were of the opinion that WTI breached its duty of loyalty and duty to disclose relevant information because the merger process happened too quickly and without decent preparation or looking for an alternative, and WTI did not appoint a committee of independent directors to negotiate about the merger. The Court of Chancery of Delaware dismissed the claim that concerned the duty to disclose and disagreed with both the company's board and shareholders regarding the duty of loyalty. It was the court's opinion that the merger was an interested transaction and not a controlled shareholder transaction, and therefore the business judgment rule applied. The burden of proof was on the shareholders.[193]

8.2. Derivative Actions in Countries

Derivative actions in countries means that any shareholder is permitted to bring an action in the name of the company against parties that cause harm to it. In Europe, derivative actions are rare. Derivative actions or lawsuits are more common in the US, the UK, New Zealand and India. In most jurisdictions, a shareholder cannot simply proceed without going through certain checks first. Certain qualifications, such as a minimum value of shares or the length of time holding those shares might be of importance.

In the **US**, corporate law is based on state law. However, each state has different laws. States where most corporations are incorporated have several barriers to derivative actions. These states are, for example, Delaware, New York, California, and Nevada. Why is this? The procedure for derivative actions according to the American Bar Association and according to the states is as follows: "First, eligible shareholders must file a demand to the board. The board may either reject, accept, or not act upon the demand. If after a period of time, the demand has been rejected or has not been acted upon, shareholders may file suit. If the board accepts the demand, the corporation itself will file the suit. If [the demand is] rejected, or not acted upon, the shareholder must meet additional pleading requirements. On the requirements being met by the shareholder, the board may appoint a 'special litigation committee' which may move to dismiss. If the special litigation committee makes a required showing, the case will be dismissed. If the committee fails to make a showing, the shareholder suit may proceed."[194] How the model is followed varies among the states. For example, in New York, a derivative action "must be brought to secure a judgment in [the corporation's] favor."[195] Delaware has again different rules, such as the demand requirements.

193 *CourtListener*, 1995. CNN, 2001.

194 Model Business Corporation Act (MBCA) § 7.42–7.44. See also *Wikipedia*: derivative suit, note 2.

195 See the judgment in *Eisenberg v. Flying Tiger Line, Inc.*

> One famous US corporate law case from 1977 is *Shaffer & co v. Heitner*. It started with a shareholder derivative action against Greyhound Lines Corporation's 28 directors and officers. Most of the directors and officers resided outside Delaware although Greyhound Corporation was a Delaware company. The case ultimately reached the United States Supreme Court. Supreme Court ruled that: "the mere ownership of property in a state is not a sufficient contact to subject the property owner to a lawsuit in that state, unless that property is the subject of the lawsuit."[196] This case overturned the previous ruling in *Harris v. Balk* (1905).

In the **UK**, the Companies Act 2006 did not reformulate the rule that was established in *Foss v. Harbottle* in 1843.[197] In the decision "an action brought by a minority shareholder may not be upheld under the doctrine[..] Exceptions to the doctrine involve exceeding one's authority and a 'fraud on the minority'." The purpose of the action is to protect the company. "Creditors, rather than shareholders, may bring an action if a corporation faces insolvency. [...] In England and Wales, the procedure slightly modified the pre-existing rules, and provided for a new preliminary stage at which case is accepted until proved otherwise. In Scotland, where there had been no clear rules on shareholder actions on behalf of the company, the Act sought to achieve a result similar to that in England and Wales."[198]

> The Supreme Court case from 2010 Roberts v. Gill & Co Solicitors dealt with a derivative action. Roberts, being the beneficiary of certain real estate, wanted to bring a derivative action against a third party. According to the court, as there were no certain special circumstances, Roberts was not entitled to bring a derivative action.199

Derivative actions do not normally take place in **Europe**, probably because the laws in Europe prevent small shareholders from bringing lawsuits. These company acts legally require a minimum share to bring a derivative action. "Larger shareholders could bring lawsuits; however, their incentives are rather to settle the claims with the management, sometimes to the detriment of the small shareholders."[200]

In the **New Zealand** Companies Act 1993, a derivative action is possible under section 165 with the leave of the court. The benefits for the company

196 *Shaffer v. Heitner*, 1977.
197 See the explanatory notes on the UK Companies Act 2006, e.g., on page 74.
198 *Wikipedia*: derivative Suit, note 7.
199 *Roberts (FC) v. Gill & Co Solicitors and others*, 2010
200 *Wikipedia*: derivative suit. Grechenig – Sekyra, 2011, 16–20. Gelter, 2012.

must outweigh the costs of acting. Moreover, the action needs to be in the best interests of the company.

In **India**, oppression and mismanagement can lead to derivative actions, but this is rare. There are clauses for these types of issues as well.[201]

9. Effects Doctrine in International Law

The **effects doctrine**[202] or extraterritoriality is a principle of antitrust and competition law. It started in the US but is now an internationally recognised legal concept. It concerns international legal relations, that is to say, (i) which court can take a case and (ii) which state law applies when there are intersections across many states. Domestically, whichever country is in question, national competition laws are applicable to foreign companies. Notably, the nationality of the companies is irrelevant. The effects doctrine covers all companies. Under normal circumstances, the damage is governed by the law of the foreign country where the damage was caused by the foreign company, unless otherwise agreed.[203][204] The effects doctrine may cause international tensions, and sometimes it is even considered as blocking legislation.[205]

201 Varottil, 2012.

202 *Grant – Barker, 2009:* "a concept relating to the exercise of jurisdiction developed first in US antitrust law whereby a State claims jurisdiction over a non-national for activities outside its territory".

203 Rome II, Article 16.

204 The principle of *ordre public* is a general principle of private international law that states that the basis of the legal order, namely the most fundamental values and fundamental principles contained in the legal order, must be protected from the effects of foreign law. *Ordre Public* means that the court may decide to disregard the law of a particular state where those provisions are incompatible with local law.

205 Milton Keynes, 2020. Michaela, 2015. Currie, 2008. "Where an anti-competitive agreement or activity outside a jurisdiction (i.e., the United States or EU) has an effect inside the jurisdiction, its authorities can take action against extraterritorial offenders and in some instances parties that suffered losses can also bring suit. The effects doctrine was broadly deplored outside the United States, where it originated, especially by politicians in Europe, where many countries enacted blocking statutes to limit its impact [...] The effects doctrine is, for example, used to enable U.S. authorities to review the merger of two non-U.S. companies, or the EU to review the merger of two U.S.-based companies, where there is substantial competitive impact in the EU or vice versa. Since a merger of two ostensibly foreign entities may have a more substantial anti-competitive impact in economies and countries other than their home jurisdictions, the effects doctrine, under whatever name it is described, is of considerable importance in many states' competitions law." *Technology and IP Law Glossary*, 2013.

> The case *Gencor Ltd v. Commission* in 1999 involved the positive acknowledgement of the effects doctrine. The case was about merger regulation where companies outside the EU's territory sent an application for a merger. The Court of First Instance said that the merger was "justified under public international law when it is foreseeable that a proposed concentration will have an immediate and substantial effect in the Community".[206]

The Brussels I regulation applies to EU-wide issues.[207] A judgment given in one EU country must be recognised in another EU country under the Brussels I regulation. This does not apply when the recognition of a judgment concerns a dispute. The judgment given at the end of the dispute must be enforced. The regulation is not appropriate for tax matters or administrative matters, nor for matters involving bankruptcy, arbitration and the legal status or legal capacity of a natural person.

9.1. Classic Swiss Watchmakers Case

United States v. Watchmakers of Switzerland Information Center, Inc.[208] involved the effects doctrine and its reach. It dealt with the scope and interpretation of the laws of two countries. All of the defendants in the case were from the United States and Switzerland. This case clarified the way in which the implementation of US law could be extended to international matters.[209] The result of the case was influenced by the Geneva Convention 1931. This convention intended to sustain and increase the dominance of Swiss watch manufacturers and their US subsidiaries in the world market.[210] Swiss watch manufacturers promised to produce Swiss watches only in Switzerland. This also meant, in practice, that none of the machines used for watch production could, for example, be sent outside Switzerland. In addition, the sale and export of watches outside Switzerland were strictly regulated. Based on the convention, Swiss watch manufacturers justified several times in the US Court of Justice their reason for not selling watches, spare parts or watch-making machines to US watch manufacturers.

The District Court stated that the Court of Justice had legal jurisdiction to deal with the issue as Switzerland's restrictions on US imports had a real, substantial and material impact on US trade. The Court of Justice decided to

206 *Gencor Ltd v. Commission* 1999, paragraphs 89–92.

207 European Community (EC) regulation no 44/2001.

208 *United States v. Watchmakers of Switzerland Info. Center, Inc.*

209 Gilioli, 1981, 481–482. Generally, there are more defendants from different countries than in this case.

210 *UN Convention. United Nations Treaty Collection*, 1931.

settle the case so that the Swiss Government had only supported the operation of the watch manufacturers and did not obligate it to do so. The court concluded that the convention provided for in 1931 does not have a foreign binding interface, nor exclusivity to decide on actions made. The US court therefore decided on the content of the foreign law.[211] The European Court of Justice decided in 2017 that Swiss watchmakers could proceed with their own repair system if it was qualitative enough. There was no need to use independent watchmakers with spare parts for Swiss luxury watches. In the long run, this means there will be fewer counterfeits of Swiss luxury watches.[212]

10. Transborder Crime in International Law

International law is also known as public international law and the law of nations, and it differs from state-based legal systems[213]. These normative guidelines consist of a common framework for issues like war, diplomacy, trade and human rights.

International law aims to give stability and consistency to international relations.[214] A set of rules refers to sources of international law, which are, for example, international custom, international comity[215] and different types of treaties. Moreover, it includes general principles of law, which are recognised by most national legal systems. All in all, we can conclude that international law, rules, norms and standards are applicable (not exclusively but primarily) to countries. It does not relate so directly to individuals.

The nature of international law is based largely on consent as no universally accepted authority and therefore it is not possible to enforce international law upon sovereign states by some external body. In this respect, not being a party to international law means that a state may even break a treaty or choose not to abide by it. However, violating customary international law and peremptory norms, i.e. committing crimes against humanity or human trafficking, might

211 "[n]ot only does the present action constitute a direct attack upon the legislation and policy of the Swiss Confederation; it further seeks to regulate conditions in Switzerland and to limit the control which the Swiss Confederation may exercise over its own watch industry. Surely, the anti-trust laws should not be applied in such a way and these laws cannot be so applied. It has always been held that the anti-trust laws do not apply to acts done in the territory of a foreign sovereign in furtherance of that sovereign's law and policy ...." Gilioli, 1981, 481–482.

212 Judgement of General Court (Second Chamber), Case T-712/14, 23 October 2017.

213 *Benton Foundation*, 2010.

214 *Farlex*; international law. Bentham, 1921, 6. Slomanson, 2011, 4–5.

215 International comity means that states have adopted certain practices to maintain good relations and mutual recognition. These include, for example, enforcing a foreign judgment.

lead to diplomatic or economic pressure and, in the worst instance, even to military intervention.[216]

As we know, states are equal and sovereign, but this is based on theory. UN Charter Article 2 (1)[217] confirms the sovereignty of nations: "If legislation is the making of laws by a person or assembly binding on the whole community, there is no such thing as international law. For treaties bind only those who sign them. The statement "[n]o state is in subjection to any other state" means that international law's relationship and interaction with national legal systems (municipal law) is variable and complex in nature.

"National law may become international law in situations where treaties such as the Geneva Convention permit national jurisdiction to supranational tribunals". These supranational tribunals can be, for example, the European Court of Human Rights or the International Criminal Court. Treaties "may require national law to conform to treaty provisions. National law or constitutions may also provide for the implementation or integration of international legal obligations into domestic law."[218]

International law is therefore dependent on the voluntary participation of sovereign states. These states formulate, participate in, observe and enforce

216 Slomanson, 2011, 4. This is called *jus cogens*. *Jus cogens* is referred to in Article 53 of the Vienna Convention on the Law of Treaties (VCLT): "[A] treaty is void if, at the time of its conclusion, it conflicts with a peremptory norm of general international law." For further reading on *jus cogens*: 1) Hossain, 2005. 2) Gastorn, 2017, 643-662 and 3) Petsche, 2010. Some lawyers (especially Roman lawyers) distinguish the law of nations, and agreements between nations. Using the view of public international law, it "covers relations between nation-states and includes fields such as treaty law, law of sea, international criminal law, the laws of war or international humanitarian law, international human rights law, and refugee law". By contrast, **private** international law "concerns whether courts within countries claim jurisdiction over cases with a foreign element, and which country's law applies." See: *Oas.org*, 2009. In the legal texts, the term "supranational law" is also used. The term refers to "regional agreements where the laws of nation states may be held inapplicable when conflicting with a supranational legal system to which the nation has a treaty obligation. Systems of supranational law arise when nations explicitly cede their right to make certain judicial decisions to a common tribunal. The decisions of the common tribunal are directly effective in each party nation and have priority over decisions made by national courts. The European Union is the most prominent example of an international treaty organization that implements a supranational legal framework with the European Court of Justice having supremacy over all member-nation courts in matters of European Union law. The term "transnational law" is sometimes used to describe a body of rules that transcend the nation state." These norms are referred to with Latin words *jus gentium and jus inter gentes*. Kolcak, 2014. Degan, 1997, 126. Blanpain, 2010, 410. Cotterrell, 2012, 500–524.

217 The Charter of the United Nations (UN Charter) of 1945 is the foundational treaty of the United Nations. There are several international organisations in addition to the United Nations. These are the World Trade Organization, the International Labour Organization, NATO, the European Union, G7 and G20, OPEC, the Organization of Islamic Cooperation, the Food and Agriculture Organization and the World Health Organization.

218 *Wikipedia*: International law. International law is divided into public and private international law.

international law. International academics have found one factor common to all the states voluntarily taking part in international law: it enlightens those states' own self-interest. Little emphasis is put on a body of law that would be higher than a state's own law. D.W. Grieg said, "international law cannot exist in isolation from the political factors operating in the sphere of international relations".[219]

> According to the Vienna Convention on the Law of Treaties "treaty" means an international agreement concluded between States in written form and governed by international law, whether embodied in a single instrument or in two or more related instruments and whatever its particular designation"[220]

There has been a lot of debate in academia, diplomacy and politics about the conflict between international law and national sovereignty. The growing trend is "towards judging a state's domestic actions in the light of international law and standards." A common view now is that the nation-state is the primary unit of international affairs and it is believed that only states may choose to voluntarily enter into commitments under international law, and that they have the right to follow their own counsel when it comes to the interpretation of their commitments.[221]

Some countries, such as India, Israel and the US, have taken a flexible and pragmatic approach to international law. This means that these countries use territorial rights universally, but in other aspects arising from treaty or custom, they might not be subject to international law at all. Also, developing countries insist on non-interference in their internal affairs (one being the standard of human rights). Developing countries support international law at bilateral and multilateral levels—for example, in the use of force, disarmament obligations and the terms of the UN Charter.[222]

> The Certain Iranian Assets (Iran v. US) case in 2019 concerned the violation of the Treaty of Amity, Economic Relations and Consular Rights. In this case, Iran tried to unfreeze and return almost $2 billion

219 Greig, 1976.

220 Vienna Convention on the Law of Treaties (VCLT), 1969, Article 2, 1(a). VCLT is an international agreement regulating treaties between states.

221 *Press trust of India*, 2013. Wikipedia: International Law: "Certain scholars and political leaders feel that these modern developments endanger nation states by taking power away from state governments and ceding it to international bodies, such as the UN and the World Bank, argue that international law has evolved to a point where it exists separately from the mere consent of states, and discern a legislative and judicial process to international law that parallels such processes within domestic law. This especially occurs when states violate or deviate from the expected standards of conduct adhered to by all civilized nations."

222 Greig, 1976.

which were held on US territory. The International Court of Justice rejected one, upheld a second and postponed a third of the objections presented by the US. The International Court of Justice agreed to a submission of a Reply brief by Iran and US Rejoinder in August 2020 and May 2021.[223]

***

The Democratic Republic of the Congo (DRC) instituted proceedings against Belgium in a case which concerned an international arrest warrant issued by a Belgian examining judge against the DRC's acting Minister for Foreign Affairs in 2000.[224]

***

The case concerning the United States Diplomatic and Consular Staff in Tehran in 1980 was widely covered. US diplomatic employees were seized by militant revolutionaries. The US brought the case before the International Court of Justice due to the Iran hostage crisis. [225]

International law can only go so far as it needs bodies created by treaties adjudicating on legal issues. Over time, numerous international bodies have been created, but only one of them, the UN Security Council, claims universal jurisdiction. Other bodies include, for example, the UN International Court of Justice and the Court of Arbitration for Sport. If a national system totally fails, cases are handled in the International Criminal Court.[226]

South American countries have built their own union. It aims to replicate the framework set by the EU with its own passport, currency and limited barriers to trade.[227] Kenya, Tanzania, Uganda, Burundi and Rwanda tried to form their own East African Community with its own supranational legal and political federation. This attempt failed.[228] Conversely, South American countries in the Andes Mountain range (consisting of Bolivia, Colombia, Ecuador and Peru) built their own Andean Community of Nations. These

223 International Court of Justice, 2019.

224 *Democratic Republic of the Congo v. Belgium*, 2000.

225 *United States of America v. Iran* - United States Diplomatic and Consular Staff in Tehran - Judgment of 24 May 1980.

226 See the UN website for more information.

227 *Wikipedia*: Union of South American Nations.

228 *Wikipedia*: East African Community.

countries follow supranational laws or, as they call them, "agreements", which are mandatory for all these countries. [229]

10.1. Transborder Crime and Competent Authorities in Transborder Crime

Crimes against one state affect the interests of another state or its administration. This means states may exercise jurisdiction over crimes committed by or against their own citizens outside state borders. This type of case might come up if a state wishes to prosecute its own citizens and the acts and omissions have taken place in another state. The citizen may also act in a way which interferes with friendly relations between two states. This citizen might be prosecuted even if there would not be any real actions taken or committed. Crimes that take place on ships or on aircraft operated by a company with a certain home country, can involve transborder (or transnational) crime and jurisdiction may be claimed. There is no relevancy as to where the craft is located at that certain time.[230]

Ultimately, the motive for transborder crime is almost always monetary and is considered a major threat to human security. Such illicit activities are hazardous to commercial, transport, communications and transnational systems. They affect free trade and the free movement of people. In addition, transborder crime influences governance structures, economic development, security and supply chain integrity. Global criminal activities can transform an international system and create new players, such as cryptocurrency dealers.

One international tool to combat cross-border crime was adopted in 2000: the Palermo Convention231 but there are also other good international normative frameworks for directors to take into account. These are the UN Convention Against Corruption (UNCAC) from 2005, International Standards on Combatting Money Laundering and the Financing of Terrorism and Proliferation.[232]

> Different European countries have different ways of handling civil and criminal matters. In Sweden, the community fine is conditional on the conduct of a criminal offence, which is punishable by a more stringent penalty. Therefore, Sweden was able to initiate a preliminary

229 *Wikipedia*: Andean Community.

230 Doyle, 2013, 1.

231 Palermo Convention or Palermo Protocol is a treaty intended to combat transnational, organisational crime. The treaty was published in six languages and has 190 parties. The Palermo Protocol is the first instrument which was globally binding.

232 UN Convention against Transnational Organized Crime 2003. Safjanski, 2017. See also United Nations Organized crime, organized responses – countering cross-border crime, 2011 and United Nations, 2016: Combating transnational crime.

investigation in 2010 against Lund's Petroleum Company. It examined whether the company committed crimes against humanity in Sudan.[233]

***

A company director (in this case defendant) may write or speak in State X, and the effects of these actions are felt in State Y. This system works well when there is a clear line of demarcation between the two state jurisdictions, or between a state and federal jurisdiction, and prosecutions may be initiated in the appropriate court. However, laws and rules are not always so clear.

In the United States, the US Constitution prevails. Since the US is a federation of states, the Constitution has general powers over the territory of the whole country and over foreign policy. It is considered as a federal government and legislature in this sense. Individual states have their own governments and local territorial jurisdictions. These are within the scope allowed by the federal constitution. The United States district courts have original, exclusive subject matter jurisdiction over the offenses that are against the laws of the United States.[234]

Federal courts investigate charges alleging federal crimes, and state courts investigate charges alleging violations of local state law.[235] According to the US Constitution, the power of the Congress is limited in enacting criminal statutes, as the federal government does not have "plenary criminal jurisdiction."[236] The Congress does not have boundless power to enact criminal laws. The US Constitution has explicit authority over Congress in three areas: (1) counterfeiting, (2) piracy and felony on the high seas and offenses against the law of nations, and (3) treason.[237] The necessary clause of the Constitution gives Congress power to enact useful or conductive laws.[238]

> "The scene of the crime ... must be determined from the nature of the crime alleged and the location of the act or acts constituting it."[239]

Certain crimes, such as those committed in the District of Columbia, in US Territories or abroad on airplanes or ships, are related to areas owned by or

233 Swedish National Council for Crime Prevention. Milne, 2018. *TMC Asser Instituut*, 2019.
234 18 USC, § 3231.
235 Maier, 2010.
236 Code, 1972, 1209-1242.
237 Doyle, 2013, 1.
238 Doyle, 2013, 2.
239 *United States v. Anderson.*

under the exclusive jurisdiction of the federal government. As the US military has its own criminal justice system for its members, any civilian "can be charged with a federal crime for acts committed on military bases". Federal courts also investigate cases against US citizens if illegal activity has taken place in another country. The Federal Rules of Criminal Procedure, Rule 18, specifies that:

> "Unless a statute or these rules permit otherwise, the government must prosecute an offense in a district where the offense was committed. The court must set the place of trial within the district with due regard for the convenience of the defendant and the witnesses, and the prompt administration of justice."

The 7th framework of the European Convention on Human Rights Article 4(1) of the Additional Protocol and Article 11 of Chapter 1 of the Penal Code define double criminality as follows:[240]

> "No one may, under the jurisdiction of the same State, re-examine or punish in criminal proceedings for an offence for which he or she has already been definitively acquitted or convicted in accordance with the laws and judicial proceedings of that State."

Parallel proceedings present a certain problem. The term refers to the "simultaneous or successive investigation or litigation of separate criminal, civil or administrative proceedings." These are usually "commenced by different agencies, different branches of government or private litigants arising out of a common set of facts."[241] This may be an obstacle to the applicability of criminal law in labour and environmental crime. For example, in the case of a human rights infringement, it can be difficult or even impossible to gather evidence. Moreover, it may take time to gather the evidence, which in turn may lead to the case becoming obsolete and never brought before a court. In civil matters, evidence should be collected within three years of the loss. The scope of jurisdiction outside country X (e.g. in Africa) may even affect the fairness of the trial. The OECD guidelines for businesses, which are important to the legal regulation of the country of destination, are discussed later in this book. If the law of the place where the offence took place does not mention these, the parent company might not be convicted of this type of offence committed abroad.

Dispute settlements have become complex due the rise of investment agreements. This means that the cases encompass multiple contracts and concern multiple parties and issues. Where can parallel proceedings then

240 The principle of double criminality precludes the initiation of new proceedings after the first proceedings have become final.

241 For further reading Weismann, 2011.

occur—e.g. in investment arbitration? Parallel proceedings may cause inconsistent and conflicting decisions. This is because domestic courts and arbitration tribunals might interpret the case differently. Do the principles where the matter cannot be raised again in the same of different court (*res judicata*) and pending lawsuits (*lis pendens*) apply in investment arbitration and could they prevent conflicting awards? Yannaca-Small says: "Investment treaties regulate and prevent the occurrence of parallel proceedings, with a particular emphasis on the consolidation of claims."[242]

With parallel proceedings it is possible to have a formal procedure in another court, tribunal or complaint mechanism which deals with the same issue and happens at the same time as the national process.[243] The OECD Guidelines' Procedural Guidance states in paragraph 26 that National Contact Points (NCPs) should not reject a case simply because parallel proceedings are underway[244].

In other words, NCPs should reject a claim which is a portion of a whole complaint if "it considers it would seriously prejudice the parallel proceeding. NCPs can and should accept all claims within a complaint that can be reviewed without causing serious prejudice to the parallel proceeding".[245]

10.2. Transborder crime examples

An interesting transborder crime took place in 1952 and concerned the Anglo-Iranian Oil Company (AIOC), which was nationalised. The company is known today as British Petroleum (BP).[246] In the case, the International Court of Justice could not investigate an alleged breach of contract concerning a private company and a state because it was outside the court's jurisdiction. The dispute concerned public international law between the UK and Iran.

242 Yannaca-Small, 2008. *Res judicata* means a matter that was adjudicated on by a competent court. It cannot be handled anymore by the same parties involved. *Lis pendens* means pending legal action.

243 *OECD Watch*: Parallel Proceedings.

244 *OECD Watch*: "When assessing the significance for the specific instance procedure of other domestic or international proceedings addressing similar issues in parallel, NCPs should not decide that issues do not merit further consideration solely because parallel proceedings have been conducted, are under way or are available to the parties concerned. NCPs should evaluate whether an offer of good offices could make a positive contribution to the resolution of the issues raised and would not create serious prejudice for either of the parties involved in these other proceedings or cause a contempt of court situation. In making such an evaluation, NCPs could take into account practice among other NCPs and, where appropriate, consult with the institutions in which the parallel proceeding is being or could be conducted. Parties should also assist NCPs in their consideration of these matters by providing relevant information on the parallel proceedings."

245 *OECD Watch*: Parallel Proceedings

246 The *United Kingdom v. Iran*, 1952 is also known as the *Anglo-Iranian Oil Co. case.*

"The court accepted the Iranian argument that the dispute was between the Iranian government and a foreign corporation, not the British government, since the dispute was not about a treaty or convention with a foreign government, it was subject to Iranian domestic law".[247]

***

In a similar case in 2003, which involved oil platforms between Iran and the US, the International Court of Justice rejected the dispute. The case concerned damage to ships hit by a mine.[248]

The world's first simultaneous settlement with four national authorities took place in an Airbus case in January 2020 regarding investigations into bribery, corruption as well as inaccurate and misleading filings (filings only concerning the Department of Justice and the Department of State, i.e. DoS and DoJ investigations). The case from August 2016 began when the Serious Fraud Office (SFO) announced it had started investigations into "Airbus SE, a company registered in the Netherlands and domiciled in France and the Netherlands." This investigation had international features since the French and US authorities were involved. The case was about potential "bribery and corruption offences in a large number of jurisdictions. The particular investigation of the Serious Fraud Office concerned bribery offences in Malaysia, Sri Lanka, Taiwan, Indonesia and Ghana".[249] Paragraphs 5 and 38 of the judgment stated the following:

"The SFO's investigation demonstrated that in order to increase sales, persons who performed services for and on behalf of Airbus offered, promised or gave financial advantages to others intending to obtain or retain business, or an advantage in the conduct of business, or Airbus SE". (5)

"In brief, persons associated with Airbus, not exclusively its employees, offered very substantial sums of money by way of bribes to third parties in order to secure the purchase of aircraft, by civil airline companies, ... and by the Government of Ghana ...". (38)

In the concluding remarks the judge said that the Deferred Prosecution Agreement (DPA) "requires Airbus to pay a significant financial

247 Kazemi, 1985, 61-65.

248 *Islamic Republic of Iran v. United States of America* - Oil Platforms, 2003.

249 *McNair Chambers*, 2020, II.

> penalty, thereby sending an important deterrent message to corporate wrongdoers. It also recognizes and rewards what Airbus has now done to address the problem by discounting that financial penalty by 50 percent. The DPA has, in addition, given Airbus the opportunity to demonstrate its corporate rehabilitation and commitment to effective compliance over the period of the DPA, without facing the potential consequences of a criminal conviction. This ensures a major UK employer continues to operate according to high ethical and compliance standards. By entering into the DPA, the SFO avoids the significant expenditure in time and money inherent in any prosecution of Airbus, and it can use its limited resources in other important work. The DPA is likely to provide an incentive for the exposure and self-reporting of organizations in similar situations to Airbus. As the SFO submits, this is of vital importance in the context of complex corporate crime".[250]

According to the Global Settlement Agreement, Airbus paid penalties of roughly €3.6 billion with added interest and costs to the French, UK and US authorities. Doing so, the company avoided criminal prosecution by the French Parquet National Financier (PNF), UK Serious Fraud Office (SFO), US Department of Justice (DoJ) and US Department of State (DOS). PNF got €2,083 million, SFO €984 million, DOJ €526 million and DOS €9 million, "of which €4.5 million may be used for approved remediation and compliance measures". The settlement was part of the Convention Judiciaire d'Intérêt Public (CJIP), Deferred Prosecution Agreement (DPA), and Consent Order.[251]

After the judgment, Denis Ranque, Chairman of the Board of Directors of Airbus, commented:

> "The settlements we have reached today turn the page on unacceptable business practices from the past. The strengthening of our compliance programmes at Airbus is designed to ensure that such misconduct cannot happen again. The agreements also reflect that the decision to voluntarily report and cooperate with the authorities was the right one. The commitment from the Board, and its Ethics and Compliance Committee, to provide full support to the investigation and the implementation of globally recognized compliance standards have paved the way to today's agreements."[252]

250 *McNair Chambers*, 2020, II.

251 By a decision handed down on 31 January 2020 in *Director of the Serious Fraud Office v. Airbus SE, Dame Victoria Sharp* (as President of the Queen's Bench Division of the English High Court) ("the Judge") gave judgment approving a Deferred Prosecution Agreement ("DPA") entered into between the Serious Fraud Office and Airbus SE. This was the seventh such DPA that the Serious Fraud Office had entered by that time. Airbus Press Release, 2020.

252 *Airbus Press Release,* 2020.

Part III Conclusions of Rules of Regulations of International Law

The principles of international law that govern questions of jurisdiction are complex and at times controversial in their application. These principles have evolved and been adapted to suit a world in which individuals and companies increasingly act and cause effects across state borders.

Through its top management, a company ensures a high level of integrity and ethical behaviour. Integrity is crucial when employees are chosen, and this also (especially) includes board members. In every decision-making process, a code of conduct is important. A lot of attention needs to put into the question of what the ethical and responsible decision-making process in the company should be. This means that the best person should always be hired for a position. Personnel should be exactly right from the company's perspective. There should also be transparency. This means that the information the organisation gives out should be timely and balanced, clear and factual.

Corporate governance aims to meet the rights of organisations' shareholders. Overall, organisations have four obligations: legal, contractual, social and market drive. In addition, corporate governance helps them exercise these rights, i.e. to communicate them effectively. Companies should also recognise their obligations towards other stakeholders—employees, investors, creditors, suppliers, customers, policy makers and communities. The board's role and responsibility are critically reviewed, especially the operations in which a company is involved.

PART IV

White-Collar Business Crime in Practice

This Part IV is the largest part of this book due to the significance the white-collar business crime cases have worldwide. Especially in this Part IV we will clearly see the double standards when it comes to dealing with business crime. This Part includes white-collar business crime issues in employment law, espionage, competition law, securities markets, tax law, embargoes and IPRs. Corruption, bribery, embezzlement, fraud, and extortion as well as money laundering, fake food industry and environmental business crimes along with previously mentioned business crime types constitutes by far the biggest losses for companies monetarily. The losses influence the companies but also on the individuals behind the white-collar business crimes cases. In the big picture, the losses affect countries economically e.g. in the form of lost tax money. The Part IV is important since directors should know these topics in their day-to-day decision-making processes. Directors cannot be the masters of everything, but they should be at least aware of these issues on a general level. One warning sign inside the companies has been aggressive sales targets with high bonuses. That has in most cases led to wrong path. In short, a general level understanding of the white-collar business crime practical matters is essential for business leaders. Why? Because by understanding the issues business leader can then monitor issues better in the organizations.

11. Business Crime in Employment Law

"PEOPLE WANT TO ENJOY FAIR AND HONEST TREATMENT, AND HAVE THEIR WORK APPRECIATED."[253]

White-collar crime in employment covers executives who, for example, do not respect human rights or commit any form of harassment or bullying. Discrimination and not respecting a company's safety and health requirements are also considered employment business crimes. In this chapter, issues of corporate espionage are also covered. Employment business crime can cause serious risks and liabilities for a company. Even more, white-collar crime in employment impacts a company's reputation and brand in the long run. In turn, this might alienate some employees, investors and shareholders. Before this happens, a CEO might carry the heaviest risk first, as was the case with McDonald's.[254]

> McDonald's CEO Steve Easterbrook had to resign in 2019 due to unethical behavior in the workplace.[255]

Employment business crime can include, for example, touching, inappropriate or offensive comments or the like, in the workplace. This might also occur by, for example, treating employees differently based on their religion or age. Treating employees differently based on their gender, sexual orientation or ethnicity is considered offensive and prohibited. Discrimination always has an impact on an employee if the discrimination used makes person discriminated against feel they are excluded from the group.[256]

> In 2020, Michael O'Leary, CEO Ryanair, was in the headlines because he wanted stricter security checks for Muslims. This was taken as a racist and discriminatory comment. And it was not the first time the CEO had been in the headlines. On a previous occasion, O'Leary had criticised overweight passengers, comparing them with monsters.[257]

Companies should provide a place that is free from discrimination, bullying and harassment. In the cases of discriminatory behaviour, companies should intervene immediately. One form of bullying is withholding information. When an employee feels they cannot use their strengths or talents, it impacts

253 Blanchard – Johnson, 1982, 8.
254 Gilbert, 2018. *Worksafe*, 2013.
255 Shiff, 2019.
256 Gilbert, 2018. *Worksafe* 2013.
257 Ellery – Ford – Thomson, 2020. Harper, 2020.

the contribution the employee can make. In the long run, it also decreases the company's morale. Bullying might also continue after the person has left the workplace. Rumours about ex-workers might severely harm their career when a false rumour becomes a prevailing truth.[258]

In 2021, the concept of wellbeing washing was introduced in a blog on the Hintsa Performance website. According to Nora Rosendahl, wellbeing washing consists of seven sins: 1) superficiality – meaning a company offers yoga classes and stand-up desks, but are they relevant if you stand up for 70 hours a week?; 2) just talk – gestures of fancy talk by experts who are rolled into an organisation to talk about wellbeing, but what happens if the employees are already burnt out or close to it?; 3) first-mover bias – accommodating the needs of the healthiest individuals in the organisation (e.g. with an in-house gym and sports activities), but what if people don't have any desire for those?; 4) shifting responsibility – highlighting the responsibility of the individual instead of the organisation; 5) misleading measurement – the workplace might be using the wrong measurement and does not understand why people are leaving; 6) one size fits all – the company finds a wellbeing service that employees use but they do not need; 7) neglecting wellbeing culture – a long-term commitment by the training company leads first.[259]

Companies should take health and safety seriously. Also, employees should seek to minimise all illnesses and take safety issues seriously. Safety should never be compromised. Therefore, compliance with all applicable laws and regulations is important.[260] The COVID-19 pandemic demonstrated precisely how important health and safety regulations are in the workplace.

In working life, employees change companies often[261], typically as a result of short-term or fixed employment contracts as well as lay-offs or resignations. The greater the rotation of people, the greater the risk there is of sharing a company's confidential information. For unfaithful employees, this offers quick wins.

Information is power. It can be borrowed, shared, loaned, given and even stolen. Theft has become ubiquitous mostly due to the internet, which in turn means that a good information security system is a must for all companies.

> In 2013, Yahoo's three billion accounts were exposed and leaked. In the same year, over 150 million Adobe accounts were breached. In 2019, the information of Alibaba's 1.9 billion users was stolen. In 2021, 700 million LinkedIn user accounts were in jeopardy. LinkedIn saw the leak on a dark web platform.[262]

258 *Worksafe*, 2017. *Worksafe*, 2013.

259 Rosendahl, 2021.

260 Gilbert, 2018. *Worksafe*, 2013.

261 It goes without saying, this is country specific. In the US, people change jobs more often than in Japan. In Finland, people would change jobs more often if there were open positions.

262 Hill – Swinhow, 2021.

Surprisingly, the biggest threat to information security is a company's own personnel, especially those who have access to confidential information of any kind. Employees may also bring confidential information from one company to another to make their own work easier. They might not realise that this information is intellectual property that belongs to their former company.

> Journalism in Germany was shaken in late 2018 when *Der Spiegel*, regarded as one of the country's most respected magazines, faced a fake news scandal. One of the magazine's award-winning journalists was found to have falsified facts and interviewed non-existent people. The scandal was a watershed moment in the 70-year history of *Der Spiegel*.[263]

An internal threat is typically not monitored as well as threats from the outside.[264] One interesting fact is that if an executive asks an employee to act against a company's instructions, the employee is most likely to obey – even if they understand that what they are doing is wrong.[265]

Trust has become a guiding corporate principle – probably now more than ever. It arises from moral and physical behaviour. In the absence of trust, great harm can be done. Leaders with a hidden agenda, might get rid of employees who are considered a threat, just by claiming a lack of trust and not seeing them as crucial to the company's operations. The possible impact to the company is a loss of a valuable human resource and the retention of a bad one. Over the longer term, the biggest loser is the company itself, as its competitiveness fails and competitors gain the upper hand. It is a question of self-awareness: some managers might see themselves as realistic, profit-minded and good corporate citizens, whereas the truth, as witnessed by employees, is something else completely.

Leaders are faced with multiple expectations. They need to communicate accurately to the personnel, media, partners, customers, consumers and other stakeholders. This is a challenge, particularly for those unfamiliar with social media. As brand ambassadors, leaders must be aware of the role of social media in modern business communications.[266]

Since business crime is ubiquitous, all kinds of information security solutions and the creation of a trustworthy cyber environment is a must. Leaders must know the possibilities and threats, and companies must evaluate, measure and interpret their own level of information security.

263 Schultheis, 2019.

264 Lautjärvi, 2018, 59.

265 Kinnunen, 2015, 124–151.

266 Lautjärvi, 2018, 29.

> In autumn 2020, Finland attracted global media attention. Finnish company Vastaamo, which provided psychotherapeutic services, suffered a massive information security breach. Blackmailers got hold of sensitive client information, for which they demanded money in return not to reveal the sensitive information. The case had over 20,000 respondents of an offence reported to the police. What was really surprising was that the CEO of the company, Ville Tapio, already knew about the security breach in 2018. He remained silent for almost two years. When the case came to public attention, he resigned immediately. The case is one of the biggest in Finnish criminal history.[267]

In employment law, effective managers are a must. But what makes effective managers tick? It is arguably their ability to listen. The effective manager's role is to help employees feel good about themselves and produce good results in the long run. Productivity includes quantity and quality.[268]

> As long as leaders produce value, they are largely impossible to stop, even if their behaviour might already seem to be detrimental to the company. This can be seen, for example, in Facebook's leader, Mark Zuckerberg. Zuckerberg was implicated in the Cambridge Analytica scandal in 2018, resulting in him losing over $16 billion dollars in just a few days, and Facebook's market value falling by $120 billion.[269]

***

> If we also look at success stories, one of the greatest success stories of all time is the Starbucks chain. This has much to do with its owner Howard Schultz, who built up the Starbucks brand from being a coffee bean seller to a global empire of 33,833 stores in 80 countries. In 2019, the brand was just behind Coca-Cola and McDonald's in 31st position in terms of value. Nevertheless, the chain has had its ups and downs. Schultz resigned in 2000, but eight years later he came back, dissatisfied with how the chain was operating.[270]

---

267 Kleinman, 2020.

268 Blanchard – Johnson, 1982, 13–21.

269 How much are these actually? Zuckerberg's loss is even more than the combined wealth of all the billionaires in Finland, and Facebook's loss represented the biggest loss in Wall Street history. The Week, 2018. Adams, 2018. These decreases in money value were not the whole story: the Federal Trade Commission also imposed sanctions on the company, amounting to billions of dollars.

270 Howard Schultz: My story, web page. Samia, 2018.

How can a company get rid of a manager who is too dominant? Paul Strebel[271] has some suggestions:

1) Lead yourself. Ideally, a dominant leader recognises themself when it's time to go. Not always, though. Alibaba's Jack Ma said for years he would step down, but he continued until 2019, having started with the company in 1999.
2) Peer group pressure. If the pressure is strong, dominant leaders are most likely to leave by themselves.
3) Revolution. The leadership team might simply displace a dominant leader. Renault-Nissan's revolution was dramatic. CEO Hiroto Saikawa gave a speech at Tokyo's financial centre, knowing that on the same morning key denunciations and revelations would lead to Carlos Ghosn's arrest for financial crimes. Famously, Ghosn fled from Japan and started life in exile in Lebanon. Two special forces soldiers helped Ghosn flee.[272]
4) Shareholders' rebellion. If the leadership team is not unified and if it is unable to displace a dominant leader, shareholders can probably do it. This was the case when Uber's Travis Kalanick was accused many times of harassment and using grey zones in different countries, but all to no effect. Finally, the five biggest shareholders required and demanded his resignation.
5) Company crisis. Without suitable top management or actions to improve it, companies often drift into crisis. This was the case with the largest bank in Switzerland, UBS. The Chairman of the Board, Marcel Ospel, is a very controversial person. He is said to have driven Swissair into bankruptcy for not ensuring enough finance for the company, while he had a huge annual salary of CHF 26 million. Ospel's mismanagement cost USB bank CHF 80 billion.

Holders of a dominant position can be divided into two categories: highly intelligent dominant position holders and gurus. Both personality traits have narcissistic features accompanied by low self-esteem, and they are both prone to self-deception. To everyone else they exhibit great optimism and self-confidence. Renault-Nissan's Carlos Ghosn and JP Morgan's Jamie Dimon are examples of the first group. Ghosn, who promised he would stay for five years in power but ended up leading the company for 20 years. A guru is typically a family patriarch, whose dominant position is feeling-based and who operates

271 Blanding, 2013. Strebel - Blanding, 2013.

272 Kostov – McLain, 2020. Greimel – Sposato, 2021. Basically, Ghosn could have been arrested because he visited Israel when he was CEO. Lebanese citizens cannot enter Israel due to a state of war existing between the countries. Lebanese law considers this a criminal act.

on the basis of what was done in the past. One example of such a guru was Lee Kun-hee (1942–2020), the Samsung family patriarch.

11.1. Human Rights

When world trade was liberated about twenty years ago in the 1990s, companies took the opportunity to produce goods with lower costs in countries where the labour force was cheap. In the US alone, the number of blue-collar workers decreased from 17 million to 5 million in under two decades. Cheaper production in countries abroad was problematic. Workers in most cases did not have any rights, the environment was misused or polluted and licenses were inadequate. This, in turn, affected company image.

Damage to a company's image may happen if it realises that there is child labour or a violation of human rights somewhere in its ecosystem, such as in its subcontracting companies. Profit maximisation has become an obsession, especially for larger corporations. All too often, large organisations strive to polish their brand image but forget to improve the quality of their products.[273] Mergers and acquisitions also provide a loophole for avoiding responsibility in cases of human rights violations.[274]

The Netherlands took a step towards corporate responsibility by enforcing the Dutch Child Labour Due Diligence Act in 2019. The Act was intended to enter into a law on 1 January 2020, but it was postponed[275]. The implementation of Dutch law is based on regulatory control. Anyone can complain about a company to the supervisory authorities by presenting concrete evidence of child labour in the company's value chain.

Upon receipt of a complaint, the supervisory authority will assess whether the company has exercised due diligence and decide on further action. The law now passed is limited to child labour, but several politicians have said it is the first step towards a more comprehensive corporate responsibility law.[276]

In Switzerland, there has been a lot of debate around corporate responsibility. The Responsible Business Initiative was first launched in 2015. Its intention was to oblige companies that operate in Switzerland to exercise due diligence in environmental, human rights matters and business relationships. The new proposal for law would also impose liability for damages. The proposal was also to apply Swiss law in situations where the legislation of other countries

273 Manninen, 2016, 77.

274 Valleala – Letto-Vanamo, 2015, 27. *UN*, 2020. *UNICEF*, 2014. Kippenberg, 2019.

275 As mentioned before, the law is accepted but not enforced in the Netherlands. The Netherlands updated its RBC politics in October 2020. This means the Netherlands will start using other laws if the directive in the EU does not proceed accordingly.

276 Jäppinen, 2019. *Ministry of Economic Affairs and Employment of Finland*, 2020. See also how the Netherlands (2017) clearly described Child Labour and its prevention. Kamerstuk, 2017.

would normally apply. This proposal was rejected, and counterproposals of a different kind have been made in 2018 and 2019.

Along with Switzerland, a lot of debate on corporate social responsibility has also been raised in Germany.[277] Moreover, the German draft law on sustainable value chains was mistakenly leaked in 2019. According to the Finnish Ministry: "the act would apply to large Germany-based companies and companies that operate themselves or through companies that they control in high-risk sectors or conflict regions. The act would also apply to the foreign operations of these companies, but it would not apply to small enterprises ... Administrative fines of up to €5 million could be imposed on a company failing to exercise due diligence. A company receiving fines of at least €250,000 could also be excluded from the award of public contracts".[278]

While Norway proposed legislation on corporate social responsibility and supply chain in late 2019, another Scandinavian country, Denmark, was still debating whether to go forward with the CSR proposal. In Norway, the obligation would depend on the size of the company's operations. Those companies that sell consumer products need to disclose information about their production sites.[279]

On the other hand, in France, the due diligence obligation is enacted and quite clear. "Legal action can be taken against a company that fails to meet its due diligence obligation. The company is given three (3) months to meet its obligation on pain of a fine. Furthermore, a failure to comply with the obligations laid down in the act may result in liability for damages with respect to harm that could have been avoided if the company had fulfilled its statutory requirements. A court may also decide to make its decision public."[280]

Companies are responsible for their adverse human rights impacts. As for subcontracting relationships based on contractual relationships the companies are not legally obliged to ensure that its subcontractors respect human rights.[281]

Companies face moral pressure to operate responsibly in their subcontracting chain. Even if the law does not regulate their behaviour, public

---

277 *German Ministry of Labour and Social Affairs*, 2020.

278 Nachhaltige Wertschöpfungskettengesetz – NaWKG. *Ministry of Economic Affairs and Employment of Finland*, 2020.

279 *Ministry of Economic Affairs and Employment of Finland*, 2020.

280 France, *Code du commerce*, Article L. 225-102-5. *Ministry of Economic Affairs and Employment of Finland*, 2020.

281 The child labour law in the Netherlands states: "Under the act, any natural or legal person whose interests have been affected by the failure of the company to exercise due diligence may submit a complaint to the supervisor [...] The supervisor may order the company to comply with the obligation to submit the pledge and to exercise due diligence and impose an administrative fine on a company that has failed to comply with the order. The maximum fine for failing to give the required pledge is €8,200, and for failing to exercise due diligence €820,000 (or 10% of the company's annual net sales)". See: *Ministry of Economic Affairs and Employment of Finland*, 2020.

opinion on the matter may be so strong that it changes the company's actions.[282] Attention needs to be paid to major country-specific differences: in the Nordic countries and in the Netherlands, for example, the monitoring of businesses is tighter than in many other European countries. It would be essential to provide regulations whereby companies are required to identify the human rights risks associated with their own activities. These would include business partners, value chains and supply chains. Moreover, by regulating these the goal is to try to prevent and mitigate adverse effects.

Extending the rules[283] on human rights beyond the jurisdiction of the state is a challenge. One reason is that states have their own sovereignty, as discussed earlier. In addition, states may fear that their legal systems will be overloaded, as evidence and prosecutions are difficult and costly.[284]

> New trends and phenomena play an important role in working life. These trends are important to understand since they have an immediate impact on company leaders too. In the latter part of 2017, the worldwide phenomenon of #metoo started. It originated around a few women and their stories of how sexual harassment and inequality is still widespread in companies.
>
> The whole MeToo phenomenon started after US Actress Alyssa Milano tweeted urging followers to share their thoughts about sexual harassment. This was the first example of public discourse at this level where people started to talk about this problematic issue. One significant example concerned Hollywood producer Harvey Weinstein's behaviour towards women. Many women spoke up about humiliating experiences they had when working with Weinstein.
>
> In 2020, Weinstein was found guilty of sex crimes and sentenced to 23 years in prison. This also resulted in the emergence of the "Weinstein Clause" in M&A agreements[285]. In Sweden, many companies terminated the employment contracts of people who harassed other employees.

282 Soon companies must prepare for mandatory reporting and compliance requirements; for example, supply chain DD is changing from optional to mandatory.

283 To mention a few: the California Transparency in Supply Chains Act (2010), the UK Modern Slavery Act (2015), the Australia Modern Slavery Act (2018), the New South Wales Modern Slavery Act, and the Netherlands law regarding child labor (Wetzorgplich Kinderarbeid (2018).

284 See more: *Ministry of Economic Affairs and Employment of Finland*, 2020.

285 Poster – Samios, 2019: "provisions typically request that a target company represents and warrants whether its officers or executives have been the subject of allegations of sexual harassment or misconduct, and if the company has entered into any settlement agreements regarding these kinds of claims."

> Worldwide, this means that leaders have an important role in stopping harassment in the workplace. Companies might need to pay damages for wrongdoing and ignorance and take a hit to their image and reputation as well. In the US alone in 2020, harassment resulted $53 million in damages being paid out by various companies.[286]

Up until 2011, attempts to resolve the possibility and willingness of companies and different countries to intervene in human rights had been ongoing for 20 years. In 2011, the UN Human Rights Council finally endorsed the UN Guiding Principles on Business and Human Rights. These were prepared by the UN Special Envoy, Professor John Ruggie.

These principles were structured in three parts: (i) the obligation of states to protect human rights, (ii) the responsibility of companies to respect human rights, and (iii) corrective measures. The acceptance of the principles was considered significant but, in fact, the work is still ongoing in some countries. The passivity (or even hostility) of some countries towards human rights and the challenge of extending legislation to issues in another country has led to growing pressure in Europe to regulate.

The internationally recognised human rights are, at a minimum, those expressed in the International Bill of Human Rights[287] and the ILO Declaration on Fundamental Principles and Rights at Work[288]. A more detailed list of some other guidelines is in the footnote[289]. The main Articles are as follows:

> UN Declaration of Human Rights Article 2: "Everyone is entitled to all the rights and freedoms set forth in this Declaration, without distinction of any kind, such as race, color, sex, language, religion, political or other opinion, national or social origin, property, birth or other status. Furthermore, no distinction shall be made based on the political, jurisdictional or international status of the country or territory to which a person belongs, whether it be independent, trust, non-self-governing or under any other limitation of sovereignty."

> UN Declaration of Human Rights Article: 3: "Everyone has the right to life, liberty and security of person".

286 Zacharek et al., 2017. Cooper – Valle, 2020. Carlsen et al., 2018.

287 *UN Universal declaration of Human Rights*, see especially article 20 (1).

288 ILO: the Declaration on Fundamental Principles and Rights at Work.

289 The ILO has eight fundamental conventions: 1. Freedom of Association and Protection of the Right to Organize Convention, 1948 , 2. Right to Organize and Collective Bargaining Convention, 1949, 3. Forced Labour Convention, 1930 (and its 2014 Protocol), 4. Abolition of Forced Labour Convention, 1957, 5. Minimum Age Convention, 1973, 6. Worst Forms of Child Labour Convention, 1999, 7. Equal Remuneration Convention, 1951, 8. Discrimination (Employment and Occupation) Convention, 1958.

UN Declaration of Human Rights Article 4-5: "No one shall be held in slavery or servitude; slavery and the slave trade shall be prohibited in all their forms." and "No one shall be subjected to torture or to cruel, inhuman or degrading treatment or punishment."

11.2. Business Crime Examples in Employment Law

In 2013, the Rana Plaza building collapsed in Bangladesh. It housed five clothing factories. More than 1,100 employees were killed and 2,500 were injured. As bodies were being pulled from the rubble, it soon became clear that not all the employees of those businesses were adults. In fact, many of them were children. Before the collapse, over 100 workers in Rana Plaza had noticed problems in the ceilings and walls and had reported them to management. The management ignored the reports and let the issue go on with fatal consequences. Later, it was revealed that the building was not built for industrial purposes and had no permissions. The collapse was caused by electricity generators placed on the roof—normally such heavy generators are located on the ground level due to the vibrations they cause. The collapse led to a dispute over child and slave labour and the treatment of employees in the clothing industry. What made the Rana Plaza case even worse was that all of this could have been avoided if the leaders had listened to their employees.

The Rana Plaza case became an international scandal also because many internationally known textile companies, such as Benetton, had operations in Rana Plaza, while their headquarters are in another country. As the disaster took place in Bangladesh, where the regulations are less strict, the case has been complicated one in terms of getting compensation paid to the families. The owner of the building was eventually sentenced to three years in prison.[290] After the scandal, Bangladesh started to move towards the ILO's Employment Injury Insurance scheme in 2017[291]. The legacy of Rana Plaza was costly – more costly than could ever be measured in money alone.[292]

Palm oil was the subject of media attention in 2014 when Finnish NGO Finnwatch revealed the poor conditions of workers on palm oil plantations—in some cases with conditions even amounting to deprivation. The report revealed that employment contracts were written in a language that migrant workers might not even understand. At the start of the work, the employer took the

290 *ILO*, 2018 I.

291 The Employment Injury Insurance scheme of the ILO is designed for the low- and middle-income-countries. The aim is to enhance working conditions in respect of occupational safety and health. The need for the ILO's own insurance scheme arose due to low compensation of employment injury compensation.

292 *ILO*, 2018 I. ILO 2018 II.

passports of migrant workers and passports were not returned for any reason. The working days were often 12 hours, and no overtime was paid. The wages paid for the work were below the minimum level. The employer could also arbitrarily decide not to pay wages if the employees felt particularly lazy for any reason. These shortcomings were addressed by a group including a non-governmental organisation (NGO) and farmers a year before. In November 2013, the NGO published a proposal on how to respect workers' values and prevent problems related to the cultivation of palm oil, such as forest deaths and land breaches.[293]

Perhaps the most famous case of image damage to countries occurred in Liberia in 1997 when President Charles Taylor sent diamonds to top model Naomi Campbell on several occasions. Taylor had traded weapons for the so-called **blood diamonds** from RUF rebels in Sierra Leone. Another name for blood diamonds is war diamonds and the aim is to finance an ongoing war or rebellion in exchange for the precious stones.[294] Blood diamonds are also often used to launder money, and there are also links to terrorism due to the ease of moving diamonds and their value. In 2010, Hollywood actress Mia Farrow, top model Naomi Campbell and model agent Carole White, testified at the Hague Crime Tribunal against Liberia's ex-president. Taylor was sentenced to 50 years in prison for trading in blood diamonds and war crimes.[295]

Shoe manufacturer Nike admitted widespread problems in 2005. An internal report showed abusive treatment in 2003 and 2004, such as restricted access to toilets, low wages, punishments for refusing to do overtime, employees working more than 60-hour working weeks and a lack of drinking water in some Asian factories.[296]

11.3. Espionage

Espionage is spying to obtain information. It is a very alarming issue both domestically and internationally, almost as worrying as how to maintain

293 *Palm Oil Innovation Group*, POIG Charter: In the DuPont-Dow merger, a large number of environmental organisations were trying to influence the Commission to ban the merger of giant players in the same industry. NGOs feared that this would have had a detrimental effect on farmers and product safety.

294 Weaver, 2010.

295 In 2017, it was reported that three African countries were planning to resign from the ICC in protest due to their perception that the Hague war crimes tribunal was focusing too much on African people or crimes committed in Africa. Former dictator of Sudan Omar al-Bashir might become the first person to be charged at the ICC for war crimes. The ICC issued an arrest warrant for al-Bashir in 2009. Former president of Yugoslavia Slobodan Milosevic was charged with war crimes but was never sentenced due to his unexpected death. Former president of Chad Hissene Habre was sentenced to life imprisonment in 2016 for crimes against humanity.

296 Teather, 2005.

military security. Surprisingly, white-collar employees have been guilty of the biggest cases of corporate espionage in monetary value. In the US alone, it is estimated that white-collar crimes cost the country about $300 billion dollars annually.[297] Companies, and especially wealthy companies, are very attractive for netspionage criminals.

Company secrets[298] or **trade secrets** are confidential practices and processes which are not known outside a company. They are what give a company an economic advantage over other companies in the markets. Trade secrets include, for example, methods, techniques, devices, patterns, processes or similar. For example, a customer list or a manufacturing process could regarded as a trade secret. Companies pay more and more attention to trade secrets. The breach of company secrets might happen either on purpose or accidently without the company really noticing. In either case, the company is affected economically. Breaching the company's core (the company secrets) might all of a sudden mean that products do not move well anymore to end customers, or the company's operations might be otherwise affected.

The EU Trade Secrets directive[299] came into force in 2018. It aims "to standardize the national laws in EU countries against the unlawful acquisition, disclosure and use of trade secrets. The directive harmonises the definition of trade secrets in accordance with existing internationally binding standards. It also defines the relevant forms of misappropriation and clarifies that reverse engineering and parallel innovation must be guaranteed, given that trade secrets are not a form of exclusive intellectual property right."[300]

> Article 2 (1) of the directive defines the term as follows:
>
> "trade secret means information which meets all of the following requirements: (a) it is secret in the sense that it is not, as a body or in the precise configuration and assembly of its components, generally known among or readily accessible to persons within the circles that normally deal with the kind of information in question; (b) it has commercial value because it is secret; (c) it has been subject to reasonable steps under

297 Nasheri, 2005, 3-5.

298 There are a couple of examples of very old company secrets: the recipe for Coca-Cola (over 125 years old) and Chanel No. 5 perfume. The most critical trade secret holders are, for example, Microsoft, whose trade secrets are crucial for innovation. If you think about Cortana personal digital assistant, what will happen if a competitor got hold of the information in Cortana? That would be dramatic!

299 Directive (EU) 2016/943 on the protection of undisclosed know-how and business information (trade secrets) against their unlawful acquisition, use and disclosure.

300 Reverse engineering is also known as back engineering. Parallel innovation means that products use the core technology of another product, but it is commercialized to the near term. European Commission, Trade Secrets.

> the circumstances, by the person lawfully in control of the information, to keep it secret..."

The Trade-Related Aspects of Intellectual Property Rights (TRIPS) agreement, Article 39, describes something as secret when (i) it is not commonly known among those who normally use such information, (ii) confidentiality has commercial significance, and (iii) steps have been taken to keep the information confidential. In different countries, the protection of trade secrets is different.[301]

Companies may use a person to spy and collect competitor trade secrets or other types of secret information. There are diverse ways of spying. For example, reverse engineering[302] creates an opportunity for competitors to find out product features and thereby make the company secret ineffective legally. The more technology develops, the faster the features of products are also revealed. On the other hand, this leads to even fewer companies which are able to protect their secret information. Product features can be further resolved. Therefore, no company is safe.[303]

> In 2019, there was a huge debate surrounding Google, which had secretly collected the patient account data of millions of people. It all started when Google entered into an agreement with large healthcare chain Ascension. The agreement helped Google access confidential patient data. In the US, this is possible without asking for permission from patients, but the data needs to be used only for the patient. In this case, Google was developing new tools and applications utilising AI and machine learning, and it used the patient data for this. That was illegal.[304] Google agreed to compensate affected patients. In the same year, Google had already paid $170 million in compensation due to a dispute which arose while acquiring personal data on children. The dispute started when YouTube (owned by Google) illegally collected information from children without their parents' consent.

***

301 WTO Trips Part II: Standards concerning the availability, scope and use of Intellectual Property Rights, Article 39, section 7 article 2 a-c: "is secret in the sense that it is not, generally known among or readily accessible to persons within the circles that normally deal with the kind of information in question; has commercial value because it is secret; and has been subject to reasonable steps under the circumstances, by the person lawfully in control of the information, to keep it secret".

302 The most famous case of re-engineering concerns the US Airforce B-29 Superfortress aircraft. Russia made the same bomber aircraft Tupolev Tu-4. See more: Wikipedia: Re-engineering.

303 Nasheri, 2005, 7–8.

304 Copeland, 2019.

In 2019, former executives of Banco Bilbao Vizcaya Argentaria (BBVA) were placed under investigation regarding a corporate spying case. The case also concerned the bank's former CEO Ángel Cano. The CEO refused to testify in the case.[305]

***

In 2021, Spain's High Court started investigations into Iberdola's CEO Jose S Galán and three of the company's executives in a case of spying, bribery, breach of privacy and fraud involving commercial documents.[306]

305 Aguado, 2019.
306 Binnie – Pinedo, 2021.

12. Computer crime

Computer crime is an illegal act where a hacker steals a company's or individual's confidential information electronically. Computer crime is also known as cybercrime, e-crime or electronic crime. Some cases are so severe that data is locked by the hacker and money is demanded in return for opening the data again. Such cases might even affect a person's life. In most cases, the motivation is money, but not always. Also, chaos lovers and demonstrating the capability for creating chaos with a "because I can" attitude might be the reason. There are many types of computer crime, including IPR infringement, espionage and fraud, to mention just a few.[307] Many of the world's biggest companies have felt the unknown threat in their businesses. For example, in 2019, Amazon, EasyJet, Facebook, Microsoft, Singapore's Ministry of Health and Zynga (known from the Farmville game) all suffered at the hands of computer criminals. In 2020, TikTok, Virgin Media, YouTube, Nintendo, Marriott International, Instagram were also attacked. To get a better understanding of the magnitude of the problem in 2020, four million records were stolen from YouTube due to the social media site's had poor security. In the same year, Clearview AI, with some 3,000,000,000 photos in its database, was hacked.[308]

12.1. From traditional espionage to cyber espionage

Corporate and industrial espionage takes place mainly in the cyber world. This is already reflected in the increased amount of writing about cybercrime.[309] One way of determining industrial espionage is the use of questionable and illegal practices aimed at obtaining important information from industry, businesses and states.[310] The difference between corporate espionage and economic espionage is that economic espionage develops as a result of government data collection measures. Economic espionage is therefore trying to create better competitiveness for countries by using open sources. Corporate or industrial

307 *Computerhope*, 2021.

308 *Wikipedia*: List of Data Breaches.

309 *Tadviser*, 2020.

310 *Wikipedia*: "The targets of industrial espionage include: product development, ongoing trade agreements, important executives, other relevant issues for the scout, such as the 'idea' of the new production method and the company's strategy. Industrial espionage includes, inter alia, recruiting a person employed by an enterprise for espionage by ideology, money, extortion or other means; intrusion into the undertaker's computer networks and acquisition of information; monitoring company traffic and determining content within the company, at home and abroad (telephones, mobile phones, Internet traffic); the installation of spy equipment (e.g. microphones, cameras, mobile phones, etc.) in important areas of the company; listening to discussions with key company staff (e.g. in hotel rooms, etc.); Stealing computers from key people in your company."

espionage is a serious crime. It is intended to adversely influence important trading, manufacturing and product development activities in another country, such as official intelligence organisations carrying out these activities.

> In 2021, a ransomware cyberattack closed 5,500 miles of a the Colonial pipeline in the United States. The pipeline is the US's largest and carries refined gasoline and jet fuel.[311]
>
> ***
>
> In 2016 in the United States, there was a dispute about building a backdoor for iPhones for law enforcement officers. The main question was whether law enforcement should have access to data on locked iPhones for criminal investigations. Apple resisted to the extent that the CEO Tim Cook sent a customer letter justifying Apple's position in the case: "Customers expect Apple and other technology companies to do everything in our power to protect their personal information, and at Apple we are deeply committed to safeguarding their data. [...] While we believe the FBI's intentions are good, it would be wrong for the government to force us to build a backdoor into our products. And ultimately, we fear that this demand would undermine the very freedoms and liberty our government is meant to protect." However, the matter was resolved in 2016 when a third party demonstrated for the FBI a way to unlock iPhones.[312]
>
> ***
>
> A hot topic in the US in 2020 was Chinese Cloud Hoppers. The term refers to Chinese hackers who find a way inside a company's IT system using cloud services.[313] The State of Cyber Resilience survey reveals a terrible situation in the cybersecurity of companies: although companies all over the world spend a lot of money on protection, only 30% of companies can be effective against cyberattacks. More than 50% of the companies interviewed took more than a month to recover from an attack. In most cases, viruses get into a company's system through partner companies.[314]

Large companies are particularly vulnerable to the loss of expertise and innovation. Even the slightest mistake is being tracked, and there is always

311 Sanger et al., 2021.

312 Segall – Pagliery – Wattles, 2016. Thielman, 2016.

313 Stauffer, 2019.

314 *State of Cyber Resilience*, 2020.

somebody who will try to benefit.[315] Competition is fierce and any means of getting an advantage are allowed, with one rule: don't get caught. Cybercriminals are no longer amateurs, and they know how easy it is to bring companies to their knees. They are also aware of how easy it is to monetize their crimes. USB flash drives, memory cards and other such devices are serious data security risks since they can be easily stolen, lost or used to spread malicious software.

The worst cybercrime threats obviously relate to the loss of life. In the worst-case scenario, a cyberattack can be targeted at a hospital or health care system. Machines can be shut down and patients, whose lives depend on these machines, may die as a result of the cyberattack. The threat may also involve the mixing or the destruction of patient data. Correcting records takes a lot of time and is also very expensive.[316]

> To date, there has been at least one recorded attack that would be classified as cyberwarfare. The cyberattack was directed at the Ukrainian energy plant Prykarpattyaoblenergo on 23 December 2015. The attack was superbly designed because the malware was built inside the energy company computer system over six months earlier using an Excel file. The energy company's computers were overloaded, which slowed down power recovery and temporarily disrupted the electricity supply to consumers. The lights went out in half of the homes in the town of Ivano-Frankivsk, with a population of 1.4 million. The break in power lasted several hours.[317]

***

> In September 2020, HAECHI-I, an Interpol operation, targeted its resources to tackle financial crime in the Republic of Korea. Later on, the operation spread to 1,400 separate investigations in several countries. Over $83 million in funds were hijacked from victims.[318]

***

315 Not all the materials on the internet are real, either. Well known fakes include deep fake, cheap fake, disinformation and misinformation. Deep fake can be used for harmful purposes and is very hard to differentiate from reality. Cheap fake is a very poor quality copy of, for example, a picture or video. Disinformation aims to mislead a user. Schick, 2020.

316 Office of the Director of National Intelligence, Economic Espionage.

317 Office of the Director of National Intelligence, Economic Espionage.

318 Mathews I, 2021.

> The COVID-19 pandemic caused a lot of "coronavirus crimes", already in the first six months of 2020. For example, the second biggest hospital in the Czech Republic faced a cyberattack in 2020. It immediately led to a situation in which the hospital's ability to test patients for COVID-19 was jeopardised.[319] All in all, COVID-19 is leading to increased cyberattacks and it will have a long-lasting impact on organised crime. A study from May 2020 revealed a 33% increase in cyber-threats during the period of COVID-19. That is a huge increase in only a few months. During the lockdown in the UK, coronavirus crimes emerged especially in the area of automated bot attacks. [320]

It is easy for a competitor to spy on a company in which the employees or management make mistakes themselves. Such errors can even be a death sentence for the company.[321] Cybercriminals are not the only threats companies need to be prepared for. A further problem seems to be that companies too often seek the most cost-effective contracts for services such as cleaning, property maintenance and security, even for lunch providers. Do companies perform proper background checks on these service providers and their workers? Do companies really know who is guarding their premises and how? Old "decent" espionage practices continue to operate alongside the modern cyber world, although they are no longer as important as they used to be.[322]

> In 2020, hackers got into the US nuclear weapons agency. To date, the case is the biggest in the history of cyberattacks. Microsoft along with other agencies were also hacked. It all started with US technology firm SolarWinds. A group of hackers got into SolarWinds' systems and were able to add a malicious code to the software system. Things started to go wrong when SolarWinds couldn't locate this code and they sent update packages to their clients with the malicious code in it. As SolarWinds had roughly 30,000 customers, the hackers were able to add even more

319 Lyngaas, 2020.

320 UK Finance, 2021. Siewert, 2020. It is estimated COVID-19 generated over $2.2 trillion in illicit trade in 2020. That, in turn, presents an emerging threat to both governments and businesses. See more Chavarria – Walker – Bahamon, 2020.

321 Ekran, 2019.

322 Until the 1990s, the FBI had a programme "DECA" (Developing Espionage and Counterintelligence Awareness), which was designed to monitor the security situation regarding economic espionage. The programme also monitored terrorism and economic intelligence. FBI, ANSIR Program. The activities of the French Foreign Intelligence Service (Direction Générale de la Sécurité Extérieure, DGSE) are an example of economic espionage. For several years, the intelligence service had a project in which it installed wiretap devices under first-class seats on aircraft. The conversations of business passengers were recorded and forwarded from Air France aircraft to DST (Direction de la Surveillance du Territoire). The programme ended in 1994.

harmful codes to the software systems of SolarWinds customers and were able to spy on companies remotely.[323]

US Financial espionage also covers issues such as payment information from the international SWIFT payment network. US authorities have access to this SWIFT data. As a result of pressure from the United States, the EU agreed in 2017 to provide the following information: amount to be paid, payer details and payee details, including account numbers and address. The information disclosed in the transfer of payment data was amended in 2019. Due to the impact of data protection legislation, Europol will in the future review US requests for any information[324]. Payment information will only be disclosed if there are reasonable grounds for suspecting the funding of terrorism.[325]

***

Since 2011, a Russian cyberespionage group has focused on companies operating in the energy sector. Its activities go by the names "Dragonfly" or "Energetic Bear". In 2014, the group installed malware on a Russian law firm's website. Customers who visited the law firm automatically received malware on their own computers, which allowed the group to collect passwords, screenshots and documents.[326]

In 2015, the UK confirmed that it had more cyber-crimes than "traditional" crimes[327]. The US and Canada have spent the most money on cyberattack prevention. They both have their own cyber policies as well.[328] According to a survey conducted by the Chamber of Commerce in Finland in 2019, the world would need 1.5 million cyber security professionals immediately[329]. This, in turn, means directly that companies need to strengthen their ability to face this unknown fear. Criminals working on the internet are already far ahead of companies. Most companies have just started to take seriously protection work,

323 Jibilian – Canales, 2021.

324 Data protection legislation, i.e. General Data Protection Regulation (GDPR) legislation. GDPR raised a number of questions. Organisations should know what data they have, how it is stored and who has access to it.

325 European Parliament B6-0042/2007. Article 4A of the Uniform Commercial Code. Swift 2017. Regulation (EU) 2019/518 of the European Parliament and of the Council of 19 March 2019 amending Regulation (EC) No 924/2009 as regards certain charges on cross-border payments in the EU and currency conversion charges.

326 Perlroth, 2014. *Infosecurity magazine.com*, 2014, *Securityweek*, 2014.

327 IRM, 2017.

328 Varonis, 2020.

329 *Finland Chamber of Commerce*, 2019.

and we know that attacks are complex. There already exists malware that is activated at a certain pre-programmed time. The purpose of such malware is to destroy production machines or re-program them remotely to carry out illegal operations.

> In 2021, hackers remotely erased Western Digital's hard drives with malicious software.[330]
>
> ***
>
> Already in 1981, the Soviet Union had tried to build a natural gas pipeline from Siberia to Eastern Europe. For the operation, the country needed software which would monitor pressure gauges and valves. After careful consideration, it managed to find a US company that sold the necessary software. However, what was not known was the software was programmed to do anti-work after a few months. It had a bug which led to a huge explosion that cost millions of dollars, which the Soviet Union could not afford.[331]

Being a cybercriminal is not very hard. There are hacking applications and other apps available for everyone at a low cost, some as low as €10. Turnkey solutions are also available on the internet. In the worst-case scenario, internet criminals can delete an entire company from the web. This is what happened to a French internet service provider OVH, whose servers crashed when 150,000 cameras were harnessed to perform a service attack.[332]

Ransomware is a particular security threat.[333] A ransomware cyberattack locks a company out of its computers. The encryption key necessary for unlocking the computers is in the hands of criminals, and without which it is impossible to unlock them. The criminals demand money to unlock the company's computers, and the payment is usually requested in virtual currency, bitcoins. The ransom demand goes up if the company does not act fast enough. Authorities in the US have estimated that criminals have earned over $1 billion in ransom, with reputational damage even greater. In 2016, US security company Datto estimated that the reputational damage for companies as a result of a ransomware cyberattack amounted to $70 billion.[334]

330 Mathews II, 2021.

331 Weiner, 2008.

332 Roberts, 2016. Baltrusaitis, 2020 conducted a survey in 2020 that estimated there are roughly 200 million cameras in China and 50 million security cameras in the US. In China, it is very hard to find the information on the number of attacks.

333 Another term for ransomware is malware. "Malware is a general term for a variety of harmful software specifically designed to attack computer systems, networks, or data." Buehler et al., 2009, 121.

334 *Datto*, 2016.

In scareware systems, the user is advised to pay for false antivirus protection. It prevents the user from working on the machine, as the Spanish security company Panda found.[335] In 2020, IT giant Cognizant, which operates in 37 countries, suffered the Maze ransomware attack. Almost all projects were put on hold for a while, and the estimated cost was roughly $50–70 million. The attack on the company was planned during the COVID-19 pandemic. The company's employees could not work from home offices because their computers were locked.[336]

The Internet of Things (IoT), where everything is connected to the web, offers great opportunities but, at the same time, great threats. There is no office anywhere in the world that has rules for all the standards IoT machines require. It is fairly easy to penetrate through the heating system to see if you are at home and in worst case scenario money is required to start your home devices again. On the positive side, new businesses will emerge and make our lives much easier. It also gives companies a way to collect information about end users. On the other hand, anything which is connected to the internet is open to hackers, as we can see from the following cases.[337]

> Over 100,000 IoT Machines were hacked in 2016 by the Mirai botnet. This was possible because the owners of machines left factory settings and passwords untouched.[338]

***

> One horror story involving excellent hacking occurred in 2011 when Sony PlayStation Network's information security wall was hacked. As a result of the data breach, the data of 77 million users was at risk. Sony was required to close its service for many weeks in order to fix its PlayStation platform. This, in turn, caused $200 million dollars in costs for the company.[339]

***

> Petya ransomware[340] closed the international operations of pharmaceutical company Reckitt Benkiser for several days in 2017. Management was instructed not to pay any ransomware demand.

335 Lawson, 2011.
336 Goodwin, 2020.
337 Burgess, 2018. Kapersky, 2021.
338 Fruhlinger, 2018.
339 Welch, 2012.
340 Petya ransomware was discovered in 2016 and targets mainly Microsoft Windows servers, PCs and laptops. Petya infects the master boot record. A new variant is called Notpetya.

Ransomware was activated inside the medical company due to old Windows operating systems.[341]

***

Ransomware Notpetya caused pharmaceutical giant Merck to lose over €1.2 billion, 7,500 servers and 30,000 computers. The company's insurance did not cover its losses at all since the company thought the attack was a declaration of war by Russia and insurance only covers peacetime losses. Notpetya also affected logistical giant Møller-Maersk's operations. All of the company's operations were taken down in 2017 and cost the company approximately $300 million.[342] Logistics giant Fedex and its subsidiary TNT Express also suffered an attack by Notpetya ransomware in 2017, and before that Fedex was attacked by Wannacry ransomware. Wannacry also affected the British National Health Service in 2017, resulting in costs of almost €110 million.[343]

As can be seen from the above, cyberattacks and different types of malware are increasing in business environments. Companies cannot be equipped to defend themselves completely, but at the very least companies should be ready for "what if" scenarios.

12.2. Company Espionage: Examples

When it comes to information leaks, there is probably no case more famous, or infamous, than that of Edward Snowden. Snowden was a computer intelligence consultant who worked for the US Central Intelligence Service (CIA) as an administrator and for the US Defense Intelligence Service as a lecturer in counterintelligence. Snowden also worked for technology giant Dell as well as the US National Security Service (NSA).[344] In June 2013, Snowden leaked thousands of secret documents a number of journalists. [345]

341 Monaghan, 2017.

342 Burgess, 2018.

343 Europol has a "No more ransom" website which is worth visiting. The website tries to eliminate ransomware effectively and offers tools to companies. Europol has a tool named "Crypto Sheriff" that can help define which ransomware has attacked company systems.

344 National Security Agency Data Collection Programs 2013. National Security Agency Data Collection Programs "Quotations from NSA Director in reply to questions asked in open hearing of the House Intelligence Committee by Representative Lynn Westmoreland (R-GA) beginning at 02:14:00 on video counter."

345 Greenwald – MacAskill – Poitras, 2013. Andrews – Burrough – Ellison, 2014. Carrol, 2014.

Julian Assange founded the company Wikileaks in 2006. In 2010, Wikileaks leaked classified documents regarding the Iraq and Afghanistan wars. The US started criminal proceedings against Mr. Assange accusing him of stealing classified documents, information hacking and espionage, to just mention a few. In what has turned out to be a very complicated case, Assange took refuge for seven years in the Embassy of Ecuador in London to avoid charges in Sweden relating to sexual assault. In 2019, following a number of disputes with the Ecuadorian authorities, Assange's diplomatic asylum was revoked and he was required to vacate the Embassy of Ecuador. Around the same time, Uppsala District Court decided that the case against Assange in Sweden had weakened and the case was dropped. This meant that Assange then faced a long court case in London where the issue of extradition to the US would have to be settled. Extradition and conviction of all charges against him, could mean Assange faces 175 years in prison. In January 2021, the court ruled not to extradite Assange. Journalists around the world wrote that if Assange were to be convicted in the US courts, it would mean the death of freedom of speech and journalism, and a possible death sentence for Assange. In 2018, there was a similar case in which Finnish hacker Lauri Love went through a long court procedure in London and won. If Love had been sentenced in the US courts, he could have gone to prison for 99 years.

Despite Love's case was hoped to be a signal for Assange's case, The UK Government decided that Assange can be extradited to the US.[346]

***

Football leaks were in the headlines in 2020. Rui Pinto, known in the media as a modern-day Robin Hood, hacked into the document systems of different law firms and accessed classified information on several famous clients. He published the information on the web. The football leaks concerned, for example, Lionel Messi and Cristiano Ronaldo, who have both been punished for tax evasion with fines. Also, FIFA's former, long-serving President Sepp Blatter and FIFA's Vice-President and UEFA's President Michel Platini lost their position due to suspected corruption and money laundering. From Football Leaks, Pinto involved himself in Luanda Leaks, which concerned Africa's wealthiest woman Isabel dos Santos who was sued in 2019 for money

346 Bowcott, 2018.

laundering, corruption and other fraudulent activity. The case against her is still pending. Blatter and Platini was found not guilty in 2022. [347]

***

In another matter, engineer Anthony Levandowski was working for Google and Uber. He attempted to steal trade secrets from Google relating to Google's self-driving car project in 2016. According to the San Jose court documents, Levandowski downloaded 14,000 engineering, manufacturing and business files. Then he launched a self-driving truck company Otto, which was acquired by Uber. Google and Google's self-driving car unit Waymo sued Uber in 2017. The case was dismissed and, shockingly, was reported to have been resolved as a settlement agreement.

Uber fired Levandowski, but he never handed over the crucial papers to Uber, resulting in Uber having to negotiate a licensing deal with Google's unit Waymo. In any case, US authorities took aim at Levandowski, who was sentenced in 2010 to 18 years in prison for theft of trade secrets. Levandowski was pardoned in 2021 by then US President Donald Trump.[348]

***

In 2019, it was revealed that Switzerland's second biggest bank, Credit Suisse's senior executive's job was to attract new customers, wealthy ones. As this was not communicated well enough within the company, it raised concerns. Which ended up Credit Suisse's COO to hire private detectives for few weeks since some workers pointed out the possibility of corporate espionage case. Some of the management knew about the new customer program, but not COO whose responsibility this was. Credit Suisse's Board of Directors ruled that the operation was "wrong and disproportionate and has resulted in severe reputational damage to the bank". Adding tragedy to the case, the private security consultant who helped the COO with this operation later killed himself.[349]

347 Aarons, 2020.

348 Isaac, 2020. Korosec, 2020. *Reuters*, 29 July 2020. According to the newspapers, Microsoft's Russian software designer gave Microsoft's confidential company secrets to a French blogger in 2014. Among those company secrets were some of the company's most valuable and most important secrets and, if revealed, would have been devastating to Microsoft. Not only this, the leak exposed Microsoft to an infringement problem. The untrustworthy employee was sued for leaking company confidential information in Seattle in the US. The software designer admitted he had done wrong but, at the same time, Microsoft was sued for phishing information and breaking into the French blogger's Hotmail account. The Russian software designer was given a three-month prison sentence and a $22,500 fine. If he had not confessed, his penalty could have been a maximum of 10 years in prison and a $ 250,000 fine. See *Slashdot*, 2014.

349 Neate – Kollewe, 2019.

The Bernard Tapie case was discussed, for example, in Finnish legal papers by professors Kurkela and Mettälä as follows. Tapie was the co-owner of German sportswear corporation Adidas through his holding company BTF. The case revealed that there were considerable differences between national legislation and norms between national and international rules on arbitration. The case of Bernhard Tapie concerns disqualifications in arbitration tribunals and highlights the importance of raising issues at the beginning of an arbitral tribunal because not doing so can lead to an annulment.

In the Tapie case, one arbitrator was found to have acted fraudulently because he used dominant procedures in favour of only one party. The arbitral tribunal concerned the restructuring of Adidas. The Société de Banque Occidentalen (SDBO) found eight buyers for Adidas. Since Tapie's Holding company faced bankruptcy, Tapie claimed the bank had persuaded his company to sell the company's shares below the market price. He started arbitral proceedings in 2007, claiming the new owner of Adidas had a secret agreement with the bank and the acquisition was based on an unlawful procedure.

The arbitration award given in 2008 revealed that the bank had acted unlawfully. It was ordered to pay €240 million to Tapie in addition to €45 million for moral damage. According to professors Kurkela and Mettälä, this was an exceptional amount under the laws of France. After the award, there were suspicions that Tapie had conspired with one arbitrator, which led to a revision of the arbitral tribunal's decision. In 2015, the Court of Appeal stated that the decision of the arbitral tribunal was fraudulent. As the period of opposition statements had already expired, the Court of Appeal could reopen the case because the case was national in nature and involved fraud. The case was heard in the Supreme Court in France (Court de Cassation). The court ruled and was of the same opinion that the case could be reopened, and Tapie was ordered to return the amount, now a sum of €404 million.[350]. If this would have been an international case, which Tapie claimed, reopening of the case would not have been possible. As the bank was owned by the State of France, Christine Lagarde being the Finance Minister in France at the time, actions went unquestioned about the arbitral award and the decision was accepted [351]. Lagarde was stated as being careless since the arbitral award was not questioned by the state. Lagarde was not charged with any crime; although one reason for that could have been that she was occupied with an international financial crisis at the time when the Tapie case was being handled.[352]

350 Kurkela - Mettälä, 2018.

351 Landon - Andelman - Breeden, 2016.

352 See Honlet - Dufêtre - Lecompte, 2016, 212-213, which states that this case involved an exceptional remedy based on an exceptional situation.

13. Business Crime in Competition Law

Fair competition refers to a free market where all can and are allowed to play. It avoids agreements and other practices that restrict competition. These can include, for example, price fixing or market sharing. In addition, abusing a dominant market position or sharing confidential market information with, for example, competitors are also prohibited. Sustaining, promoting and following international and local competition laws (referred to as antitrust laws in the United States) is crucial for companies. An understanding of the concept of 'fair competition' is essential.[353] The image below shows the different and most important types of Antitrust Law violations:

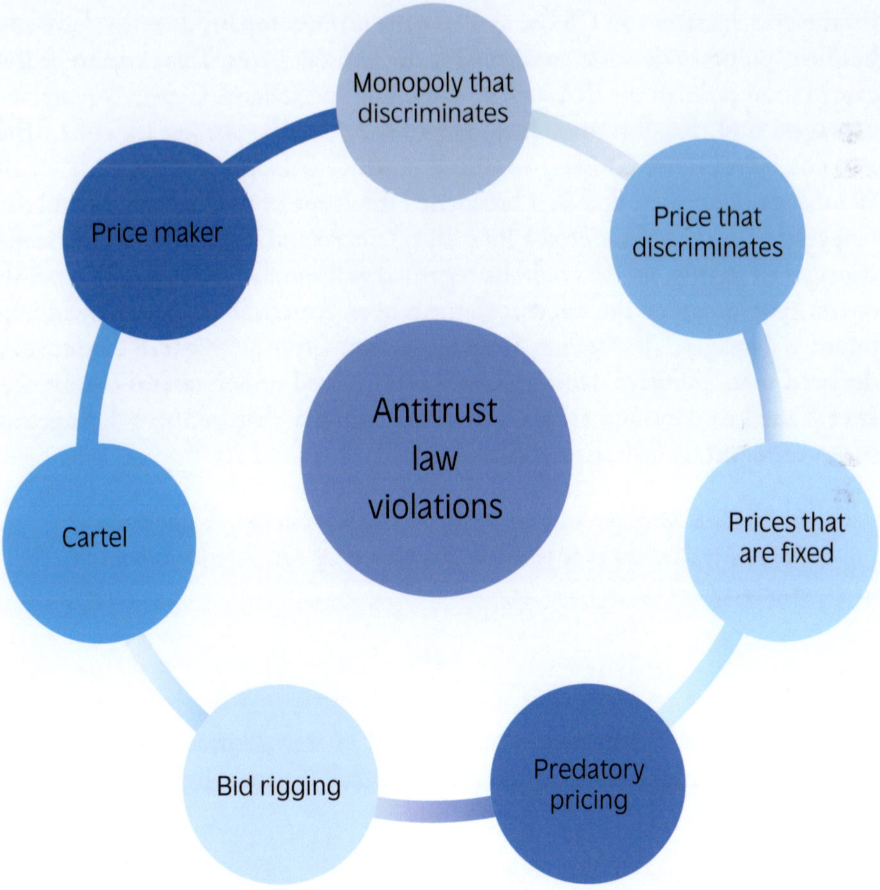

Image 5. **The image shows the different and most important types of Antitrust Law violations.**

353 See United Nations Note by the UNCTAD Secretariat: The role of competition policy in promoting sustainable and inclusive growth, 2015.

Violations of competition law (or Antitrust Law) by directors and/or other parties can involve personal liability, such as lengthy prison sentences and substantial fines for directors, especially in the US and the UK. In addition, a company may have treble responsibility with treble damages over the party in the United States, as stated in the Clayton Act and the RICO Act. For example, if the US Government is defrauded, it is entitled to recover treble damages. Compensatory damages mean that damages cover the loss suffered, but these type of treble or punitive damages "can be awarded in addition to compensatory damages". Punitive damages exceed the value of the harm and are awarded if the defendant is considered to have acted fraudulently, wilfully, maliciously or similarly.[354] Also, if the case concerns, for example, wilful patent infringement, treble damages may be awarded.

If competition restrictions have an impact on the United States, liability for the breach arises and US law applies even if the company does not have any business, property or other contact with the United States. This can also be the case in some parts of the EU, such as in the UK and Ireland, Cyprus (exemplary damages) and, for instance, in Singapore. At the beginning of 2021, The People's Republic of China introduced punitive damages, for example, in all IP infringement cases, that is, it broadened the scope of the Patent Law and the Copyright Law (implemented 1 June 2021). In Poland, courts may direct some damages to charity, which could be regarded as exemplary damages[355]. Spanish courts have "accepted the full enforcement of an American judgment including punitive damages." The Italian Supreme Court, *Corte Suprema di Cassazione,* declared that "punitive damages could be enforced under certain conditions after it used to consider, as Japanese courts still do, that punitive damages as such were contrary to Italian public policy"[356].

> In 2017, a Singapore court ruled in *PH Hydraulics & Engineering Pte Ltd v. Airtrust* that punitive damages were available for breach of contract.[357]

***

> In 2016, the US Supreme Court decided in *Halo Electronics v. Pulse Electronics,* a patent infringement case, that if patent infringement

---

354 Congressional Research Service, 2010.

355 Coleman et al, 2014. Branton, 2008. Note that this does not mean that automatically all white-collar crimes are criminal cases. They can also involve civil cases. Swiss Reinsurance Company, 2012. Mae Koo, 2021. Note that while this damages option exists it is used very rarely. Waelbroeck et al, 2002.

356 Elbalti, 2021.

357 *Airtrust (Hong Kong) Ltd v. PH Hydraulics & Engineering Pte Ltd.*, 2015.

is wilful, a company is liable to pay treble damages. This decision was based on the US Patent Act, section 284, which states: "[the] court may increase the damages up to three times the amount found or assessed."[358]

***

In 2011, executives at Furukawa Electric Company entered into an international agreement to fix prices. Furukawa was a supplier of automobile parts in Tokyo and the practice had been taking place for more than 10 years. The agreement had a dramatic effect on US trade, which meant US law applied. The Furukawa executives were sentenced to eight months in prison and the company was fined $200 million.[359]

***

In 2002, 64-year-old Betty Bullock, a US citizen with inoperable lung cancer, successfully sued tobacco company giant Phillip Morris for negligence, strict product liability and fraud. The case resulted in the largest amount of punitive damages awarded against the tobacco industry in history. The case lasted for nine years. In 2011, a Los Angeles court ruled that Bullock be awarded damages amounting to $28 billion. Sadly, Betty Bullock died in 2003 years before the final ruling.[360]

***

When talking about agreements in competition law, an agreement is considered to be any type of oral or written agreement expressing mutual consent. Also, passivity or informality can be interpreted as consent to an agreement. It is important to keep in mind that a breach of agreement in competition law may take place even if the agreement is not implemented. As seen from the cases below, joint actions and parallel conduct are also regarded as breaches of competition law.[361]

In practice, it is impossible to achieve completely free competition. In Europe, for example, the EU is made up of many member states, which means that although competition policy objectives can be drawn up more generally the national characteristics of the various member states remain strong and preclude the possibility of the EU becoming a community market such as is in the United States.

358 Seidenberg, 2016.

359 Clarkson – Miller – Cross, 2018, 451.

360 *Thomson Reuters*, 2019 II.

361 Pietruszewska, 2020.

The US Sherman Act (2 July 1890) prohibits cartels between companies (US Code, Title 15, Chapter 1 §1): "Every contract, combination in the form of trust or otherwise, or conspiracy, in restraint of trade or commerce among the several States, or with foreign nations, is declared to be illegal. Every person who shall make any contract or engage in any combination or conspiracy hereby declared to be illegal shall be deemed guilty of a felony, and, on conviction thereof, shall be punished by fine not exceeding $100,000,000 if a corporation, or, if any other person, $1,000,000, or by imprisonment not exceeding 10 years, or by both said punishments, in the discretion of the court."

> In 2012, four executives of the Yazaki Corporation were charged and pleaded guilty for breaching Antitrust Law. Fines for two companies, Yazaki Corp and Denso Corp, amounted to the second largest criminal penalty ever, $548 million. The case concerned price fixing of automobile parts and conspiracy to rig a bid decision. Four Japanese executives were sentenced to prison terms ranging from 15 months to two years.[362]

In 2002, the EU Commission completely reformed merger control.[363] As a result of the reform, competition law decision-making powers were transferred to national competition authorities, companies' own responsibility increased, controls tightened and sanctions became stricter.[364] This was due to the Commission's willingness to focus on cases in the EU area which were felt to be of great economic and legal importance for the single market. Cases which do not fulfil EU-wide significance are dealt with by national authorities. As a result of this reform, the role of national merger control was further emphasised.[365]

The Commission's competition policy has, from time to time, been questioned. In particular, questions have been raised over whether it is fair in markets of different sizes. Indeed, it seems that the Commission would use unfair competition policy to put small and large markets on an unequal footing

362 The US *Department of Justice*, 2012.

363 European Commission Green Paper on Merger Regulation.

364 In the Nordic countries, there are also differences. Sweden has harmonised its laws in a very similar way to EU competition law, while Denmark and Finland have national specificities in competition law.

365 If successful, the acquisition would seem to have far-reaching consequences. These include, for example, improved market efficiency, increased consumer welfare, operating profits and better long-term profitability of companies. The acquisition will also contribute to the improvement of scale and efficiency, so that those with a larger market share will also succeed in the market better than others. Admittedly, opponents of acquisitions believe that acquisitions could lead to higher consumer prices. Thus, the acquisition affects market structures, market performance and market behaviour. The acquisition may lead to higher prices if market imbalances are found and if the continuing demand for the efficiency of the companies and the reduction of competitors as a result of the acquisition are considered.

by imposing conditions on small markets that are not imposed on large ones, and thus creating a so-called **false positive** situation.[366]

In large markets, the Commission accepted acquisitions which should have been prohibited in the first place—and this is called a **false negative** situation.[367] This is reflected in the comparison between European and US competition law, as the EU practice is very strict, while practice in the United States might be sometimes more flexible. It could be questioned whether the EU's strict internal competition policy prevents the growth and success of large companies. For example, in France, the Siemens/Alstom merger failed due to the European Commission blocking Siemens attempted acquisition of Alstom.

In the EU common market, the abuse of a dominant position by one or more undertakings is prohibited if it affects trade between member states. This may include, for example, limiting production to the detriment of consumers and imposing excessive purchase and selling prices. The dominant position is assessed entirely by considering the company's market share, size and number of competitors.[368] A business corporation may have a dominant position if the group's cooperation is deliberately structured to be dominant on a permanent basis.

> The United Brands Company case from 1978 is regarded as one of the most significant European competition law cases concerning the abuse of a dominant position in the relevant product market. United Brands Company (UBC) sold bananas to different member states at different prices. UBC restricted the distributor business so that distributors were bound to buy certain banana brands only from UBS and not anybody else. If UBS did not have certain brand, distributors could not sell those. UBC sold mainly Chiquita bananas and fixed its prices weekly. This meant that different member states paid different prices. The Commission and the ECJ concluded that the company's actions violated Article 86 (now Article 102) and were clearly an abuse of a dominant position and the company's behaviour was therefore unlawful. This case became the leading ruling in the ECJ.[369]

Collaboration between competitors always carries a risk. On the face of it, collaboration is acceptable; however, when it starts to restrict or distort competition, it then turns illegal and the collaborators are then seen as a

366 Oinonen, 2011, 136.

367 Oinonen, 2011, 133.

368 Kuoppamäki, 2008 I. See also Mentula et al., 1998, 37. Kuoppamäki criticises the Treaty of Rome, as it is based on the situation in the 1970s, which distorts the efficiency aspects of the market today. This is particularly evident when comparing European and US competition law, as the practice is very strict in the EU, while abuse controls in the US are loose. Kuoppamäki, 2008 I, 1097-1099.

369 Preliminary ruling in the ECJ Article 267 (previously 177).

cartel, which, in competition law, is considered the most serious risk to fair competition and is therefore heavily fined. Cartels can operate price fixing and also market and customer sharing. In addition, if a company limits production without an acceptable reason or shares sensitive information with commercial value among competitors, it is guilty of operating a cartel. Such a situation might occur if new product development projects or investments are revealed. Only publicly available information is acceptable for acquiring information. It is worth bearing in mind that boycotting certain customers or suppliers knowingly or operating biased tendering processes are also illegal. [370]

Relevant markets should always be defined on a case-by-case basis. They form one of the key issues in the application of competition rules. This means that a relevant market in competition law is different from a relevant market commercially. Some attention should be paid to the decisions of competition authorities. A dominant position as such is not forbidden; however, when a company's market share exceeds 40–50%, it is seen as having acquired dominant market power,[371] which then needs to be controlled. For example, dominant companies cannot tie or bundle products or services or set prices that are too high or too low. They can always recommend to their customers non-binding prices, but they cannot force any company to set prices at a certain level. It is also illegal to use contract terms that are unreasonable or deny the supply of goods or services to certain customers.[372]

In the past twenty years or so, countries are gradually tightening sanctions, i.e. criminal penalties. For example, **Belgium** and **New Zealand** have tightened their criminal sanctions in antitrust legislation, especially when proven to be serious in nature. In Belgium, individuals can now be fined up to €10,000. New Zealand has tightened its legislation to include criminal penalties and also imprisonment for serious antitrust cases. Basically, a company is liable if its management commits the crime. In some countries, a company might be criminally liable if its employees commit a crime and management lacks compliance.[373]

Given that sanctions for violating competition rules can be serious, monitoring and competition compliance audits are strongly recommended. Fines can be huge – up to 10% of group-wide turnover! And that's not all: investigations and legal proceedings also take time and money. Settling claims, court cases and media headlines affect a company's image. Moreover, after a court case, agreements can be declared invalid, which in turn might further lower a company's reputation. This in turn might negatively affect shareholder

370 Dunleavy, 2010. Ezrachi, 2012. In 2019 Microsoft and Google started collaboration in standardisation.

371 Please see case *Irish Sugar plc v. Commission*, 2001.

372 Dunleavy, 2010. Ezrachi, 2012.

373 Coleman et al, 2014. Branton, 2008.

value. Huge amounts have been paid to settle claims by, for example, direct or indirect customers or competitors.[374]

Negative publicity can have a greater impact than all of the above. Employees and directors who know about the existence of a cartel may lose their jobs or, in the worst-case scenario, they might even find themselves in prison. Almost everywhere in the world competition laws have extraterritorial reach. Extraterritoriality becomes an issue if the actions relate to the country in question. Even if companies only attempt to enter an anti-competitive agreement, they can be fined. This happens regardless of whether the actions are effective or not. In this context, competition authorities have developed a "leniency" programme whereby the first party to inform the competition authorities about a cartel is given full or partial immunity when it comes to fines.[375]

In the United States, criminal sanctions have been imposed in cartel and predatory pricing cases.[376] Sanctions are defined, for example, in the US Foreign Corrupt Practices Act.[377] The Act also mentions corruption, such as bribing a foreign official or a political party official. The jurisdiction of the US authorities often extends beyond US borders.[378] The scope of criminal law may also be global.

The Sherman Antitrust Act[379], the Clayton Act and the Federal Trade Commission Act form the basis in US antitrust laws. The Sherman Antitrust Act and Clayton Act[380] describe three types of situations where the US Federal Government may address restrictions of competition arising in economic businesses. First, it prohibits any arrangement restricting inter-state trade and market organisations with a restrictive effect on US foreign trade, such as cartels or agreements between undertakings prices and production restrictions. Second, it restricts an arrangement that has a negative effect on competition. Third, the creation of a monopoly in one business area is prohibited in the United States. The federal court has the right to dissolve such a company if it is established that the company is in breach of the above provisions in the United States. For example, Standard Oil was split into 34 separate companies back in 1911. It was also necessary to dismantle information technology and telephone company AT&T so that only the parent company continued to provide service in the United States. Also, the merger of chemical industry giants Dow and

374 Dunleavy, 2010. Ezrachi, 2012.

375 Dunleavy, 2010. Ezrachi, 2012.

376 According to *Wikipedia*, predatory pricing is: "the undercutting by a company to eliminate a competitor entering the market and to cover costs at higher prices after the competitor has left. It is used to defend a dominant position." Several companies can hold dominant positions simultaneously.

377 Public Law 19 December 1977. 15 USC. § 78dd-1. 95-213. Known also as FCPA of 1977.

378 Please see effects –doctrine Chapter.

379 The Sherman Antitrust Act, 1890.

380 The Clayton Antitrust Act, 1914.

DuPont was approved in the EU in 2015 but with the obligation to sell off some of its operations.

If infringements are noted, a court may issue a fine or even recommend imprisonment. Similarly, victims may claim treble damages. They can also claim rationalised legal fees. These requirements are imposed by the Clayton Antitrust Act. At the time of the adoption of this law in the early 20th century, the US Federal Trade Commission was also set up to investigate offences contrary to competition laws and to prohibit anti-competitive measures. Both are more public law than civil law. This is particularly relevant where the court hears an action which is linked outside the United States. In civil matters, the action may lead to the applicability of foreign law in the United States.[381]

The UK system combines features of British and European regulation[382]. Both The UK Competition Act 1998 and the Enterprise Act 2002 have features from UK legislation but also the EU has influenced UK laws. The functioning of competition in the UK is assessed by a separate Competition and Markets Authority (CMA). In the UK, cartels, predatory pricing, binding and the abuse of a dominant position are prohibited.[383] In the UK, there are also criminal penalties for, for example, predatory pricing. A large number of cases are also settled out of court.[384] While the UK was still in the EU, it was obligated to align its domestic legislation with EU law. One very important case in the application of UK law and EU competition law is Courage Ltd v. Mr. Crehan in 2001.[385]

> The case concerned a lease agreement between Courage Ltd and Mr. Crehan, a pub landlord, which was subject to the condition that Crehan should purchase a certain quantity of beer from Courage. Courage did not receive a 'minimum fee' and therefore brought an action against Crehan. Crehan defended himself arguing that the agreement was not valid under Article 81 of the EU Competition Act. In addition, Crehan claimed that Courage even sold beer at a lower price to those with whom it did not have a similar exclusive distribution agreement. English law did not allow damages to be claimed if the contract had been unlawful (even if it was contrary to EU law). Nevertheless, the Court of Justice of the EU ruled that Crehan may rely on Article 81

381 Gilioli, 1981, 474–475.

382 Few years ago the UK has left the EU. As the issue is not valid in terms of white-collar business crimes, this will be not considered in this book.

383 We shall see how Britain's exit from the EU will affect Competition Laws and their progress in the UK. What is certain is there will be more expenses in trade, more bureaucracy and tougher competition. Trade will take place according to the WTO's rules and guidelines. This has already had an impact on multinational companies, which have moved their business away from Britain.

384 ICN Cartel Settlements 2008, Appendix A.

385 C-453/99, *Courage Ltd v. Bernard Crehan*, 20 September 2001.

in such a conflict and it must be complied with, regardless of what is provided for by national law.[386]

It remains to be seen how the UK's exit from the EU will affect competition. At least it directly affects those companies which have business with the UK. Brexit will most likely indirectly increase bureaucracy and competition, but it will most probably raise the costs of mutual trade as well. It remains to be seen what Brexit means for Sweden, Holland, Finland and Germany, which have the greatest volume of exports and imports with the UK. Customs formalities are the first issue to solve. Trade will be conducted according to WTO agreements in the same manner as with Russia. The UK needs to renegotiate all of its trade agreements.

13.1. Examples of Competition Law and Antitrust Law

The following are examples of business crimes.

In 2020, Facebook rivals and defunct app developers submitted a 107-page complaint and antitrust lawsuit against Facebook claiming it was "one of the largest monopolies ever seen in the United States." As a result of the lawsuit, Facebook founder Mark Zuckerberg was forced to sell his controlling share in the company. New York University's Professor Fox considered the remedy not to be normal as Facebook had over time acquired significant power over the US economy.[387]

In 2020, Apple was hit with sanctions amounting to €1.1 billion following a violation of competition law in France. In this case, Apple did not permit any independent stores to sell its products at a lower cost than Apple stores. Therefore, Apple used its dominant position unlawfully. The dispute originally began in 2012. First, the company had agreed that its wholesalers would not compete. Second, independent retailers could not, without risk, sell the company's products cheaper than Apple stores, leading to price uniformity. Third, the company abused vendors' financial dependence on the company by imposing on them unfair financial terms that were worse than those issued to its own dealers.[388]

Apple also violated antitrust law by colluding with publishers to raise e-book prices in a UK court.[389]

386 *Courage Ltd v. Bernard Crehan and Bernard Crehan v. Courage Ltd and Others*, 20 September 2001.

387 Gandel, 2020.

388 *BBC*, 16 March 2020. *The Guardian*, 16 March 2020.

389 Raymond - Stempel, 2013.

In 2017, AT&T/DirecTV's acquisition of Time Warner Inc. was blocked due to the fact that the merger would have had a negative impact on competition. The US Department of Justice ruled that the merger would have resulted in higher bills and weakened innovation.[390]

In 2012, the cartel involving Phillips, LG Electronics and Panasonic was fined $1.9 billion over its cathode-ray tube. In fact, two cartels were suspected to have operated for a decade. The EU Competition Commission considered in its ruling that companies from two continents started to fix prices and carve up the TV and computer monitor cathode-ray tube markets. The companies and their company executives met for 10 years in different cities and played golf at the same time. Joaquin Almunia, who was the EU Competition Commissioner stated: "These cartels ... feature all the worst kinds of anti-competitive behaviour that are strictly forbidden to companies doing business in Europe." Also, Samsung, Toshiba Corp and French Technicolor were fined separately. In 2012, the fine was the biggest antitrust penalty in the European Commission's history. Before this case, the biggest penalty had been a fine of €1.38 billion imposed on a car glass cartel four years earlier.[391]

Microsoft was fined €899 million for abuse of its dominant position and non-compliance with a previous decision in 2008. Microsoft had ignored previous sanctions. Competition Commissioner Neelie Kroes wrote in his statement that "Microsoft was the first company in 50 years of EU competition policy that the Commission has had to fine for failure to comply with an antitrust decision." [392]

390 *The US Department of Justice*, 20 November 2017.

391 Yun, 2012.

392 *Reuters*, 27 February 2008.

14. Securities Markets and Business Crime

"Financial crime is first and foremost a market, thriving and structured, ruled by supply and demand."[393] Securities fraud is one form of white-collar crime and can be committed in a variety of forms but primarily involves misrepresenting information investors use to make their decisions. Securities fraud can also include embezzlement by stockbrokers, stock manipulations and front running.[394]

Business crimes previously referred to in this book mainly concerned the falsifying of corporate information and using confidential company information for self-dealing. This section is about influencing the decision-making process by giving misleading information to markets, for example. The perpetrator of such a fraud can be a stockbroker, brokerage firm, company, investment bank or similar.[395]

It is important for a CEO and board members to remember that traditions and practices differ according to cultures. In the US, for example, CEOs in the past were used to managing their companies almost alone. The board mainly watched from the sidelines, while CEOs made incomprehensible and unbelievably wrong-headed decisions contrary to the interests of the company. In Russia, for example, a CEO can decide alone whether the company is listed or not. A lot has changed after many of the big cases involving business crime.[396]

> The CEO of Enron had clearly mismanaged communication inside the company but was able to communicate perfectly with people outside the company. Amazingly, less than a year before Enron finally crashed in 2001, the company was selected as the most innovative company in the United States. From the Enron case, it can be concluded that scandals not only destroy customer relationships but also affect the morale of the company's own employees. In the United States, sectoral scandals and the Sarbanes-Oxley Act (SOX) have contributed to improving the communication between management, mainly between the government and the CEO. Prior to this, there were many vague, even illegal, executive decisions, such as those made in Irish Tyco International

393 de Brie, 2000.

394 Chen, 2019.

395 FBI White-Collar Crime. Investment fraud is becoming more common according to Europol in 2020. The size and nature of fraud is increasing and becoming more international. In governance, information security is a "hot potato."

396 Tiihonen, 2007, 17.

(2002), American WorldCom (2002), American Xerox (2002), American GM (2014) and American Kodak (2012).[397]

If we look at investment frauds, they have one feature in common, they offer high rates of return with little or no risk. These investments might concern, for example, commodities, securities, real estate or other types of categories. Ponzi and pyramid schemes work so that they "draw upon the funds furnished by the new investors to pay the returns that were promised to prior investors caught up in the arrangement." This scam needs more and more people or victims to keep it going and to keep funds flowing in.[398] Securities market fraud is one form of white-collar crime, as it aims to gain finances from investors by misrepresenting information. In racketeering, only the person who is normally offering the service can benefit, and the others will lose. The system is created with a fraudulent or illegal service to resolve some problem.[399]

The FBI has also noted other types of investment fraud concerning short-term debt instruments. What they all have in common is that instruments are issued by a "never heard of" company and the promise is to pay out large profits with little risk. Commodities fraud is one example. It is based on the sale of raw materials or semi-finished goods, but it is illegal. Typically, the goods are uniform, and the payment is, for example, gold, pork bellies and coffee. Often the perpetrator creates an artificial account statement that has an impact on the purported investments. Notably, these investments have never happened.

Broker embezzlement concerns actions that are illicit or unauthorised. Here, the broker steals directly from the clients typically by forging client documents, doctoring account statements, unauthorised trading or funds transfer activities or other conduct that amounts to a breach of the broker's fiduciary duties. [400]

Market manipulation involves artificially inflating "the price of lower-volume stocks on small over-the-counter markets." This is also called a *pump and dump* scheme. In pumping, investors are recruited with false or deceptive sales practices, public information or corporate filings. According to the FBI, bribed brokers use pressure on sales to get many investors onboard with the aim of raising the stock price value. Eventually, when the target price is achieved, the perpetrators start dumping the shares for huge profits, leaving innocent investors to foot the bill.[401] This form of securities fraud is most common with

397 Tiihonen, 2007, 17. One notable website is Principles for Responsible Investment (PRI), which offers guidance in ESG matters. It is supported by the United Nations. https://www.unpri.org/. ESG (environmental, social and economic) factors (also known as people, planet and profit or TBL, triple bottom line) are at the core of PRI's actions.

398 *Investopedia*: Ponzi scheme.

399 Chen, 2019. Seth, 2020.

400 *FBI*, 2020.

401 *FBI*, 2020.

small cap cryptocurrencies and very small corporations because the competition at that level is hard. Very small corporations are also called "microcaps".[402]

Market fraud may also consider rumours and leaks which falsify the outcome. When are rumours and leaks considered violations of the rules and regulations? The Market Abuse Directive offers some guidance:

> "Therefore, if and when the relevant publication or the rumor relates explicitly to a piece of information or information that is inside information within the issuer, the latter is expected to react and respond to the relevant publication or rumor as that piece of information or that information is *sufficiently accurate to indicate that a leak of information has occurred and, thus, that the confidentiality of this inside information is no longer ensured*. In such circumstances, which should be the exception rather than the rule and *should be examined by the issuer on a case by case basis*, a policy of *staying silent or of "no comment" by the issuer would not be acceptable*. The issuer's reaction or response should be made publicly available in the same conditions and using the same mechanisms that were used for the communication of inside information, so that an ad hoc announcement has to be published without undue delay." [403] (emphasis added).

14.1. Securities Market Fraud in the US

US Rule 10b-5 offers guidance concerning market fraud in the US[404]. Rule 10b-5 provides an implied private right of action to recover damages based on material misstatements or omissions, or manipulative and deceptive devices, in connection with the sale or purchase of a security. It targets securities fraud as follows:

> "It shall be unlawful for any person, directly or indirectly, by the use of any means or instrumentality of interstate commerce, or of the mails or of any facility of any national securities exchange, a) To employ any device, scheme, or artifice to defraud, b) To make any untrue statement of a material fact or to omit to state a material fact necessary in order to make the statements made, in the light of the circumstances under which they were made, not misleading, or c) To engage in any act, practice, or course of business which operates or would operate as a

402 Wikipedia: Pump and Dump Schemes. See also the website of the US Securities and Exchange Commission: pump and dump schemes.

403 *CESR* (2009): Market Abuse Directive.

404 Securities Exchange Act of 1934. SEC Rule 10b-5, C.F.R. 240. Cornell Law School.

> fraud or deceit upon any person, in connection with the purchase or sale of any security."

The usefulness of Rule 10b-5 is that it states precisely what the most important issues in a securities exchange are. Thus, "acting in bad faith [...] the trading partner is severely liable for damages and in criminal liability to society," as free competition is distorted.[405]

The parties are, of course, bound by other obligations that involve contractual aspects, such as damages, cancellation and invalidity of the agreements. These also include the buyer's reporting obligations and the seller's disclosure obligations.[406]

> There are several levels of regulation of disclosure requirements:
>
> a) information acquired by the buyer at his own risk (the buyer is responsible for the quality of the product; also known in legal texts as *caveat emptor* rule (let the buyer beware);
> b) the provision of information is not obligatory (but, if provided, must be accurate); and
> c) important or relevant information should be provided. [407]

Following the Sarbanes-Oxley Act, the United States established in 2002 under the US Securities and Exchange Commission the Public Company Accounting Oversight Board (PCAOB). The PCAOB started to oversee audits and auditors' activities to ensure the accuracy and completeness of a company's periodic reports. In addition, the Sarbanes-Oxley Act requires the appointment of an Audit Committee, a committee of the board of directors to which the board delegates its responsibilities for audit functions, financial reporting and internal control over financial reporting, for each listed company.[408]

Key sections of the Sarbanes-Oxley Act for leaders are: (i) A public-sector auditor (PCAOB) is established. (ii) Public companies have an obligation to evaluate and publish the suitability and effectiveness of their internal control systems.[409] In addition, corporate auditors should provide an opinion on the accuracy of the published estimates. (iii) It is the responsibility of CEOs and CFOs to confirm the financial statements of the companies. (iv) Provisions to

405 Kurkela, 2003, 18–19.

406 Rudanko, 1998, 327.

407 Kurkela, 2003, 15.

408 Ahokas, 2012, 133.

409 Sarbanes Oxley Act and SEC/Sarbanes Oxley Act. These articles from SOX are most relevant for white-collar workers: *302, 303, 304, 806* ja *906*. Article 303 sets out provisions for the prevention of abuses. Article 304: *forfeiture of certain bonuses and profits*. Article 806: *whistleblower protection*. Article 906 sets out that a mistake could result in fines or even 20 years in prison.

increase the independence of auditors that prohibit auditors from certain types of engagement with their client companies. (v) Obligation for listed companies to set up fully independent audit committees to oversee cooperation between the company and its auditors. (vi) Prohibition of personal loans made by companies to their key personnel. (vii) Faster reporting of insider trading. (viii) Extended and tougher criminal and civil penalties for breaking the law.[410]

> In 2019, the Department of Justice and Securities and Exchange Commission were investigating a bid-rigging and bribery scheme. Microsoft had sold software licenses to Hungarian governmental agencies. Microsoft and its Hungarian subsidiary settled the case for $25.3 million.[411]

In the US, securities fraud or allegations are investigated by the SEC (Securities and Exchange Commission) and the NASD (National Association of Securities Dealers). The FBI is also involved in most cases. It is common for state authorities to investigate investment scams as well.

> In this respect, Utah was a pioneer where Ponzi scheme perpetrators targeted their actions at tightly knit cultural and religious groups in the state. Utah launched an online registry for white-collar criminals in 2016 with images and descriptions of the crimes perpetrated.[412]

Securities violations or fraud have been reported in the United States in, for example, the following cases:

> In 2019, Galleon Group founder Raj Rajaratnam was convicted in an insider trading case. Rajaratnam was convicted in a criminal case in 2012, and in in a civil case in 2019, where Rajaratnam was fined $96 million. This case is a good example of how it is possible to be convicted in parallel cases in the US. What makes it exceptional is that under the Securities Exchange Act, Section 21A, individuals can be charged both in civil and criminal cases to a maximum amount. Rajaratnam's case is related to the cases of McKinsey & Company senior executives Anil Kumar and Rajat Gupta. All three men were charged and convicted for insider trading and conspiracy. Kumar testified against Rajaratnam and Gupta after he pleaded guilty. Rajaratnam faced a total of 14 charges and 11 years in prison, and over $150 million in fines. Robert Moffat

410 *SEC*: Sarbanes Oxley Act.

411 Jaeger, 2019.

412 Lam, 2016.

was also implicated in the case, ending his journey to becoming the next CEO of IBM even before it started[413]

***

In April 2017, Tesco overstated its profits and gave false and misleading accounting information. The company got caught and it received £129 million in fines and £3 million to cover the costs of the investigation. This Deferred Prosecution Agreement (DPA) was greatly criticised because individuals who would have faced criminal charges avoided criminal proceedings when the company paid the fines.[414]

***

The second biggest fraud of all time took place in 2012. Robert Allen Stanford was sentenced to 110 years in prison for operating a Ponzi scheme. He stole money over 20 years from his company SIB. The Ponzi scheme cost his company roughly $7 billion. He misinformed approximately 50,000 investors, of which 18,000 never got any of their money back. He used the money for his luxurious lifestyle. Stanford was convicted for fraud.[415]

***

In 2009, there was wide abuse of insider trading in Silicon Valley, involving many IT companies as well as financing companies. Companies such as IBM and Intel as well as their lawyers and leaders were also accused of crimes. SEC charged three New

---

413 Ellman-Golan – Sandick, 2019. See *Securities and Exchange Commission v. Raj Rajaratnam*, 2019. In 2018, Jesse Litvak was convicted for securities fraud in the US. He worked as a securities trader for investment bank Jefferies & Co in the US. *United States v. Litvak* concerned whether Litvak was considered a fiduciary agent falsely or not. The case is significant, not for the amount but the expectation level. What expectations are there between traders and customers, and what is the government role? See more: Schwartz – Sandick, 2018. *United States v. Litvak*, 2018.

414 *BBC*, 28 March 2017. Tesco was not the only one. The US oil company Halliburton was also accused of mis-accounting. The company had increased its profits by adding cost surpluses to profits in shareholders' reports. The company itself considered its accounting as standard practice in the industry. The scandal grew because the Vice President of the United States at the time, Dick Cheney, was one of Halliburton's leaders. He resigned from the company in 2000. Halliburton admitted in 2003 that its subsidiaries had given Nigeria $2.4 million in bribes in order to have favorable corporate tax treatment in Nigeria. Theater, 2004. Mojeed, 2015.

415 *Investopedia*: Allen Stanford. The US Department of Justice, press release, 14 June 2012. See *United States v. Stanford*, 2015.

York-based attorneys at the law firm Ropes & Gray LLP for tipping inside information in exchange for kickbacks and six Wall Street traders and a proprietary trading firm involved in a $20 million insider trading scheme. The SEC alleged that the three lawyers tipped material non-public information about confidential corporate acquisitions by firm clients to a network of traders and hedge fund managers in exchange for kickbacks. This concerned the merger of IBM and Google. The wrongdoers used prepaid phone numbers, and they transferred money in bags and envelopes.[416]

14.2. Market Manipulation in UK Banks

Barings Bank was the UK's oldest investment bank, with a history that dated back 200 years. In 1995, it went bankrupt due to rogue trading activities of one of its star derivatives traders, Nick Leeson, who lost $1.4 billion of the bank's money in fraudulent and unauthorised stock market trades. From 1992, Leeson started to involve himself in risky derivatives trades. Ultimately, it was his doubling strategy, i.e. every time he lost money, he would bet double to recover the lost amount, that led to his and the bank's downfall. Initially, everything went well. At the age of 27, he was considered to be one of the top derivatives traders in Singapore. He made a lot of profit and earned a bonus of $200,000. However, his luck changed, before he realised what was happening. In 1995, he made a catastrophic error. On 16 January 1995, Leeson had bet that the Japanese stock market would not move significantly overnight. The next day, the Kobe earthquake hit Japan and the markets were severely hit. Realising the magnitude of the problem, tried to make a correction by making another risky trade, but things just got worse. Leeson fled Singapore, leaving a note at the company reading simply, "I'm Sorry". He fled the country leaving behind him losses of $1.4 billion, which were double Barings' trading capital. At this point, the bank was beyond saving. Dutch Bank ING bought what was left of the bank. Leeson was sentenced to six and a half years in the prison. His marriage ended and he was diagnosed with cancer.[417]

***

In 2012, twelve banks operating in London (including Barclays, Citi, Deutsche Bank, UBS, Credit Suisse, HSBC, JPMorgan Chase, Royal Bank of Scotland, Societe Generale) were reported by the press to have manipulated Libor rates.[418]

416 Shah, 2009. SEC I and II, 2009.

417 Leeson, 2016. *Investopedia*: Nick Leeson.

418 *Financial Times*, 12 July 2012.

What is more shocking than the ubiquity of this crime is the reporting of many similar offences in the media in 2019 and 2020. In 2021, similar cases also appeared the media.

In 2012, the media questioned how the largest banks in the world had been able to influence the market levels of money, currency and commodities. The manipulation of the Libor interest rate did not mean small transactions in euros, as all the banks involved were able to increase their market value by 16–19%. In monetary terms, this meant approximately €15 billion. When the banks were caught, their market manipulation eventually resulted in fines of nearly $10 billion in the United States. The amount was relatively small, as it was expected the banks would receive fines of up to €34 billion for currency manipulation. The OECD commented that, for example, the UK alone was facing the biggest economic scam in the world.[419] Martin Wheatley, who at the time served as the FCA's Chief Market Officer in the UK, said: "Today's record fines mark the gravity of the failings we found, and firms need to take responsibility for putting it right. They must make sure their traders do not game the system to boost profits or leave the ethics of their conduct to compliance to worry about".[420] Apparently though, nothing was learnt from the 2012 case. Seven years later in 2019, the same happened again. This time the scam centred on a pension fund in Hawaii.[421]

How did the banks end up in this situation? It all started with the manipulation of reference rates in Libor and Euribor.[422] The determination of the price of money was no longer based on free market pricing, as the authorities had thought. The banks had been able to set their own interest rates before 2009. Reference rates had also been manipulated almost daily, even in a cartel between banks. In 2009, a debate between London banks leaked to the public. In the debate, Lloyds and HBOS were planning one- and three-month Libor interest rates. In this way, brokers had also secured their big bonuses and a good life for themselves. The management of the banks had not been completely in the dark either. They had ordered their employees to give lower-than-actual Libor estimates. Therefore, the level at which the bank assumed that it would "obtain a loan from the market" had been a lie. If this had not been done, the real situation of the banks and their difficulties in obtaining soft loans would have been revealed.

419 Beioley, 2019.

420 Beioley, 2019.

421 Burton, 2019.

422 Euribor is the average interest rate at which banks lend money to each other. Libor is the average interest rate at which banks *assume* that they will receive the loan in question. Libor interest rates also use several different currencies. Libor and Euribor interest rates are used for, for example, derivatives markets, housing markets and consumer credit markets. The amounts in euros that can be affected by these interest rates are therefore large.

A message from one employee of the RBS banking chain was published in 2007. A manager who worked at RBS Bank said that yen-Libor was a cartel and wondered how much money the manipulation of the Libor interest rate brings in. As an example, one Citibank employee made a profit of nearly $100,000 in half a minute for interest rate manipulation.[423]

As we can see from the above, the manipulation of Libor and Euribor interest rates shows total disregard for the law and government actions. Proof of this criminal disregard is seen, for example, in the fact that interest rate manipulation was taking place at the same time as there was an ongoing investigation into the bank's loan markets.[424]

US dollar to British pound is one of the most widely used exchange rate ratios. Investigations by British and US authorities also revealed shortcomings in these "free" market determinations of exchange rates. Bank employees had agreed between themselves on exchange rate manipulation. When new members were admitted to this ring, willing to increase both their banks' and their own personal income, the conditions were harsh: "If you do something wrong, you might want to sleep with one eye open in the future," a Citibank employee warned.

The official investigation extended from interest rates and currencies to raw materials. Authorities began to looked into why banks such as Goldman Sachs, with 1.5 million tons of aluminium, and Morgan Stanley, with 100 oil tankers and 55 million barrels of oil and 60% of copper owned by JPMorgan, suddenly started to buy coal mines, gas pipelines, aluminium stocks and uranium trading companies. According to the authorities, by owning such raw material companies, the banks received a big advantage in the financial markets because they receive inside information and are able to manipulate the prices paid by consumers. The investigations revealed that the price of silver had been influenced by three banks and that of gold by five banks.

The resources of the authorities were limited. The aim was to curb bank abuses under the antitrust section of the Competition Act. The authorities also had to make concessions. For example, they offered amnesty to the banks that came forward to expose their rivals. The EU Commission was obliged to conclude that it did not punish UBS in Switzerland and Barclays in the UK. The authorities also had to mediate fines, which was like a lottery win for the banks. The banks were never fully held accountable for their activities. However, on the other hand, under US law, UBS and Barclays were in more serious trouble. UBS received a $700 million fine from the US market authority CFTC. Barclays decided to pay €360 million in compensation to the US and UK authorities for interest rate manipulation. The CEO of Barclays had to resign due to the Libor interest rate manipulation scandal.

---

423 *BBC*, 28 July 2014. Hawkes, 2017. Sokala, 2015. Strotkamp, 2019.

424 Jones, 2021.

The matter was not fully closed at that time, as there were still separate investigations into derivatives trading. This meant that cartel investigations were progressing in the EU. The EU imposed €485 million in fines on Crédit Agricole, HSBC and JPMorgan for participating in a cartel in euro interest rate derivatives. In addition, in future lawsuits, banks may be ordered to pay further compensation to those parties, such as municipalities, who have suffered financial losses. In any case, investors have and will lose billions of euros. If the banks are found guilty of operating a cartel, fines could have a significant impact on their turnover. The fines imposed on the banks amounted to 10% of their annual turnover but were reduced 10-100% due to a leniency notice and settlement. On 2 December 2021, the Commission fined UBS, Barclays, RBS, HSBC and Credit Suisse €344 million for participating in a foreign exchange spot trading cartel. As Credit Suisse did not cooperate with the investigation, it received no reductions.[425]

14.3. *Market Manipulation in German Banks*

The International Monetary Fund (IMF) has identified Deutsche Bank as one of the riskiest banks in the world.[426] By 2016, the bank had paid more than €9 billion in compensation and fines for its own misconduct and was preparing for an additional €5 billion. The bank marketed and sold misleading mortgage-related securities to clients and bought its own products and packaged parts into new products. This Collateralized Debt Obligation (CDO) investment scam[427] was said to have some similarities to a pyramid scam. Deutsche Bank's operations in the United States alone resulted in billions in compensation.[428]

CDO investment products are not the only problematic issue for Deutsche Bank: it has also had problems with stockbrokers who liked to game with trading. A stockbroker who worked at Deutsche Bank's Russian branch bought Russian shares worth tens of millions of rubles from its customer Igor Volkov's Russian company. This took place almost every day between 2011–2015. The same shares were sold on the London Stock Exchange in the name of a tax haven company, which was also a Volkov company. The rubles were thus exchanged for other currencies. This single act of misconduct almost led to the

425 For antitrust cases, see European Commission, 2 December 2021. All chapters above: European Commission Press release, 7 December 2016. See Vaughan, 2017; *CFTC*, 2014; *European Commission*, 4 December 2013 and 21 October 2014; *FBI*, 2014; *FSA*, 27 June 2012; FSB, 2014; *Gov.uk*, 2014; Valladares Rodríguez, 2014, *United States Ministry of Justice*, 2012; *United States Senate*, 2014.

426 *Global Financial Stability Report Press Conference*, 2016. Landon, 2016.

427 CDO, i.e., Credit Default Obligation. CDO was very popular in the early 2000s, but demand ended in 2008 due to the financial crisis.

428 The same kind of situation caused the US recession in 2018, which impacted European Markets as well. *The Economist*, 7 September 2013. *YouTube*, 2020 I.

collapse of Deutsche Bank in 2016. Since then, the bank has used substantial funds to pay off various fines and damages.

By 2015, Deutsche Bank had not organised its internal controls, despite comments from the authorities. The authorities found that Deutsche Bank's stockbroking activities violated at least money laundering rules. For these so-called gambling transactions, the bank had to pay the US Banking Supervisor fines amounting to around €400 million. In the UK, the bank was expecting an additional fine of around €190 million at the time. The bank did not recognise the characteristics of money laundering, although shares bought in rubles were sold almost immediately through the bank's own branches in London and New York. Authorities have stated that these trades could, at worst, have led to tax evasion and breaking or even abusing the law.[429]

Deutsche Bank faced even more scandal in 2016. Money laundering, espionage, interest rate scams, the prosecution of management and much more all damaged the bank's reputation and ruined its brand. Additionally, investor confidence was lost and the bank's market value plummeted. The Russian money laundering scheme cost the bank over $20 billion in 2019, and it is estimated it will cost more when the US and UK authorities finish their investigations. Worse yet is the fact that Deutsche Bank had no idea what was going on, and the bank first heard about the accusations from the Organized Crime and Corruption Reporting Project (OCCRP).[430]

In 2021, the German banking giant was once again in headlines. Deutsche Bank agreed to pay $130 million to settle bribery and fraud allegations. In this case, Deutsche Bank's activities violated the rules of commodities markets in three countries. The bank was accused of funnelling bribes to clients through Saudi Arabia and the United Arab Emirates.[431]

429 Freifelt – Schuetze, 2017. *The US Department of Justice*, 2017.
430 *OCCRP*, 2020. Saudelli, 2018. Harding, 2019.
431 El Mansouri, 2021.

15. Business crime in Tax law

With effective tax planning, companies aim, as much as possible, for preferential taxation by legal means. Aggressive tax planning may be morally controversial, but it is not illegal. Companies and tax authorities might have different views on general taxation, and the authorities might impose taxes, tax increases and possibly give penalties for delays. Still, effective tax planning is not a crime. It becomes one if the company fails to notify the authorities of the amount of money it has raised. One must recognise the difference between legitimate tax avoidance permitted by tax laws and illegal tax evasion punishable under criminal laws. Aggressive tax planning can be seen as tax avoidance but still is not tax fraud. Tax fraud is typically linked to a deliberate cover-up of income, while tax avoidance is designed to maximise profits and minimise taxation. When a company or its executives are convicted in court of tax-related crimes, we are talking about illegal tax planning: at that point it turns into tax evasion or tax fraud.

Good governance in companies should also be followed in taxation worldwide.[432] Tax planning should take the following into consideration: (i) there are business reasons for the arrangement, (ii) the arrangement is genuine real, and (ii) the arrangement aims to minimise taxes[433], which is not the main reason for the operation. It can be seen from numerous legal opinions that an overall assessment is crucial.[434]

> In 2019, Finnish oil company Neste received tax relief from the US due to its use of bio gasoline. The relief amounted to hundreds of millions of euros in 2019 and for the next three years. This was perfectly legitimate.[435]

***

> In Ireland v. the European Commission in 2016, the court ruled that the authorities in Ireland granted Apple tax relief it should not have since it was considered illegal state aid. The Irish government does not accept the ruling.[436]

An EU-wide project to list those countries that do not respect tax rules started in 2018. The project aimed to encourage all people and businesses to avoid countries where tax fraud is constantly detected or who do not otherwise follow

432 *European Council*, 28 April 2009.

433 Note that this is not an aspect that must be met.

434 Helminen, 2012, 118-121.

435 Neste corporate website, 2019.

436 *European Commission*, 30 August 2016.

good administrative tax procedures. The obligation to notify will continue to apply to such aggressive tax planning arrangements that extend to any of the countries outside the borders.[437]

International taxation relies greatly on two anchors "1) tackling tax avoidance [...] and 2) promoting transparency and exchange of information among jurisdictions for tax purposes". The OECD/G20 Base Erosion and Profit Shifting (BEPS) project relates to the first. Needless to say, these would be pointless if these tax solutions were not accepted and implemented universally. However, this debate has proven to be lengthy. It started in 2009 with an issue concerning bank secrets, where the OECD/G20 developed a restructured agenda for a fight against non-co-operative jurisdictions including tax havens and stated bank secrecy was over. [438]

Countries agreed to fight against cross-border tax evasion together. The international standard for Exchange of Tax Information on Request (EOIR) was committed to the law. Countries also joined a restructured Global Forum on Transparency and Exchange of Information for Tax Purposes.[439]

Global tax transparency was also in focus later, notably in 2014. OECD development included then the global Common Reporting Standard (CRS) for Automatic Exchange of Information (AEOI). By 2016, 101 jurisdictions had committed to implementing it by the beginning of 2017. According to the OECD, this standard will "minimize the compliance burdens for both governments and financial institutions and result in an increase in voluntary compliance, as demonstrated by the over $48 billion already collected through voluntary disclosure programs aimed at encouraging taxpayers to report income and wealth previously hidden from their tax authorities."[440]

Since then, the OECD has worked with G20 countries and with the Global Forum[441] to provide all jurisdictions participating in OECD country workshops with the tools and guidance for consistent global implementation. In 2016: "the OECD's Forum on Tax Administration (FTA) agreed a Common Transmission System (CTS) creating the first global bilateral exchange system to make operational automatic exchanges in a truly transformative way. The cornerstone of the CTS was data security, with leading industry standards of encryption applied to each transmission. The FTA members funded its development but will make the system available to developing countries."[442]

437 *European Council*, 2016. *European Parliament*, 2018. In 2021, a new leap in this respect was taken. The OECD considers that the corporate tax haven system is coming to an end soon because a minimum corporate tax rate of 15% was introduced. See the OECD's website.

438 Saint-Amans, 2016.

439 Saint-Amans, 2016.

440 Saint-Amans, 2016.

441 According to the OECD's own website, Global Forum is "a network of policymakers and stakeholders from member and partner countries created by one or several OECD Committees".

442 Saint-Amans, 2016.

The literature on the subject refers to the intermediate community by writing about CFCs (Controlled Foreign Corporations). As there is no such CFC legislation in, for example, Russia, this absence of legislation allows Russians to make investments in, for example, the British Virgin Islands. In practice, Russians do not need to report such investments unless the money is withdrawn. In Russia, investments are transferred to other countries mainly for non-fiscal reasons, such as political risk.

One of the most important pillars for investigators to tackle illicit financial flows was established in the OECD's Oslo Dialogue in 2018. The critical part of this dialogue was the **OECD International Academy for Tax Crime Investigation**. The intention of this programme was to improve the ability of developing countries to detect and investigate financial crimes, and recover the proceeds of those crimes, by developing the skills of tax and financial crime investigators through intensive training courses. Almost 1,000 investigators from over 95 countries have received training as part of this initiative.[443]

> It is undeniable that tax arrangements and tax planning are part of business life. For example, in 2015, Facebook paid only $6,187 in business tax on its $3.4 billion earnings in the UK. British Barclays has 249 subsidiaries in the British-owned tax haven islands. Of Britain's 100 largest listed companies, almost every single one takes advantage of aggressive tax planning. Of these, there are 8,492 subsidiaries in tax havens, which means almost 100 companies in tax haven countries per listed company.[444] As a result, countries receive less and less tax revenue. If countries have less tax revenue, it also means less tax revenue for EU Member States – around EUR 60 billion each year.
>
> All of this cannot be blamed solely on companies, because the countries also use tax planning. Moderate state-wide tax planning can attract several large global companies to the country. This happened in 2014 in Luxembourg when the so-called information leak LuxLeaks took place. It was revealed that the state of Luxembourg itself had concluded tax agreements with large companies, among others, by allowing large companies to transfer funds to Luxembourg when the corporate tax rate was 1%. The LuxLeaks papers show that companies like Ikea, PepsiCo and Burberry, as well as Deutsche Bank from the banking sector, have accepted these good deals. Previously, we saw how well Starbucks

443 *Tax Crime Academy*, 2020.

444 Wong, 2016.

handled sustainability but when it comes to tax planning it has not been so successful (see page 62).[445]

In 2017, the world's largest leak of information came to be known as the "Paradise Papers". Various entities, such as Apple, Facebook and Nike, had been circumventing taxes using legal methods. The companies had been looking for gaps in tax legislation and had paid taxes to countries with low taxes for years. The media used the term "tax avoidance". It has been inferred from the information leaked to the media that some cases even involve criminal activity. Tax haven services were originally provided by the companies Appleby and Asiaciti Trust. Tax haven services were mainly directed to the Cayman Islands, the British Virgin Islands, Bermuda, the Isle of Man and Jersey. The information leak affected a total of 25,000 companies and 180 countries. The Paradise Papers leak included over 13 million leaked documents and around 70 years' worth of documentation.[446]

The following directives are currently subject to corporate taxation: (i) the Parent-Subsidiary Directive, (ii) the Interest Royalty Directive (iii) the Merger Directive and (iv) the EU Anti-Tax Avoidance Directive.[447] These mention, among other things, the tax advantages for companies. The Interest Royalty Directive does not hinder the application of national law or tax treaties if taxation is aimed at tax evasion or tax fraud. This means that the benefits mentioned in the directive are not met if the measures taken are intended for tax exemption or tax evasion. The Merger Directive is similar in nature. Its tax advantages do not apply if the transaction is aimed at tax evasion or avoidance. The Parent-Subsidiary Directive does not preclude the application of such rules where tax evasion or fraud is prohibited.[448]

In 2014, the Accounting Directive was adopted[449]. It aimed to "ensure the clarity and comparability of financial statements, other than international financial reporting standards (IFRS); limit administrative burdens and provide for simple and robust accounting rules, especially for small and medium-sized enterprises (SMEs); and increase transparency of the payments made by the mining and logging industries to governments."

445 *Financial Times*, 23 June 2017.

446 *Wikipedia*: Paradise Papers. Wikipedia: European Union Tax Haven Blacklist.

447 Council Directive 2011/96/EU of 30 November 2011. Council Directive 2003/49/EC of 3 June 2003. Council Directive 2009/133/EC of 19 October 2009.

448 Helminen, 2012, 49.

449 Comparable and clear company financial statements across the EU, Directive 2013/34/EU on the annual financial statements, consolidated financial statements and related reports of certain types of businesses.

The European Parliament wanted to tighten up the reporting of the tax footprint so that the OECD rules would become part of EU legislation. This would mean that a company pays tax to the country where it actually operates and makes a profit. The proposal for a directive progressed in early 2016. The proposal concerned multinational companies with a turnover above the threshold of €750 million who would become mandatorily obligated to notify authorities of their tax footprint. This would mean that if the proposal is accepted, companies must report the taxes received and paid separately for each member state. In addition, they must report profit before taxes, turnover and the number of employees, as well as the size of their business outside the EU. This legislation moved forward in the European Parliament in 2018.[450]

In 2016, the European Commission also proposed amendments to taxation, including tax evasion. This was done after the Panama Papers[451], i.e. those funds deposited in Panama to be safe from the tax authorities. In addition to taxation, changes were required to the Money Laundering Directive[452]. The Commission's proposal would guarantee tax authorities access to due diligence checks[453] and establish who are the beneficiaries of such companies and foundations.

In addition, the Commission wanted greater transparency in taxation. The Commission therefore proposed an amendment to administrative cooperation. A Due Diligence Review (DDR) would be carried out on new and existing accounts. The purpose of the checks was to prevent any accounting operation used for illegal activities. The countries that have been caught with, for example, inadequate money laundering and terrorism guidelines, would also be subject to harmonised checks of their financial flows by banks.[454]

The Commission wants taxation to become transparent, regardless of the state. It wants to focus on this because tax evasion is generally international in nature. In the long term, the aim is to find a situation where EU countries can, for example, exchange ownership information related to tax effects. So far, individuals and companies have been caught mainly through whistleblowing. Therefore, the Commission also wanted to protect better whistleblowers who report breaches in the EU[455]. The Commission has also noted that certain tax advisors and financial intermediaries may have eased tax evasion. This

450 Manninen, 2016, 52. *European Parliament*, 2018.

451 Garside – Watt – Pegg, 2016. Harding, 2016.

452 Directive (EU) 2015/849 of the European Parliament and of the Council of 20 May 2015.

453 Due Diligence is a preliminary review and investigation of a company's risks and responsibilities. Due Diligence is usually used to determine the audit of an acquisition.

454 *European Parliament*, 17 December 2019.

455 Directive (EU) 2019/1937 of the European Parliament and of the Council of 23 October 2019 on the protection of persons who report breaches of European Union law.

disadvantage was also addressed by providing information on the activities of tax advisors and preventing aggressive and illegal tax planning.[456]

In July 2017, Google was released from massive post-tax sales in France. The case concerned the French State's argument accusing Google of tax evasion. It based its argument on the fact that Google had recorded profits in Ireland, a lower tax country. The matter was re-examined as the French State was not satisfied with the decision. In July 2017, the EU adopted a directive aimed at making large companies more specific about the taxes they pay in all countries. Finally, in the latter part of 2019, Google decided to pay to French authorities $1 billion to settle the investigation into fiscal fraud.[457]

***

In 2017, The Formula 1 owner Delta Topco avoided payments of €900 million through tax evasion. Delta Topco, which manages Formula 1, paid €115 million in taxes instead of a €1 billion tax. In the UK, corporate tax would have been 20%, but the country's tax laws allow legal tax evasion. When Delta Topco took out large loans from the owner companies, they generated an accounting loss by recycling the money through Jersey[458]. Delta Topco gave up its shares when the American Liberty GR Cayman Acquisition Company acquired Formula 1. The new owner and the new management have promised to operate a tax regime as effectively as the previous owner.[459]

Not everything always ends up as a "loss" to the tax authorities. For example, bank giant **JP Morgan Chase** received billions of additional taxes due to tax speculation in 2012.[460]

Before the JP Morgan Chase case, **Goldman Sachs** had also been found guilty of, for example, the distortion of the price of shares and bribery. In the tax speculation case in 2012, the bank giant Goldman Sachs was also caught by instructing its staff to act illegally in relation to at least 21

456 *European Commission*, 21 June 2017. PWC, 2020.

457 *Reuters* 3 January 2019. Carraud – Rosemain, 2019.

458 Jersey is considered one of the world's most popular tax havens. Some fictional companies in Jersey have given England the title of being one of the world's biggest banana producers.

459 Sylt, 2017. *The Guardian*, 21 January 2017.

460 Hawthorne - Magu, 2018. *JP Morgan*, 2012.

customers. The problem was that the bank paid fines and the case never made it to court.

To compound matters, the managers responsible for the scheme had received bonuses in the same year, revealing a contradiction in the matter. David Viniar, Chief Financial Officer of Goldman Sachs, admitted that the banking giant had deliberately sold unsuitable products to investors. When these products were traded on derivatives markets, the banking giant made a profit. It was quite easy because the bank knew the value of the products it had sold to investors. Indeed, the US Stock Exchange Supervisor (SEC) fined the bank for sharing misleading securities market information. At the time, the fine was the highest issued by the SEC ($550 million). Surprisingly, despite this historic event, investors reacted positively to the situation and the bank's stock market price increased.[461]

461 David Viniar's testimony. Mandis, 2013. SEC, 2010.

16. Embargoes and Business Crime

Why is an embargo relevant to business leaders, especially in the context of business crime? As such it is not, but an embargo has **consequences** which in turn relate to business crime and white-collar crime activities - one of them being smuggling and the other playing with dirty money.

An embargo (economic sanctions) is an official government trade restriction that forbids trade or other commercial activity with another country. This means that trading (in full or in part) is illegal. An embargo is imposed by one country or several countries acting together. It has wide effects on all the countries involved in or impacted by the embargo. The aim of the embargo is to force the targeted country to act in accordance with the demands or wishes of the country or countries imposing the embargo. It could be said an embargo is an ideological war that targets economical balance and avoids the use of military force. An embargo could include blockades to strengthen the effects of the embargo, such as an embargo on weapons against a country at war. Less restrictive measures may include product export embargoes or visa restrictions.[462]

Embargos have a comprehensive impact on all the economies involved. It means that a particular country's trade is considered partially or completely prohibited using commercial, political, military, social or financial penalties. In practice, sanctions may include trade barriers, tariffs, restrictions on financial transactions, limiting or banning exports or imports, creating quotas for quantity, imposing special tolls, taxes, banning freight or transport vehicles, freezing or seizing freight, assets, bank accounts, limiting the transport of particular technologies or products, no-fly zones and naval blockades. Typically, an embargo is targeted at a sovereign state, but it can also be targeted at groups and individuals, domestically or internationally. The aim of the embargo is to use strong diplomatic measures imposed in an effort and "by the imposing country, to elicit a given national interest result from the country on which it is imposed." An embargo differs from a blockade in that it is considered a barrier to trade rather than an act of war. An embargo can lead to a closed economy and its effectiveness depends on its international nature and participation. Long-lasting embargos can lead to the self-sufficiency of countries.[463]

462 *Investopedia*: Embargo.

463 Berkheimer, et al., 2013. Greenwood, 2010. Enrich, 2020. One of the most famous embargoes in the world was the decades-old US embargo off Cuba. Ongoing embargos can be seen on the BAFA's website: embargos. Also, the UN has an updated list of countries under embargo: Consolidated United Nations Security Council Sanctions List.

16.1. EMBARGOS AND UN

Embargos may also be imposed by entities such as the United Nations. The UN Treaty (the Charter), sets out the main principles of international relations. In addition to these, the Charter also contains the objectives that the UN seeks to achieve. The UN has four objectives: 1) the UN maintains peace and security at an international level and resolves disputes peacefully; 2) the UN is constantly developing relations between nations to ensure, for example, that every person has the same rights and respect for them; 3) the UN's objective is to address economic, social, cultural and humanitarian problems and to promote human rights; and 4) the UN also seeks to serve as a hub for different nations.

Therefore, the 193 UN member states all have rights and obligations, such as peaceful dispute resolution[464]. In practice, UN member states may violate the principles laid down in the UN Charter. The UN seeks to exert a political influence on state decision-making so that all states' activities are "acceptable to international law". The various declarations are an example of a political expression of will for the member states, although they are not as such mandatory or binding. The UN may also intervene in the actions of other countries if such serious deficiencies or features are identified in their operation which pose a threat to international peace and security.[465] This happened in Myanmar when the UN called for an arms embargo in the summer of 2021.[466]

> In 1993, the UN Security Council established the International Criminal Tribunal for the Former Yugoslavia, the first war crime tribunal in peace-time since the end of the Second World War. A total of 161 indictments and convictions were recorded. Previous international war crime tribunals took place immediately after and in response to the Second World War at Nuremberg and Tokyo. The purpose of such international war crimes tribunals is to secure justice for the millions of victims and their families who have suffered war crimes and in which state leadership has often been involved. Another major UN war crime tribunal was established in 1994 following the Rwandan genocide.[467]

By 2020, UN member states have voted in the UN General Assembly almost 20 years in a row to cancel UN embargos. The United States and Israel have opposed such cancellation and, as a result, the proposal has been rejected every time. Total embargos no longer actually exist; those that continue mainly concern export restrictions or import restrictions or financial sanctions. Sanctions are only to be used if international peace and security are

---

464 The UNRIC library is the perfect place to start reviewing the international principles given

465 *United Nations*: FAQ.

466 *Deutsche Welle,* 18 June 2021.

467 United Nations: FAQ. Wikipedia: International Criminal Tribunal for the former Yugoslavia.

threatened. Such a threat would include, for example, terrorism or human rights violations.[468]

16.2. Embargos and US

The US has imposed economic sanctions quite many times. Also, such embargos have lasted very long. In 2014, the restrictions concerning one of the world's (and history's) longest embargoes between the US and Cuba were reduced. This meant that after 50 years, cruises and flights between US and Cuba were once again possible. The trade policy blockade of the United States against Cuba was aimed at hindering the development of the Cuban economy. The embargo was also intended to affect Cuba's foreign policy and was in force from 1962 until 2014. However, the embargo did not change Cuba's political system. The embargo not only hampered trade between Cuba and the United States but affected all companies that were subcontractors or using Cuban raw materials or semi-finished products in their own activities. For example, the car manufacturer Toyota previously got into trouble during the embargo because its subcontractors were not allowed to use Cuban nickel in Toyota's spare parts.[469]

> In 2019 Huawei faced a major boycott operation from the US and its allies. Huawei's phones were said to have contained a surveillance system for the Chinese government. This in turn reflected negatively on Huawei's part in 5G wireless network involvement. As the evidence against Huawei was quite minimal, Huawei effectively accused the US government of harassment, chasing the company and starting legal proceedings against it for political reasons. The boycott was very complex in nature and included allegations of corporate espionage and theft of intellectual property. It also included allegations that Huawei had wilfully exported technology of US origin to Iran and violated US sanctions at the time.[470]
>
> In 2019, the US refused cooperation with Chinese companies. For the Chinese technology company Huawei, this meant it could no longer enter US markets. The world started to talk about a Huawei boycott. Facebook, for example, blocked Huawei from adding its applications automatically to new Huawei phones. Not only did this apply to the Facebook app but also to WhatsApp and Instagram. This was done after the US Government said Huawei was allegedly using its devices for espionage purposes. This turned into a technological war with more losers than winners.

468 Finnish Ministry of Foreign Affairs: international embargo.

469 MacAskill, 2011. Kanninen, 2015.

470 Magee, 2019.

> Based on this decision, the US caused losses of up to 15% for American companies like Qualcomm and Intel, who produced chips for Huawei. The losses could actually be even bigger when considering future 5G investments. 5G is seen as important since it represents a huge leap forward in communications technology—along with AI, a hospital doctor might one day be able to perform surgery remotely and parcels could find their destinations without human assistance. Leaps in technology also come with many threats, of which cyber threats are the biggest.
>
> In the dispute between the US and China, there are also winners: the longer the dispute between the US and China prevails, the better companies like Sweden's Ericsson can improve their profitability due to easier access to US markets. We also need to remember that the relationship between China and the US is more complex than simply a trade war. The US imports much more from China than vice versa. Moreover, the US owes China as much as $1 trillion in state loans. Interestingly, the US has warned its citizens about the cyber threat from China, but Europe is being built mainly on Chinese 5G platforms.[471]

16.3. Embargos and Iran, North Korea, Russia and China

In 2007, the European Union sanctioned Iran for its nuclear programme and the country's poor human rights situation.[472] The EU tightened the sanctions in 2012 and continued them until April 2021. The sanctions imposed in 2012 were also based on sanctions imposed by the UN Security Council. It maintained, among other things, the ban on imports and exports of arms.

Many countries and international bodies have imposed bans on North Korea. One of them was imposed for the export of certain products after North Korea was found to have placed a bomb on a South Korean airplane in 1987. At present, the sanctions rule for investment and financial markets in North Korea prohibits, among other things, the creation, maintenance and operation of joint ventures with North Korean communities, the granting of finance to North Korean communities, North Korean investment in commercial activities in the European Union, and the opening of new accounts in financial institutions.

> In 2021, the Department of Justice and the Office of Foreign Assets Control (OFAC), settled violations in a case where a global supplier knowingly sold products to North Korea. Indonesian company PT Bukit Muria Jaya sold cigarette paper to North Korea through an

471 Yun Chee, 2019. *Global Times*, 18 August 2020.

472 Nichols - Charbonneau, 2012.

> intermediary located in China. As the Indonesian company used direct payment using a dollar account, although the account was not a US bank, it still led to almost 30 wire transfers through the US banks. According to the embargo, corresponding banks are not allowed to transfer money to North Korea. PT Bukit Muria Jaya was fined almost $2 million for conspiracy for bank fraud.[473]

Extensive sanctions have been imposed on Russia following the invasion of Ukraine in February 2022. The sanctions included, for example, travel bans for important people as well as import and export bans in trade. In 2014, the West condemned the occupation of the Crimean Peninsula and imposed sanctions on Russia as a result. Russia, for its part, responded to Western sanctions by imposing its own embargo. The sanctions have had an impact on world trade. For example, the sanctions drove down the value of the ruble, which caused an economic crisis in Russia. The West, for its part, is estimated to have suffered losses of around €100 billion. In addition to sanctions, the West has sought to resolve the situation, by excluding Russia from the G8 summit and transferring the meeting place from Russia to Brussels. In addition, the EU froze EU-Russia summits.[474]

> Around this dispute, Siemens was suspected in 2017 of violating EU sanctions. The company had, according to lawsuits, supplied Crimea with turbines. Siemens denied all accusations and argued that the turbines arrived in Crimea by accident. The company explained that the turbines were supposed to be delivered to the Russian city of Taman but somehow ended up in Crimea. This resulted in Siemens totally shutting down its energy production unit deliveries to Russia at the end of 2017. Moreover, Siemens gave up its 40 percent share in the Russian energy sector company.[475]

The world witnessed a trade war and many embargos between the US and China in 2019, continuing into 2022. This also had larger consequences, including the effect on countries' currencies. In just over 10 years, the Yuan went lower compared to the dollar. China allows this because it wants its competitiveness back. This in turn might lead to a larger issue: a currency war or, at the very least, a crisis. This might mean slower economic growth in the US, which could lead the Federal Reserve to lower interests more aggressively. This might affect the value of the dollar and international subcontracting chains. This means when countries face embargoes there are always those who want to benefit from that situation – and play with dirty money.[476]

---

473 Volkov, 2021.

474 *European Commission,* 26 July 2016; *European Union Newsroom*, 10 March 2016.

475 *CNBC*, 5 August 2017.

476 *UNCTAD*, 6 November 2019.

17. IPRs and White-Collar Business Crime

A company's most valuable assets are its Intellectual Property Rights (IPRs). Nowadays, bad faith and various copying methods represent a huge risk factor for companies and directors. Intellectual Property (IP) is a broader concept than IPR. IP consists of brand, technological inventions, service concepts, data, knowledge and know-how and business secrets.[477] IPR, on the other hand, consists of patents, trademarks, designs and copyrights. The image below explains the differences:

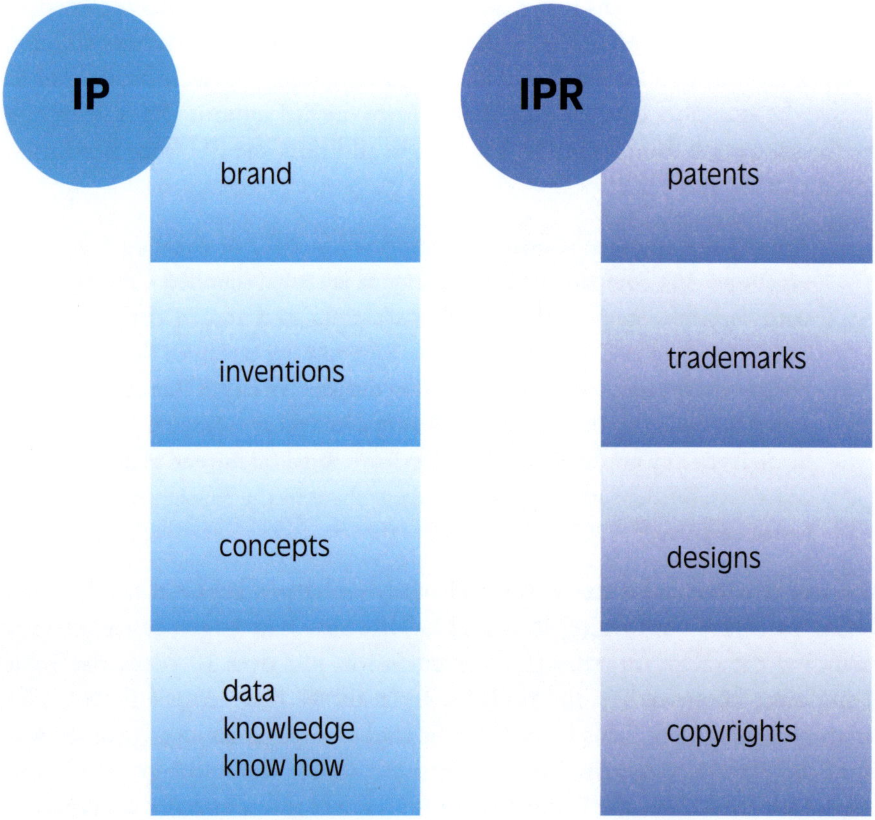

Image 6. The image shows the differences between Intellectual Property (IP) and Intellectual Property Rights (IPR).

477 Leskinen, 2021.

Intellectual Property Rights (IPRs) are intangible assets. The growing importance of IPRs is reflected in particular in increased investment protection and increased awareness of IPR content. IPRs are often problematic due to their diversity. They are national in nature, even though the business environment is international. For example, US IP law has evolved to reflect what the United States' own interests have been. Also, as in the case of patents, the United States joined international agreements much later in when compared to other countries. Interest and nationality explain, to some extent, why the United States differs from the EU in intellectual property law. The protection of inventions and copyright is mentioned in the United States Constitution. Federal authorities have jurisdiction over these matters. Trademark protection is largely based on state law[478]. In practice, Western and developing countries will also certainly always have different perspectives on the level of intellectual property protection.

Good and prudent protection is particularly emphasised in international trade and in various political contexts.[479] Companies spend a lot of money on protecting intellectual property rights, but less attention has been paid to fighting against copycats within the company. Also, it is important to remember that, for example, trademark registration is vital if the company intends to sell or market items in China; otherwise, there is a serious risk that the brand will be hijacked.

In addition, products might not be sold to local online stores or through social media, as these operators might check if the trademark is registered. Marketing might be prohibited if the registration is missing. This is not always the case though. In November 2019, there were changes that came into force in China's trademark law as they tried to strengthen the scope for tackling speculative and bad faith trademark registrations.

In the United States, the execution of trademark law is not, in principle, as accurate as in the EU. For example, the Supreme Court of the United States, in its ruling in 1988 on retail store K-Mart, stated that the trademark right is lost in the US if products are exported outside the US by the trademark holder or company that the trademark holder controls (controlled undertaking).[480]

In Japan, the case with Parker Pen revealed a similar decision. In this case, the court decided that parallel imports could not be banned in Japan if the proprietor of the trademark did not create a distinctive goodwill value in Japan for its trademark.[481]

478 *WIPO*, 2020.

479 Hurmelinna, 2001, 4.

480 Directive 89/104/EEC - Exhaustion of trade mark. *K Mart Corp. v. Cartier, Inc.*, 1988. See also *Silhouette International Schmied GmbH & Co. KG v. Hartlauer Handelsgesellschaft GmbH.*

481 Parker Pen case: *N. MC. Co. v. Schulyro Trading Co.*, 1970. See Tozzi, 2011: the U.S. and Japan Differ in Court Analyses of Gray Market Goods, But Yield Same Result.

If we compare a patent to a business secret, the patent includes a requirement for inventiveness and novelty, unlike a business secret. Business secrets can include financial information and can be unlimited in terms of time. There is no such feature in patents. For example, computer software that has only limited patentability features can be protected as a business secret. Depending on the country, the maximum validity period for the patent is 20–25 years, and business secrets are in principle valid for a lifetime unless the secrets are publicly disclosed.

A business secret is not limited to a specific area, which is the case with patents, and does not require government approval or a certificate of registration. The patentee has a right of prohibition over others, but business secrecy does not confer similar exclusivity. A business secret relates only to unauthorised disclosure and use. This situation does not preclude a competitor from coming up with the same business secret or just by chance finding information, for example, about the products on the market. A business secret is, on the other hand, easier to lose than a patent. Patent law contains provisions on liability and infringement of a patent.[482]

> In Finland, leading textile manufacturer Marimekko found Dolce & Gabbana products that infringed its Unikko design. In 2008, both parties agreed to sign a settlement agreement and withdraw all lawsuits against each other.[483]

Intellectual Property crime is committed if "someone manufactures, sells or distributes counterfeit or pirated goods, such as patents, trademarks, industrial designs or literary and artistic works."[484] The counterfeited product business is not a small business. The share of counterfeits was 6.8% according to EUIPO in 2019. This means 6.8% of all items imported into the EU. Counterfeiting represented 3.3% of world trade in 2016.[485]. In 2013, the percentage was 2.3%, which equals €338 billion. For comparison, that is the equivalent of the whole GDP of Austria or the combined GDPs of both the Czech Republic and Ireland. The impact is higher in the European Union area. Europol estimates that lost sales to industry represent about €2.3 billion in toy counterfeiting, €43.3 billion in clothing counterfeiting and about €9.5 billion in cosmetics and personal care products. According to WHO, annual lost tax revenue amounts to roughly $45 billion in the tobacco and cigarette industry every year. Of all sectors affected, counterfeiting alone is estimated to affect 518 000 lost jobs in the EU. So as counterfeiting continues people continue lose their jobs. IPR

482 Vapaavuori, 2019.

483 *Fibre2Fashion*, 15 October 2008.

484 *Europol,* Intellectual property crime.

485 *EUIPO,* 2020. Fighting organised crime, especially intellectual property crime, which is ranked as one of the top ten priorities at the EU level. *EUIPO*, 2021.

crime casts a long shadow. For the most part, it affects businesses but may well also result in the loss of jobs or other costs. These other costs might even affect health since some products, such as counterfeit medicine products, might be dangerous in terms of safety and health. However, all of this may come with other illegal activities and might affect governments on a larger scale and their ability to invest in innovation and create wealth.[486]

In 2016, Samsung accused another electronics manufacturer, Huawei, of infringing its technology patents in China. Huawei had previously sued Samsung in China and in the United States. Huawei won the dispute in October 2017. [487]

Various patent disputes can adversely affect a company's market value. Samsung's patent dispute affected Samsung's market value so badly that it lost $10 billion.[488]

***

Europol launched two operations, OPSON V and Silver Axe, starting in 2014. The first operation was targeted at health and safety, and in which over 10,000 tons and one million litres of hazardous fake drinks and food were seized. The second operation took place in 2015 and ended with the seizure of 190 tons of illegal or counterfeit pesticide.[489]

***

A gang of metal thieves caused over €1 million of damage to SNCF (the national railway company in France) and were eventually caught in 2020. The case concerned train robberies in Romania. The network listed 57 thefts of metal components weighing a total of 38 tons.[490]

***

486 *Europol*: Intellectual property crime. Europol gives one example: "clothing counterfeiting in the EU costs business €43.3 billion in lost sales, governments €8.1 billion in lost revenue and 518,281 people their jobs."

487 *ChinaDaily*, 12 October 2017.

488 Miyoung, 2012.

489 *Europol*: Intellectual property crime. COVID-19 pandemic caused even more counterfeits in the EU area.

490 *Europol*, 13 February 2020.

> In 2020, a pan-European operation targeted counterfeit medicine. The operation ended in the arrest of 165 suspects in 12 countries, €7.9 million seized and almost 36 million units of medicines seized.[491]

Despite the differences between intellectual property and business secrets, intellectual property rights can all too easily lead to litigation if the opposing party can be drawn into a class action. All too often, companies accede, forget fact-checking and fall for false claims. In addition, negative publicity and costly legal proceedings are a major cause of anxiety. A good illustration of this is related to some iconic songs known all over the world:

> Warner / Chappell claimed for a long time, even decades, that it owned the copyright to the song "Happy Birthday to You". The company also generated millions in revenues each year from the use of these words in various films and other publications, which is why production companies often preferred the song "For He's a Jolly Good Fellow". In 2015, in the United States, a court ruled that there was no copyright by Warner. The company settled the dispute by paying $14 million in damages.[492]
>
> ***
>
> In the *Intel v. Via Technologies*[493] case, 2002, Intel sued Via Technologies for infringement of its five patents. Intel had also refused to license its patents to Via Technologies. The Court of Appeal took the view that an infringement of competition law was possible and, in some respects, even probable in such a case. The decision could be compared to *CSU v. Xerox* Federal Circuit USA, 2000. In that matter, it was stated that the patent confers far-reaching immunity, but with three exceptions. There is no such far-reaching immunity if: (i) the patent was obtained by fraud, (ii) the patentee sues to disrupt the competitor, and (iii) the case is subject to unlawful tying. The restrictive effect on competition is acceptable if the restriction is not illegally extended beyond patent rights.
>
> ***
>
> The operations of a file search service called The Pirate Bay were the subject of a European Court of Justice ruling in 2016. Anybody was able

491 *Europol*, 6 March 2020.

492 Loomis, 2016.

493 *Intel Corp. v. VIA Technologies, Inc.*, 2002.

to download copyrighted files through The Pirate Bay. In the view of The Pirate Bay, the company did not infringe the copyright in any way because it did not retain the copyrighted files but merely provided the so-called tracking files. Tracking files were used to direct users to other users' platforms from which copyrighted files could be downloaded. The issue was multidimensional as The Pirate Bay was based on the same idea as Google's YouTube. YouTube, though, is not primarily responsible for the uploading of illegal content. The European Court of Justice ruled that The Pirate Bay's activities were illegal and therefore the company committed copyright infringement.[494]

***

Choosing the correct intellectual property right should be done carefully. The practical significance of the design law in different countries and regions can sometimes be surprising for companies. The shoe manufacturer Crocs became aware of this in 2010. The company had to give up its EU design right because its shoe model called "Beach" had already been published long before its registration and thus no longer met the novelty requirement of the design right.

In the court's opinion, the overall impression did not differ sufficiently from the manufacturer's own footwear that was already on the market. In practice, the exclusive right was invalidated because the company had published the new model before registering the design and had already protected some models which were too similar to the new one. Crocs could not, therefore, prevent others from using the shoe design.[495]

***

Google has been accused of several copyright infringements of unauthorised copying, mainly for copying Java code. Oracle sued Google for copying the Android operating system. The dispute escalated to a level where evidence was found against Google. If Google had been found guilty of copyright infringement, Android distribution in the United States could have been prevented. This would have been a huge loss for Google. Prior to the final decision, market rumours suggested

494 *Stichting Brein v. Ziggo BV* and *XS4ALL Internet BV. Wikipedia*: Pirate Bay.
495 OHIM appeal board confirms design for the Crocs plastic sandal invalid, Crocs Inc v. Holey Soles Holdings Ltd, 26 March 2010.

that the case would end in royalty payments to Oracle. This did not happen, as Google won the lawsuit in 2016 and successfully argued its use was "fair use"[496]

***

A slightly different infringement case is that of Grumpy Cat. In 2018, Grumpy Cat's owners were awarded $700,000 in damages for infringement. Grumpy Cat became one of the most celebrated cats after its grumpy face appeared on Reddit and went viral. The cat owners sold books, t-shirts, and other collateral with the cat's face. They licensed IP rights to Grenade Beverage for coffee products. The company launched a new product without agreement from the cat's owners, which ended in the owners suing the company for copyright and trademark infringement.[497]

***

In October 2019, Scientist Ian Shanks won a case against his former employee, Unilever, over a 13-year battle in the UK courts. Eventually, he received compensation of £2 million for his blood glucose sensor invention. Section 40 of the UK Patents Act states that employees can receive additional compensation from their companies for inventions of outstanding benefit. The Supreme Court of the UK, despite Unilever's argument, ruled that profits had been significant and substantial. The invention stood out in comparison to profits made from other patents as well.[498]

Poor knowledge of IPRs or a lack of time to review IP rights in mergers and acquisitions might cause huge problems for companies. The case of Rolls Royce is a perfect example of this:

British luxury car manufacturer Rolls-Royce Motors produced the brands Rolls-Royce and Bentley. Vickers Plc acquired the company in 1980 and was about to sell it in 1998 to BMW since BMW already supplied components to these luxury cars. BMW lost out to Volkswagen Group, which bid £90 million. The deal included, among other things, the rights to the world-famous *Spirit of Ecstasy* bonnet ornament sculpture synonymous with Rolls-Royce.

---

496 Please see the Google decision, 16 June 2016.

497 *NPR*, 2018. *MIP*, 2020.

498 *MIP*, 2020

One issue the negotiators forgot to check was that the Rolls-Royce brand name and logo were not controlled by Rolls-Royce Motors. The owner was Rolls-Royce plc, which decided to license the RR name and logo to BMW for £40 million. This in turn created a chaotic situation, Volkswagen bought the rights for the grille and Spirit of Ecstasy and BMW retained the RR logo and name for car building purposes.

After negotiations, the companies reached a solution whereby VW had the right to use the RR name and logo until 2002 and, from 2013, only BMW had the right to use the name RR for its car production, and VW would produce Bentley cars.[499]

17.1. Brand Protection

There are other ways for a company to lose value other than through wrong decisions or white-collar crime. One of these is negligence. For example, if brand equity[500] crashes or even breaks, a company may suffer immeasurable losses. In 2010, Finnish telecommunication giant Nokia lost 58% of its brand value in one year, worth $20 billion in cash.[501]

Brand value can also be lost without enough oversight of brand protection, which allows similar products to enter the market. The most worrying thing here is that the same customers, distributors, or subcontractors may buy both original and copy products for their store shelves without realising the difference.[502]

Consumers' appreciation of sustainable products has risen greatly compared to, for example, the 1980s. Production has responded to demand as companies have seen the importance of consumers in sustainable development products.[503] For a long time, it was incorrectly believed that consumers would say they wanted buy sustainable products but in reality they would not. A US study in 2019 found that 50% of purchased consumer packaged goods are actually sustainably produced. This means consumers really are conscious about how they use their money.[504]

499 Feast, 2003. See the DPA between SFO and Rolls-Royce.

500 The brand value is difficult to measure. Generally, a strong brand suggests a higher market volume and increased sales.

501 *Brand Minds*, 2018.

502 Berr, 2013.

503 *The State of Sustainable Markets*, 2015. BBC, 3 September 2019.

504 Whelan - Kronthal-Sacco, 2019.

Ikea reported in 2016 that it intended to use only sustainably produced wood in its business by the end of 2020. In 2016, 50% of the wood used by Ikea was sustainably produced, FSC-certified wood. In 2020, 98% was either certified or recycled wood.[505]

Damage to image has resulted in, among other things, states taking better care of their investments. States have started to pay attention to this issue more to secure their investments in the future as well as to minimise their involvement in scandals. Scandals or negative publicity might occur if investments are made that hurt a company's public image. Paying attention to working conditions as well as international recommendations, such as the UN Global Compact recommendations, is important.

For example, a Norwegian pension fund began to ensure the ethical aspects of its investments. The pension fund listed 120 companies in which it no longer invests. It abandoned companies that were developing components for nuclear weapons and bombs in 2015. These included companies like Boeing and Airbus. In 2009, the pension fund gave up tobacco companies. Also, its investments in Wal-Mart stopped due to the company's use of child labour in its operations. The pension fund also noted that Wal-Mart did not appear to comply with occupational safety regulations. In 2015, the Norwegian pension fund left mobile phone maker ZTE off its investment list due to continuous suspicions of corruption.[506]

Brand protection has challenges in almost all aspects. For one thing, the terminology is not the same worldwide. As markets vary greatly from each other, brand protection practices also vary. What is absolutely needed is to find ways to make brand protection in digital platforms easier. Therefore, ISO 22386 was introduced in 2021 to standardise enforcement actions globally.[507]

17.2. IPRs and AI

Generally, **artificial intelligence (AI)** means algorithms or other computational techniques for modelling and decision making, and it is worth protecting. AI has a great impact on how people buy, for example, branded products. This in particular put pressure on trademark law, which then had to adapt to reflect the

505 *FSC*, 2016. IKEA, 2020. FSC means that the raw wood is from an FSC-certified forest. FSC-certified raw material and products can be traced, if necessary, from raw materials to end users.

506 *Wikipedia*: Government Pension Fund of Norway.

507 *DH Anticounterfeit*, 2021.

changes. Trademark law is considered very practical and adaptable in form. This is especially true if we look at the changing commercial landscape.[508]

In recent years, the number of commercial applications like maps and route planning, keyboard word prediction, self-driving cars and targeted online advertising has exploded. The ultimate goal of better algorithms is better products. In terms of IPR, algorithms are the rules and models that drive the invention. Data, on the other hand, is used to train these rules and models.

Patents and trade secrets can be used for algorithm protection. Patents are useful for marketing purposes and the patent holder can have a 20-year right to prevent others from using the invention, which causes some concerns. It requires publication of the algorithm, has limited territorial effect and infringement is often difficult to detect.

Copyright can be used for protecting data as well as trade secrets. It does not require registration or publication in the EU. Detecting copyright infringement is difficult.

As trade secrets do not require publication, they can prevent better algorithms and data from copying. Those might be better choices, for example, in India or in Brazil where, due to backlogs, it can be difficult to obtain patents quickly and effectively. There are some issues to consider also regarding trade secrets: they do not prevent reverse engineering or competitors coming up with it on their own. Total secrecy and ongoing care are needed to maintain confidentiality. Trade secrets are also very difficult to enforce.[509]

> Google's search algorithm is a good example of AI. Google still has protection in its algorithm just by keeping it secret. Google's self-driving car division Waymo is an example of when things go wrong. An engineer who used to work for Waymo stole thousands of confidential documents and sold them to Uber (as previously discussed on page 72). Waymo's company secrets are lost forever.[510]

Artificial intelligence is already advanced in terms of IPRs.[511] Virtual platforms already greatly affect the European Digital Single Market (DSM). Global investments in AI are expected to reach £150 billion by 2025. The AI market grew from $8 billion in 2016 to more than $47 billion in 2020. In 2016– 2017, investment in AI increased by more than 300 percent.

Five themes play an important role in combining AI and IPR: 1) IP protection for AI technology, 2) regulation of information and data used as

508 Curtis - Platts, 2020.
509 Nielsen, 2019. Narula – Pandey, 2019.
510 Korosec, 2019.
511 Lai, 2020.

inputs for AI, 3) ownership and protectability of AI's output, 4) Digital Rights Management (DRM), and 5) IP enforcement through AI[512].

> The EU wants to tighten AI supervision. The EU's mission is to ensure that the systems are safe and secure enough for consumers. The Chairman of the EU Commission, Ursula von der Leyen, said in February 2020: "AI is a huge opportunity to Europe; therefore, we want that consumers can trust these systems."[513]

Europe and the US have different standards for patentability, with the US being more lenient. It is possible to have a patent for an AI invention in the US although it would have most likely been rejected in Europe.[514]

The problem that arises with AI is the question of liability. If a machine makes a decision according to how it was designed, whose fault is it if the algorithm starts to malfunction[515]? Who is liable for damages and which party to the contract party is liable for the AI's mistakes, or even crimes? What happens if a company's executives make a decision based purely on AI algorithms? Who is then liable for the mistake? I believe there is still no clear answer to this issue.

17.3. IPRs and Darknet

Darknet, or the dark network, is associated with anonymous networks. These allow anonymity and access to sources of information that cannot be accessed directly from the internet. Darknet sites can be found in web browsers or standard search engines. Darknet operates within the structures of the public internet, but access requires some action. The Darknet network is anonymous. This means that it encrypts network traffic and routes network traffic through multiple "knots". Darknet is basically used by people who are strict in their privacy and freedom of expression.

It is possible to access Darknet, for example, via TOR software, I2P or Freenet. It is important to remember that Darknet has both legal and illegal features. Citizens of closed countries, such as North Korea, use Darknet to communicate with the world. The purpose is mainly to prevent their internet behaviour from being monitored and page blocking problems. Darknet has evolved into a large-scale establishment used by criminals. On Darknet, the

512 Frosio, 2019.

513 *European Parliament*, 23 January 2020. See also the European Commission's White Paper on Artificial Intelligence, 19 February 2020.

514 Nielsen, 2019.

515 In 2021, Tesla cars crashed with the autopilot on in, for example, Australia and the US, killing the passengers.

illegal side is linked, among other things, to arms caches and illegal goods, often paid for with Bitcoins.[516]

Darknet is used as a marketplace for counterfeit and pirated products. Counterfeiting means, for example, manufacturing or selling goods under a false trademark. The intention is to secure monetary gain using the brand without permission. In piracy, someone is making unauthorised copies of the products protected by IP. Darknet may also combine genuine and counterfeit products. The genuine products are sold both on Darknet and on the internet. The price for counterfeit products is usually very low; for example, a counterfeit Rolex costs about $40 and a genuine Rolex can cost more than $10,000. Big profits and agile distribution are very favourable to Darknet. Some consumers might not be aware of the security and health issues and the only issue they are interested in is how much money they can save.

Darknet also sells pharmaceutical products. Europol has estimated the profits earned by a single trader selling the Xanax pharmaceutical product at $152,000. Xanax is a trademark of Pfizer Inc. Piracy software and eBooks are sold for a sixth of their actual price. The most alarming issue is that the prevalence of Darknet in IPR violations has not yet been understood. Illicit tobacco markets are also a concern for consumers.[517]

> In the summer of 2017, two of Darknet's largest marketplaces, AlphaBay and Hansa, were shut down. AlphaBay reached up to 200,000 users and 40,000 subcontractors through Darknet. The company had 100,000 copies of various counterfeit or suspicious services on Darknet, which it transmitted and sold.[518]

> The usage of Darknet was reported to have grown in 2020 due to the COVID-19 pandemic. As there are more and more Darknet users, Europol started to monitor the marketplace more carefully. In late 2019, Europol found that counterfeit products and items were sold on illegal platforms. This led to 11 arrests in the EU area.[519] In early 2019, Canadian, European and American officials joined forces to combat Darknet. This international law enforcement effort resulted in 61 arrests and the closure of 50 illegal websites. The counterfeits seized amounted to roughly €6.2 million.[520]

516 *Europol*, 2017 I. Levin, 2017.
517 *Europol*, 2017, II.
518 *Europol*, 2017 II.
519 *EMCDDA*, 2020. *CEPOL*, 2020. *Europol*, 2019 II.
520 E*uropol*, 2019 I.

18. Corruption, Bribery, Embezzlement, Fraud and Extortion

"People trust me with their secrets. But who do I trust with mine?"[521]

In the developed world, the biggest problems in business are bribery and corruption. In developing countries, the problem is usually the corruption of public officials – which is a serious problem causing obstacles to development. Companies should have appropriate anti-corruption guidance to inform their own operating environment. These guidelines should include the measures used in the company to combat corruption.

The most successful guidance addresses those areas that are the most vulnerable to bribes and the risks of bribery. The guidance should be kept up to date, as it must be based on existing legislation. In the case of an international company, it is not enough that the parent company in, say, Sweden has taken care of the instructions. The code of conduct should be created for each of the group's subsidiaries in each country of operations due to the different domestic legislation, although the principles in the ICC[522] are well aligned.[523]

521 Judi Dench's line in the movie *Notes on a Scandal.*

522 ICC International Chamber of Commerce is an international co-operation society.

523 By way of comparison, the OECD Convention does not mention 'subsidiaries or joint ventures'. Neither does the FCPA make any direct reference to subsidiaries or joint ventures, although the US Department of Justice has announced that it will also review the status of joint ventures despite ownership interest. This same statement has been made by, for example, the US Market Supervisors SEC in some of its cases.

According to the 2019 Global Anticorruption Survey, as much as 94% of respondents said their business is exposed to the risk of corruption. Over 300 senior executives in three continents (Europe, Asia and the US) responded to the survey. Almost 40% of respondents said the risk is considered significant. Over 50% said their companies have been hit by losing business due to illicit payments to government officials. The risk of corruption is already seen in companies so that over 60% of survey respondents said they would avoid doing business in a country in which the risk of corruption is involved. As much as 75% said they have stopped or delayed acquisition due to the risk of corruption.[524] These numbers are alarming and concern businesses globally. Corruption affects economic growth and security.

When a company creates an anti-bribery programme, it is not the job of just the company's board or management to combat corruption. Employees and their representatives should be involved in drafting the guidance. This ensures that the guidance also reflects the employees' perception of the company's realistic and appropriate measures and development needs. When consensus is reached, as a result of the negotiations, it is easier for the employees to follow these guidelines. The guidelines should consider the views of stakeholders. Usually, it is through the stakeholders that the company learns what is right.

> Regina v. Skansen Interiors Ltd, 2018, is a case of bribery that shows that management must be committed to and monitor compliance. It is not enough to set a rule on employees, but management needs to ensure that the rules are adopted, monitor compliance and assess their adequacy. Section 7 of the case said that "adequate procedures" were not enough.[525]

18.1. Bribery

Bribery, alternatively referred to as a **kickback** or **extortion** and **embezzlement**, is the improper use of gifts and favours, such as money, company shares, employment or political benefits, in exchange for personal gain. Bribery is a form of corruption. It aims for personal gain and "from the personal gain that is given can be anything from actively giving preferential treatment to having an indiscretion or crime overlooked."[526]

Basically, bribery can be anything in the form of cash, hospitality, entertainment, promotional expenses, facilitation payments, political or charitable contributions. It can also be indirect and happen through third

524 *AlixPartners*, 2019. *Clifford Chance,* 2019.

525 R v. Skansen Interiors Ltd., 21 February 2018.

526 Stenzel, 2017.

parties. A company may be held liable for bribery or corruption that is attempted or committed on the company's behalf by a third party. Businesses need to ensure that they are compliant with applicable anti-corruption laws in each of the countries in which they operate as well as with applicable international anti-corruption legislation with extraterritorial reach, such as the US Foreign Corrupt Practices Act and the UK Bribery Act.[527]

Bribery can sometimes form part of the systemic use of corruption for other ends, such as to perpetrate further corruption. It can make officials more susceptible to blackmail or extortion. Bribery is evidence that a company has failed to perform the legal or proper duties of the job. Moreover, it can be illegal, unethical in nature or even include biased operations made in bad faith.

Corruption, of which bribery is one part, has wider consequences. It can be seen as a barrier to entry into the formal sector, and it governs firms operating at a smaller scale: it affects growth. Corruption always has a negative impact on product innovation. This in turn means less productivity. Corruption is a "symptom" of poor governance since it soon starts to be the rule rather than the exception. It could be tackled by increasing coordination between governments, businesses and civil societies.[528]

One excellent description of corruption comes from Finland. Researchers determined levels of corruption as follows: "Heavy (widespread) corruption forms include: (i) promising, taking, requesting, giving kickbacks, and accepting corruption of bribery; (ii) misuse of public funds by theft, fraud or backfire; (iii) the sale or exploitation of public property or equivalent interests without the power to do so; and (iv) abuse of public authority and status. Other forms of corruption include: (i) inappropriate gifts, inappropriate medium-term; (ii) distortion of the facts; (iii) misuse of confidential information; (iv) manipulation of the documents and the manipulation of the game rules; (v) maintenance of the favorite system; and (vi) illegal monitoring and surveillance". Mismanagement and maladministration are forms of corruption as well. These are "(i) failure to perform duties; (ii) breach of trust and procrastination of matters; (iii) intentional insufficient information; (iv) the protection and secrecy of bad governance; (v) mismanagement: indifferent management and neglect of subordinates; and (vi) the use of drifting and distorted means in management.[529]

In 2010, a large kickback scheme began at Bank of America. For five years, Palestine Ace, her husband and her associate embezzled over $2.7

527 Salminen – Mäntysalo, 2013, 24–48.

528 *Wikipedia*: Corruption. Legvold, 2009, 197. Forgues-Puccio, 2013.

529 Salminen – Mäntysalo, 2013, 24–48. The text is freely translated from the Finnish text.

> million. They used a marketing budget and made fraudulent donations to non-profit organisations.[530]

The terms 'petty corruption', 'grand corruption' and 'systemic corruption' are sometimes also used in the literature. Petty corruption occurs in the public sector, for example, in a registration office, state licensing board or similar, and it is smaller in scale.[531] Grand corruption refers to countries or governments with a strong dictator or authority.[532] Therefore, many countries have separated the powers of the state into legislative, executive and judicial branches to ensure no single branch exercises too much power.[533] Systemic corruption normally starts when a company has lost its transparency in operations or uses monopolistic powers or even conflicting incentives. A company like this also has low payments and a culture of impunity.[534]

Bribery and lobbying often overlap, although bribery is illegal and lobbying is not. Some have even said that lobbying is "bribery in a suit" because it can have massive impacts on economies and businesses. The similarity is that both aim to ensure a favourable outcome. With lobbying, influence is used by offering financial contributions, such as trying to shape laws and legislation. With bribery, a monetary contribution is used to gain power and to ensure a certain result. In the US and according to the Lobbying Disclosure Act (1995), lobbyists need to register with the Secretary of the Senate and the Clerk of the House.[535]

> In 2021, China's top banker, former Chairman of the China Huarong Asset Management, Lai Xiaomin was sentenced to death for taking bribes worth $277 million.[536]

***

> In China, Interpol's ex-boss Meng Hongwei confessed in 2020 to having taken bribes to the value of €1.9 million. Hongwei was sentenced to thirteen and a half years in prison.[537]

***

530 Paxton, 2020, 30.

531 North Carolina State Board of Dental Examiners v. Federal Trade Commission, 2014. *United Nations Office on Drugs and Crime*, 2016.

532 Alt – Lassen, 2008. Cernkovich – Giordano – Rudolph, 2000, 131-170.

533 *Anti-Corruption Resource Centre*, 2020.

534 Alcazar, 2001, 135–136. Znoj, 2009, 53–54.

535 *Investopedia*: The differences between bribery and lobbying.

536 Deng, 2021

537 Buckley, 2020.

> Retail Company giant Walmart was accused of bribing government officials, among others, in Mexico. The company was suspected of trying to obtain new permits faster so that they could open stores sooner in 2019. After seven years of a federal bribery investigation, Walmart settled its cases involving Mexico, Brazil, China and India at a cost of $283 million. SEC's Chief Charles Cain said: "The company could have avoided many of these problems, but instead Walmart repeatedly failed to take red flags seriously and delayed the implementation of appropriate internal accounting controls."[538]
>
> ***
>
> Consumer healthcare company Johnson & Johnson (J&J) paid a settlement of $70 million in 2011. By doing so, the company avoided civil and criminal fines by the SEC brought under the Foreign Corrupt Practices Act (FCPA). The case concerned bribing government doctors in Greece, who eventually selected the company's surgical implants. Moreover, the case concerned bribing hospital administrators in Poland to get contracts and Romanian public doctors in order for them to prescribe J&J pharmaceutical products. In the SEC's announcement, the companies' subsidiaries used kickbacks in Iraq and obtained 19 contracts under the United Nations Oil-for-Food program (OIP).[539]

There are many international agreements to combat corruption and bribery: African Union Convention on Preventing and Combating Corruption,[540] EU Civil Law Convention on Corruption,[541] EU Criminal Law Convention on Corruption[542] and UN Convention against Corruption,[543] to mention just a few. More details about the FCPA, OECD and ICC rules can be found later in other chapters. Overall, there have been several reforms of bribery rules in different countries. For example, in France, the Anti-Corruption Agency (known as l'Agence Française Anticorruption, AFA) [544] published the final version of its practical guide to "anti-corruption checks in the context of mergers-acquisitions" in January 2020. This was created because the AFA thought compliance is becoming a real strategic issue in external growth operations. [545]

538 Meyersohn, 2019.

539 Gardiner, 2011.

540 *African Union*, 10 February 2020.

541 *Council of Europe*, 2003.

542 *Council of Europe*, 2002.

543 *UNDOC*, 2004.

544 Founded under Sapin II law on 9 December 2016 (French: Loi Sapin2).

545 Agence française anticorruption, January 2020. Initially, the professionals had criticised the AFA's recommendations for their lack of realism in view of operational constraints. In this new version

The Bribery Act 2010 (the 2010 Act) in the United Kingdom reformed bribery and corruption in the UK because the previous legislation was considered territorial and was the subject of much criticism. The new Act intended "to cover bribery both in the United Kingdom and abroad." It also "created new specific offences of bribery of a foreign public official (Section 6 in the Bribery Act 2010) and where a commercial organization fails to prevent bribery (Section 7 in the Bribery Act 2010)." Available figures indicate that between 2014 and the second quarter of 2018, the Crown Prosecution Service (CPS) had launched 107 proceedings under the Prevention of Corruption Act 1906, compared with around 42 for all offences under the 2010 Act.

The first conviction of a corporate entity under the new Section 7 (failure to prevent bribery) took place in December 2015 against Sweett Group Plc, which had pleaded guilty. Deferred Prosecution Agreements (DPAs) are not part of the 2010 Act, but rather were introduced in the United Kingdom by the Crime and Courts Act, 2013 (effective from February 2014). Under the DPA regime, a company accused of an offence under the 2010 Act may be able to enter into a discretionary agreement with the Serious Fraud Office (SFO) pursuant to which prosecution of the offence is suspended for a finite period. Such an agreement requires court approval. If the company complies with the provisions of the DPA, the offence will not be prosecuted at all. While still relatively uncommon in the UK, DPAs have been used to a far greater extent in the United States (where they have been in use for significantly longer).[546]

> The first DPA was used in 2015 between the Serious Fraud Office and Standard Bank. The bank "was charged with an offence of failing to prevent bribery contrary to Section 7 of the 2010 UK Act. In the course of securing $600bn project financing by the government of Tanzania from the respondent bank and its sister company, an additional 1% fee was paid to a 'local partner', a Tanzanian company of which two of three directors and shareholders were current and former Tanzanian government officials. There was no evidence that the 'local partner' had provided any services related to the transaction. The withdrawal of the $6m in cash from an account at the sister company led to a report by staff which generated a self-report to the SFO within three weeks, full disclosure of the internal investigation to the SFO and full

---

of the guide, the AFA took into account the criticisms, and the guide is more suited also to the reality of merger-acquisition operations. Sapin II helps companies prevent and combat breaches of probity. Above all, it ensures that the subject entities comply with their obligations and, if necessary, sanctions them. The AFA recalled that the Sapin II law does not impose "the evaluation of a company whose acquisition or merger is envisaged" and that its recommendations are not legally binding.

546 *McNair Chambers*, 2020, I. The most comprehensive source is the UK Bribery Digest published by Ernst & Young, 2018.

> cooperation." The terms of the DPA included: "(a) payment of $6m compensation to the Tanzanian state plus interest; (b) disgorgement of profit on the transaction of $8.4m; (c) payment of a financial penalty of $16.8m; (d) past and future cooperation with relevant authorities in all matters relating to the conduct arising out of the circumstances of the draft indictment; (e) at the respondent's expense, commissioning and submitting to an independent review of its internal anti-bribery and corruption controls, policies and procedures regarding compliance with the act and other anti-corruption laws; and (f) payment of the SFO's costs."[547]

18.2. Examples of Bribery

In 2020, FC Barcelona started court proceedings against its Vice President Emili Rousaud. He accused FC Barcelona of corruption, a claim the club refuted. The club said it takes such accusations seriously and, as a result, started a court case to back up its employees and restore the honour of the club.[548]

In 2018, Swedish telecommunication company Telia settled with a penalty of $1 billion in a bribery case.[549] According to the indictment, Telia's management had paid millions of dollars in bribes. The trial was held in Stockholm and concerned three of Telia's executives. Telia's CEO Lars Nyberg, Director Tero Kivisaari and one lawyer were accused of corruption and bribes in Uzbekistan in 2007–2010 when Telia made a deal in the country. The purchase price was suspected of having been directed to the daughter of Uzbek's dictator. In 2017, Telia agreed to pay a settlement fee of $965 million to US and Dutch authorities.[550]

Ukraine's former president Viktor Yanukovych had a massive amount of assets. He had a private zoo and a 137-hectare estate, just to name few of his properties. The president fled with his family to Russia in 2014 at the start of a deadly revolution in his country. He left behind documentation which made it evident he had enriched himself at the expense of the country's citizens. He had used Ukrainian public funds for his and his family's luxury life. The president was held liable for the disappearance of $40 billion in state assets. In his absence, he was convicted and sentenced to 13 years in prison. It came as a total shock for Ukrainians when Swedish public broadcaster (SVT) reported the receipt by a Swedish bank a bribe of $3.7 million in 2011. Moreover, the

547 *McNair Chambers*, 2020, I. *Ernst & Young*, 2018.
548 *FC Barcelona*, 13 April 2020.
549 *TheLocal.Se*, 22 September 2017.
550 *RFERL*, 15 February 2019. Lynch, 2021.

bank was involved in two other transactions with a total value of $18 million in 2007 and 2014.[551]

One of the biggest bribery trials in 2016 involved a fine of almost €780 million paid by the engine manufacturer Rolls-Royce (RR). By paying the amount, the company avoided a trial concerning the company's aircraft trades. The company was accused of various types of corruption in the trade, including China, Brazil, the United States and Indonesia.[552] The amount paid was the biggest ever approved by the UK Court of Justice in 2017.[553] RR's Deferred Prosecution Agreement (DPA) is considered one of the most significant DPAs when considering financial penalties and contributions towards the SFO's costs. However, if RR had not paid the amounts and demonstrated extraordinary cooperation with the SFO and its investigators, the matter could have been much worse. After paying "(i) £258,170,000 to reflect the profits that Rolls-Royce made as a result of criminal conduct; (ii) £239,082,645 as an additional penalty; and (iii) £13,000,000 towards the SFO's costs of its investigation" the case was settled.

Perhaps the most famous corruption case of all is the Watergate scandal. In 1973, US President Richard Nixon issued a mandate to investigate allegations of abuse and corruption to his associates. Ultimately, Nixon himself was forced to resign because he was personally suspected of corruption. Prior to this, he had dismissed the person to whom he had given authority to investigate the issue. After Nixon, President Bill Clinton was forced to respond to concerns about Whitewater real estate deals. The person who investigated the case committed suicide.[554] When it comes to countries dealing with corruption, **Italy** has perhaps suffered more than most.[555] Bribes and corruption between the country's political and economic elite were so commonplace that Milan came to be known as *Tangentopoli*, the city of bribes. One of the world's most famous corruption cases was uncovered in Italy in the early 1990s when members of the country's parliament were involved in a corruption scandal. At the time, more than half of Italy's members of parliament were indicted, with a total of around 1,200 people convicted. The number of arrests was around 3,000.[556] After the corruption scandal, Silvio Berlusconi became Prime Minister of Italy and was subsequently convicted of tax evasion in 2013. In his time, corruption in Italy increased.[557] The Italian mafia is a largely discussed topic. Ultimately, the nature

551 Kozyreva – Jason, 2018.

552 Evans – Watt – Pegg, 2016.

553 *Deutsche Welle*, 17 January 2017. Rolls Royce revised the company's code of conduct following corruption and bribery cases against the company. Those can be found on the company's website.

554 *History*, 16 July 2015. *Investopedia*: Watergate; Freeland, 2017.

555 There is a master's thesis written about Silvio Berlusconi's dirty politics and clean hands in 2016. Wallius, 2015.

556 *Wikipedia*: Tangentopoli.

557 *BBC*, 29 May 2019.

of its activities has become "invisible". Previously, the mafia's activities spilled out onto the streets as gunfights and drug dealing. Today, the mafia works more in the background and uses its power covertly. For example, it funds refugees by offering them hard-hitting assistance.[558]

Today, there are probably more headlines about bribery involving **Russia** than anywhere else in the world. Bribery and, to some degree, corruption is endemic to the country's culture.[559] Corruption also sustains the grey markets and black economy. The situation is not made easier by unclear legislation and problems of interpretation of Russian law.[560] Shell, Mitsui and Mitsubishi were forced, for example, in the framework of the Sakhalin 2 energy project, to give a majority of shares away to the Russian state-owned Gazprom.[561] The head of the anti-corruption department provided an interesting nuance to the fight against corruption in Russia when he was personally suspected of taking exceptionally large bribes worth $120 million.[562]

The Winter Olympics also played their part in 2016. A Russian general was suspected of receiving €15 million in so-called 'threshold money' for the plot allocation in connection with the Sochi Winter Olympics in Russia.[563]

CEOs of the world's largest companies have also been found guilty of taking bribes. The CEO of Samsung admitted some of the charges related to a bribe of over $30 million. The bribe was intended for a friend of the President of **South Korea** for the support of the National Pension Fund for the merger of two Samsung partners. On 25 August 2017, one of Samsung's heirs, along with four of his executives, received prison sentences of five years for bribery, embezzlement and false testimony. The President of South Korea was forced to resign in March 2017 as a result of the scandal.[564]

In 2011, the President of France received a suspended prison sentence for allegedly misusing public funds to the tune of €1.4 million. The case involved hiring the president's political supporters for posts he himself invented for them. The charges were from the years 1977 to 1995, when the president served as Mayor of Paris.[565]

Japan faced a huge scandal involving copper market manipulation in 1995. Through the company Sumitomo where he was a copper trader, Yasuo Hamanaka controlled copper markets in Japan mostly due to a favourable

558 Burtsov, 2014. Grabianowski, 2020.

559 Kuorsalo et al., 2007, 125–126, 128, 108. Bribes are estimated to be about two and a half times times greater compared to the budget in Russia.

560 Salmenniemi - Rotkirch, 2008, 103–109.

561 Green, 2007.

562 *The Telegraph,* 13 September 2016. Transparency International has estimated that corruption is a threat to Russian democracy.

563 Hakala, 2016. Azzali, 2016, 1-21. Simona, 2016.

564 *ChinaDaily*, 12 January 2017.

565 ITV, 13 January 2014.

market situation. However, as the markets changed dramatically in 1995, his short hedging became untenable. Hamanaka was found guilty of forging the signatures of his company's supervisor for various trades, and eventually he was convicted. This, however, did not save his company as its name and reputation were severely damaged. The case was complicated further when Sumitomo also blamed JP Morgan Chase and Merrill Lynch for keeping up the scheme and giving continuous loans to Hamanaka without the company knowing about it. Eventually, all companies were found guilty.[566]

In 2009, the mining company Rio Tinto was rocked by bribery claims when four of its employees were shown to have bribed officials at Chinese steel mills. In return for bribes, the employees received steel-related production data, that is, information intended to influence global market prices. The four were charged with stealing state secrets and industrial espionage. The cost of this instance of industrial espionage was estimated to be about $120 billion.[567]

18.3. Good Faith

Good faith (bona fide) is an important concept in law. The following is an excellent description of Good faith in paragraph B of UCC 2-103:

> "**Good faith** in the case of a merchant means honesty in fact and the observance of reasonable commercial standards of fair dealing in the trade." (emphasis added)

Cooperating parties must be able to trust each other. Sharing or giving wrong information or concealing information resemble a mistake, fraud or deception. Good faith is often integral to contract processes. International law is based on a commonly known definition, emphasising truth and good faith. Good faith is considered, for example, in insurance matters if a person's intentions were fair, sincere and honest no matter what the outcome.[568]

Also, the UN Convention on Contracts for the International Sale of Goods (CISG) or the Vienna Convention, which is not applicable to stock trading nor consumer trade, provides guidance: if the damage has been known or foreseeable, it should be compensated (CISG Article 79). The CISG aims to ensure certainty in international trade, which, at the same time, lowers transaction costs. Without it, there could be more room for uncertainty and the possibility for disputes. It means that the CISG aims to fill the gaps in contract language and consider points that were not considered in the contract. The

566 Beattie, 2019.

567 *ChinaDaily*, 10 August 2009; *Financial Times*, 30 March 2010.

568 *TransLex*, 2020. Good Faith as an international principle of law.

main purpose is to have a uniform and fair convention for international trade.[569] However, the CIGS is not applied if there is a situation where "a purchaser supplies the majority of materials required for manufacturing and supplying the end product."[570] The CISG is used if the contracting parties operate in different countries. About 90 countries have ratified the CISG. If the parties enter into an agreement that they will, for example, be bound by the laws of the UK, the CISG is not applicable since the UK is not on the list. Similarly, if Nordic countries enter into an agreement, the CISG does not apply. Also, if the contracting parties specifically agree not to use the CISG, they can agree to be bound by the law of another country. This might come into consideration if the parties feel the provisions of the CISG do not protect their interests.

As with other laws, there are differences between trade law, the CISG and legislation. The biggest difference is the liability for damages. The CISG does not distinguish between direct and indirect loss and does not mention reasonable aspects of damages. It does not cover "a provision regarding equitability of damages". In international agreements it is important to agree especially on limitations of liability. [571]

In 2011, the UK High Court expressed the implied duty of good faith in a distribution agreement in *Yam Seng Pte Ltd v. Int Trade Corp Ltd.* [572] This case involved fragrance distribution to many countries and bad faith practices. The court ruled in section 125 as follows:

> "The New York Court of Appeals said in 1918: 'Every contract implies good faith and fair dealing between the parties to it'[573] The Uniform Commercial Code, first promulgated in 1951 and which has been adopted by many States, provides in section 1-203 that 'every contract or duty within this Act imposes an obligation of good faith in its performance or enforcement.' Similarly, the Restatement (Second) of Contracts states in section 205 that 'every contract imposes upon each party a duty of good faith and fair dealing in its performance and enforcement'."
>
> In section 127: "In Australia the existence of a contractual duty of good faith is now well established, although the limits and precise juridical basis of the doctrine remain unsettled. The springboard for this development has been the decision of the New South Wales Court of

569 Convention on International Sale of Goods (CISG). Obligations of the seller are in Articles 30, 33, 35, and 42. Obligations of the buyer are listed in Articles 53, 56, and 60.

570 *Fondia*, 2020.

571 Convention on International Sale of Goods (CISG). *Fondia*, 2020. CISG Contracting states can be found in CISG webpages.

572 *Yam Seng Pte Ltd v. International Trade Corp Ltd.*, 2013.

573 *Wigand v. Bachmann-Bechtel Brewing Co.*, at 277.

Appeal in *Renard Constructions (ME) Pty v. Minister for Public Works* (1992) 44 NSWLR 349". (emphasis added)

In section 128 the court ruled that: "there has been clear recognition of the duty of good faith in a substantial body of Australian case law, including further significant decisions of the New South Wales Court of Appeal in Alcatel Australia Ltd v Scarcella (1998) 44 NSWLR 349, Burger King Corp v. Hungry Jack's Pty Ltd (2001) NWSCA 187 and Vodafone Pacific Ltd v Mobile Innovations Ltd (2004) NSWCA 15." (emphasis added)

Section 129 court noted that: "In New Zealand a doctrine of good faith is not yet established law but it has its advocates: see in particular the dissenting judgment of Thomas J in Bobux Marketing Ltd v. Raynor Marketing Ltd (2002) 1 NZLR 506 at 517." (emphasis added)

And in section 130 the court said: "Closer to home, there is strong authority for the view that Scottish law recognizes a broad principle of good faith and fair dealing: see the decision of the House of Lords in Smith v. Bank of Scotland, 1997 SC (HL) 111 esp. at p.121 (per Lord Clyde)." (emphasis added)

In 2014, the Supreme Court of Canada declared that good faith was a general organising principle: see the ruling in the *Bhasin v. Hrynew*. In section 131, the court ruled that: "Under English law a duty of good faith is implied by law as an incident of certain categories of contract, for example contracts of employment and contracts between partners or others whose relationship is characterized as a fiduciary one. I doubt that English law has reached the stage, however, where it is ready to recognize a requirement of good faith as a duty implied by law, even as a default rule, into all commercial contracts. Nevertheless, there seems to be no difficulty, following the established methodology of English law for the implication of terms in fact, in implying such a duty in any ordinary commercial contract based on the presumed intention of the parties."[574]

18.4. Old Boys' Networks

Old boys' networks (in some countries known as good brother or good sister networks) are informal systems where the wealthy or elite from the

574 *Bhasin v. Hrynew*, 13 November 2014.

same backgrounds help each other. Such networks are generally accepted. However, they stray into becoming illegal where the network operates in grey areas. This can happen, for example, with cartels and when using a dual role in a decision-making process. The network is corrupted if it shares or starts to share unreasonable mutual benefits. Also, if the network is closed, i.e., outsiders cannot join, network loyalty is based on reciprocity and favouring the network is considered as corruption. It is considered illegal if a corrupt network allocates funds to private interests and/or public interests allocate funds to private interests.[575] It may be noted that Enron and other business examples presented in this book are examples of the simultaneous occurrence of these threats. Image 7 below demonstrates how unhealthy old boys' networks slowly erode a company from the inside out.

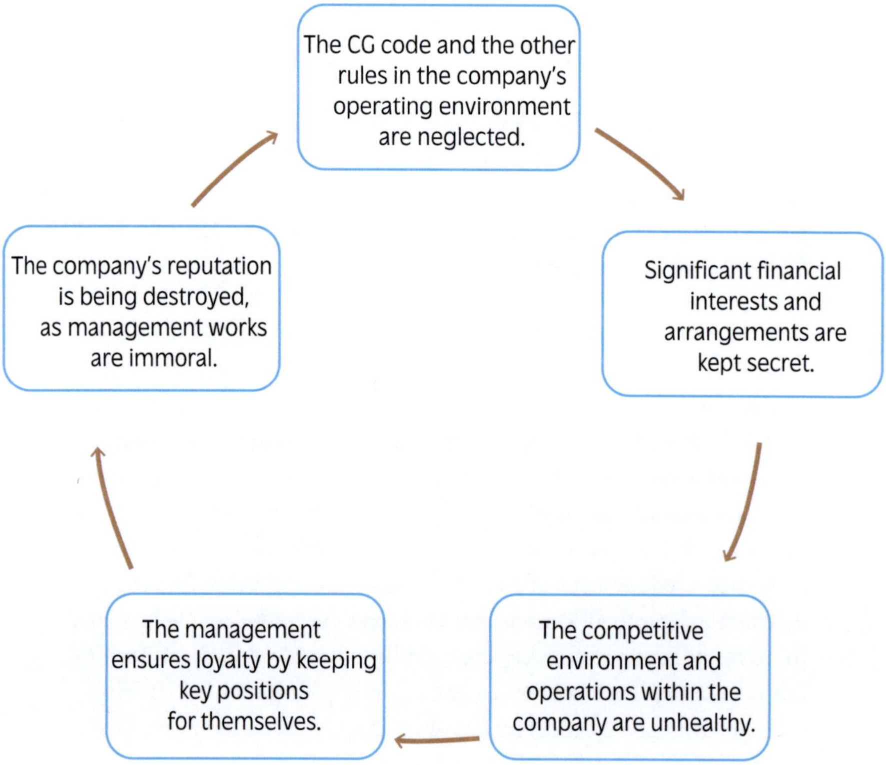

Image 7. Old boys' networks are not by definition illegal, but they might become illegal and they might be a threat to businesses. The image shows how the threat evolves (original source: Mäntysalo, Salminen, 2014).

575 According to Transparency International, 2019, "certain bribes paid abroad were technically tax deductible in German companies until 1999. These fees were categorized as 'useful expenditures', as long as those expenses were not incurred in Germany and there were no foreign state officials involved."

The abuse of discretion might mean that, for example, a judge uses their power in a criminal case to influence the outcome. If an individual favours a friend or family or other connections of any kind, this is a form of a good sister/brother network, nepotism and clientelism.[576] This type of networking can be used, for example, in job seeking. Individuals may use their connections to gain a competitive advantage over others and exercise influence using personal connections in the job markets. This is considered an "attempt to corrupt the formal hiring process" and is therefore considered a form of corruption because not all are given the same and equal opportunity to demonstrate their merits in the selection process. In this process, the job seeker is using a non-meritocratic advantage over others, which does not give an opportunity for the best candidate to be chosen for the position in question.[577]

> Spain's biggest corruption scandal, its own Watergate (Gürtel), was exposed in 2018. The scandal involved hundreds of corrupt politicians and businessmen. Eventually, when the magnitude of the scandal was clear, it shattered the entire Spanish political system, even reaching as far as the office of the president. In this very complex case, the main player was a businessman Francisco Correa Sanchez. He was sentenced to 51 years in prison. The treasurer of the former president, Mariano Rajoy, was fined almost $50 million. Rajoy's government also collapsed in 2018.[578]
>
> ***
>
> In Peru, former president Alberto Fujimori used 75 percent of the National Intelligence Service's unsupervised budget for bribing politicians, judges and the media. The corruption was revealed in 2019. Fujimori was sentenced to 30 years in prison.[579]
>
> ***
>
> Tunisia's former president Ben Ali created laws which ensured that companies were obliged to direct money to certain sectors if they wished to do business in Tunisia. This law was in place from 1987 to 2011. It meant, for example, that the government prevented McDonald's from entering Tunisia because McDonald's did not pay the ruling family. This

576 Thorburn, 2008, 1070–1130. Some states, though, do not forbid these forms of corruption.
577 Lambsdorff, 2006.
578 Edwards, 2019.
579 Quigley, 2019.

not only affected McDonald's but also other businesses, meaning that competition was practically shut out.

By 2011, Tunisia was run by 220 family monopolised businesses in telecommunications, transport and real estate. These sectors produced 3 percent of Tunisia's economic output in 2010. It also took 21 per cent of private sector profits in the same year. Also, the Ben Ali family amassed $13 billion in 2010. "Tunisians paid a heavy price for this and missed out on employment opportunities, while new entrepreneurs and unconnected investors continued to fail. Ben Ali fled the country in 2011." In the same year, "550 properties, 48 boats and yachts, 40 stock portfolios, 367 bank accounts, and approximately 400 enterprises were seized" from Bel Ali's family. Tunisia has been at the crossroads after the revolution and has all the ability to build up an open economy.[580]

18.5. International OECD and ICC Anti-Bribery Rules

The OECD and the ICC have issued guidelines on international bribery offences. The International Chamber of Commerce (ICC) has published various guides and guidelines on bribery and anti-corruption that are worth reading for corporate management. For example, the rules can be exported to a different country in the form of a book from a company without being considered as a gift.[581] The following outlines the guidelines of the ICC and the OECD.[582]

According to the ICC, a company should prohibit, in any form:

> "With respect to Third Parties subject to the control or determining influence of the Enterprise, including but not limited to agents, business development consultants, sales representatives, customs agents, general consultants, resellers, subcontractors, franchisees, lawyers, accountants or similar intermediaries, acting on the Enterprise's behalf in connection

580 Rijkers – Freund – Nucifora, 2014 I. Some researchers identified 662 firms that had some link, direct or indirect, to Ben Ali's family during his period as president. See: Rijkers, Freund – Nucifora, 2014 II.

581 When it comes to good guidelines for companies, here is a recommended list: "Resisting Extortion and Solicitation in International Transactions", "Fighting Bribery - a corporate practices manual", "ICC Guidelines on Agents, Intermediaries and Other Third Parties", "ICC Guidelines on Whistleblowing", "ICC Guidelines on Gifts and Hospitality" and "ICC Rules on Combating Corruption".

582 See "ICC Guidelines for Managing Corruption" and "ICC Anti-Corruption Clause". See also "ICC Rules on Combating Corruption 2011", "ICC Guidelines on Agents, Intermediaries and Other Third Parties", "ICC Guidelines on Whistleblowing" and "ICC Resisting Extortion and Solicitation in International Transactions".

with marketing or sales, the negotiation of contracts, the obtaining of licenses, permits or other authorizations, or any actions that benefit the Enterprise or as subcontractors in the supply chain, Enterprises should: *instruct them neither to engage nor to tolerate engagement in any act of corruption; not use them as a conduit for any corrupt practice; hire them only to the extent appropriate for the regular conduct of the Enterprise's business; and not pay them more than an appropriate remuneration for their legitimate services.*" (emphasis added).[583]

Article 1 of the ICC rules mentions **prohibited practices.** Usually, a suggestion of such prohibited practices is made by a corrupt-minded employee and rarely is the company management aware of this.[584]

Article 4 of the ICC rules mentions, among others, **political parties and corporate donations and sponsorships.**[585] It is not recommended

583 ICC Anti-Corruption Clause, Paragraph 2.2 f.

584 ICC Anti-Corruption Clause, Article 1: " Enterprises will prohibit the following practices at all times and in any form, in relation with a public official at international, national or local level, a political party, party official or candidate to political office, and a director, officer or employee of an Enterprise, whether these practices are engaged in directly or indirectly, including through Third Parties: a) **Bribery** is the offering, promising, giving, authorizing or accepting of any undue pecuniary or other advantage to, by or for any of the persons listed above or for anyone else in order to obtain or retain a business or other improper advantage, e.g., in connection with public or private procurement contract awards, regulatory permits, taxation, customs, judicial and legislative proceedings. Bribery often includes (i) kicking back a portion of a contract payment to government or party officials or to employees of the other contracting party, their close relatives, friends or Business Partners or (ii) using intermediaries such as agents, subcontractors, consultants or other Third Parties, to channel payments to government or party officials, or to employees of the other contracting party, their relatives, friends or Business Partners. b) **Extortion or Solicitation** is the demanding of a bribe, whether or not coupled with a threat if the demand is refused. [...] c) **Trading in Influence** is the offering or solicitation of an undue advantage in order to exert an improper, real, or supposed influence with a view of obtaining from a public official an undue advantage for the original instigator of the act or for any other person. d) **Laundering the proceeds of the corrupt practices mentioned above** is the concealing or disguising the illicit origin, source, location, disposition, movement or ownership of property, knowing that such property is the proceeds of crime. [...]"

585 ICC Rules on Combating Corruption: *"Political and Charitable Contributions and Sponsorships* a) Enterprises should only make contributions to political parties, party officials and candidates in accordance with applicable law and public disclosure requirements. The amount and timing of political contributions should be reviewed to ensure that they are not used as a subterfuge for corruption. b) Enterprises should take measures within their power to ensure that charitable contributions and sponsorships are not used as a subterfuge for corruption. Charitable contributions and sponsorships should be transparent and in accordance with applicable law. c) Enterprises should establish reasonable controls and procedures to ensure that improper political and charitable contributions are not made. Special care should be exercised in reviewing contributions to organizations in which prominent political figures, or their close relatives, friends and Business Partners are involved."

that companies use direct or indirect support for a political party and non-governmental activities that gain business benefits. If a company seeks to influence policy through support or bribery, such support should be made publicly. This does not apply to all countries. In some countries, political support can even enable the country's democratic development or keep political parties alive and is therefore legal and considered good practice in such countries. In these countries, companies usually have instructions on how to provide support and donations for political activities. If the company's reputation is damaged by such political support, the company should forbid donations. This can happen, for example, if the company suspects that the donation target has changed.

Donations very quickly turn into abuses. It must be remembered that the ICC Guidelines do not prohibit the legal donation of political activities in which a company is not registered. Attention should be given to the regulations of the country concerned. The OECD Convention does not explicitly prohibit donations to foreign political parties or their employees. The OECD mentions one exception: bribery may not be carried out in a country where there is only one party and the politician in question is in public office and / or a member of a single party. The Foreign Corrupt Practices Act (FCPA) in the United States[586] has denied and criminalised any payments, offers or promises made by American companies for the promotion of their business to a foreign political party, its employees or candidates for election.

Charitable contributions have been recognised in the ICC rules as contributing to the general good of society, such as education. Their main purpose must not be a condition or expectation of reward for their own business. Charitable contributions are not payments that give benefits to the company, such as visibility in advertising used by the charity. Similarly, situations in which a company is given the opportunity to promote itself by advertising, such as by highlighting its name, are not considered charitable.

There are many ways to perform charity, such as giving money and company products. Charities must be decided in advance. Ex-post controls include reporting and ensuring that the sponsorship has been channelled correctly. Management should ensure that such payments are reviewed and reflected on and support the mission and vision of the company.

This provides an assurance, for example, by asking the company to report on how and for what purpose the sponsorship and charity money was spent. Sponsorship donations should not be covert bribery and should not take the form of individual donations either. At its worst, sponsorship takes place, for example, in the bidding phase, where conflicts of interest may arise, such as with regard to the ability to evaluate. Management should take care of the business aspects of the sponsored subject, making sure that the organisation to which the money has been given is able to use the money for a pre-agreed purpose.

586 The Foreign Corrupt Practices Act (FCPA) was accepted by the US Congress in 1977.

Article 6 of the ICC rules prohibits **small payments or so-called 'emoluments'**.[587] Using this kind of facilitation payment to speed up the job is in principle illegal. Still, these are widely used. The ICC has encouraged companies to abandon such charges, as they may be part of a large body of corruption. Facilitation payment can be, for example, part of an abuse. The OECD Convention and the FCPA have not taken a clear position on how to deal with facilitation payments (though not accepted, but not forbidden), although they generally consider the giving of such money to be a minor form of corruption. There is one exception in the FCPA. Payment is possible if the routine performance of state administration is accelerated and assured. In this case, emoluments must be reported and documented with sufficient accuracy to be considered legal, such as in the United States.

Facilitation payment can also undermine companies' operating principles and proven practices. Often, the facilitation payment is given in cash, which makes it very difficult to track it afterwards. In companies, a facilitation payment is recognised as part of representation or other expenses, as it is often considered illegal. In any case, it is clear that there is a problem with the accounting of the facilitation payment money: if the company records the payment openly in the financial statements in a named account, the company appears to be making illegal payments. If it fails to mention the payment, the company can be found guilty of an accounting offence and simultaneously even tax evasion.

Facilitation payment is a problem if companies are not prepared for it in any way. If the company does not pay the facilitation payment in some countries, the business may even be at risk. On the one hand, this can be seen as blackmail but, on the other hand, if a business in the country is jeopardised by a low fee, is the scale then disproportionate?

> Ikea was in major trouble in Russia when it tried to fight against corruption in 2009. Ikea refused to buy electricity from Russian companies because they were, according to Ikea, corrupt. So, the company decided to rent diesel engines that supplied electricity to Ikea's Russian store. According to Ikea, the person who managed the generators took bribes from the company that leased the generators. The agreement drastically raised rents. Ikea calculated that the cost of

587 "Facilitation payments are unofficial, improper, small payments made to a low-level official to secure or expedite the performance of a routine or necessary action to which the payer of the facilitation payment is legally entitled. Facilitation payments are prohibited in most jurisdictions. Enterprises should, accordingly, not make such facilitation payments, but it is recognized that they may be confronted with exigent circumstances, in which the making of a facilitation payment can hardly be avoided, such as duress or when the health, security or safety of the Enterprise's employees are at risk. When a facilitation payment is made under such circumstances, it will be accurately accounted for in the Enterprise's books and accounting records."

> this fraud was €134 million. Ikea terminated the contract and sued the company in a Russian court. The court found Ikea guilty of breach of contract and ordered Ikea to pay damages to the diesel generator rental company.[588]

In such countries where slush money is seen as a ”compulsory must for the company's sake”,[589] an action plan should be made with this in mind, even if it is not easy. The problem here is that it is difficult for management to know where facilitation payments are actually used if they are disguised as part of a larger whole. Employees can provide tips on where the company uses facilitation payments. The internal audit or security department may also disclose items and situations more accurately. The management is also in favour of a network of companies working in other similar business sectors in the country to learn about local habits, for example, whether there are officials who always require bribes. Such situations usually relate purely to the fact that the official wants more 'salary', which is used to support their family. In this case, the company rarely has any other means than trying to influence local legislation, diplomats or policymakers in order to change the rules prevailing in that country over time.

In Article 5 of the ICC rules, the **performance or reception of gifts and hospitality-based payments** is prohibited if it affects the outcome of any of the transactions at hand.[590] In contrast, the OECD convention does not expressly mention the gift or hospitality. The starting point of the FCPA is more permissive in cases where the payment remains reasonable, it is a "natural expense" and the gifts are intrinsically linked to business, sales or marketing between companies, such as a travel expense. As an additional requirement for gifts and hospitality charges in the FCPA, payments must relate, for example, to the "promotion of a product or service". These include, among other things, reasonable[591] marketing and promotional costs.

---

588 *Russia Monitor*, 4 April 2010.

589 A few indexes are useful for companies. For example, they can be used to investigate which business sectors and countries may have high levels of corruption. Transparency International Bribe Payers Index lists nine biggest OECD bribe export countries. Moreover, it publishes information about bribery generally.

590 ICC Guidelines on Gifts and Hospitality: ”Enterprises should establish procedures covering the offer or receipt of gifts and hospitality in order to ensure that such arrangements (a) comply with national law and applicable international instruments; (b) are limited to reasonable and bona fide expenditures; (c) do not improperly affect, or might be perceived as improperly affecting, the recipient's independence of judgment towards the giver; (d) are not contrary to the known provisions of the recipient's code of conduct; and (e) are neither offered or received too frequently nor at an inappropriate time."

591 For example, a reasonable and genuine expense is travelling, and accommodation costs incurred by a customer when inspecting US manufacturing facilities. It may also be a small sample of the product provided by the manufacturer.

> The International Athletics Federation (IAAF) dealt differently with ICC Article 5. In this case, the management level applied for advantages by tightening up the economic performances of athletes who were caught doping. As a counter service, leaders promised that the doping would never become public. For many years, the IAAF promised it would do everything it could to eradicate doping, but the leadership of the IAAF worked differently. For many sports leaders, signalled the end of their careers. Corruption at FIFA or the bribery scandal at the International Olympic Committee in 2002 regarding the winter competition application were relatively small violations compared to the activities of the IAAF.[592]

When creating anti-corruption guidelines, local habits and cultural aspects are important.[593] The guidance should include detailed corporate instructions as toon when gifts, expenses and hospitality demonstrations are considered bribery and when not, as, for example, when it is the reasonable maximum amount accepted by the company in the context of business activities. The guidance should be readily available to all employees.

The guidance should give employees and managers a clear description of the company's full ban on the provision and receipt of gifts (such as money, goods, services, and loans). Prohibited activities are particularly those where gifts might influence contracts or contractual negotiations, even if they are used to demonstrate that the relationship is valued. The purpose of the gift should be such that it is based on a business relationship, does not include a counter obligation or expectation of a reciprocal gift, is open or in the nature of the company's advertising or marketing. A good rule of thumb is that if a company informs any interested party about the gift and if such a party does not regard the issue as problematic and the gift is not regular and complies with the legislation in force, such hospitality is hardly evidence of bribery.[594]

592 Transparency International, 2016. *Wikipedia*: 2015 FIFA Corruption Case. Pandey, 2015.

593 The Council of Europe Criminal Law Convention (ETS 173) defines bribery in Article 12 (Trading in influence) as follows: "Each Party shall adopt such legislative and other measures as may be necessary to establish as criminal offences under its domestic law, when committed intentionally, the promising, giving or offering, directly or indirectly, of any undue advantage to anyone who asserts or confirms that he or she is able to exert an improper influence over the decision-making of any person referred to in Articles 2, 4 to 6 and 9 to 11 in consideration thereof, whether the undue advantage is for himself or herself or for anyone else, as well as the request, receipt or the acceptance of the offer or the promise of such an advantage, in consideration of that influence, whether or not the influence is exerted or whether or not the supposed influence leads to the intended result."

594 Lautjärvi, 2018, 277. A company's board of directors must comply with anti-bribery principles and it is responsible for the firm's guidance on corruption. The managing director is responsible for the implementation of guidance and daily supervision. In their own conduct, senior management must ensure that the principles are also respected by the leadership.

The representatives of the company should sign a consent in which they undertake to comply with the company's guidelines, including those relating to bribes. One of the grounds for termination of an agreement with a representative could be that the agent does not refuse a bribe. The company should also explicitly communicate the consequences of non-compliance with the anti-corruption programme to its own personnel. The sanctions used by the company should be fair, and they should be consistently and equally respected throughout the organisation and at all organisational levels. Particularly at risk is the company's sales and marketing, as the achievement of annual sales targets demands the winning of deals. Competitors may even be ready for a bribe to obtain an agreement. If a contract is lost to a competitor, the company should encourage its employees and not punish missed opportunities. It is also inappropriate to justify past trades with anti-corruption guidelines.[595]

Article 8 of the ICC rules provides an important role for **human resources management.**[596] Proper orientation and training on anti-bribery guidance for the entire company's staff is extremely important. Training should be organised periodically.

It is not enough to organise training, for example, only in the induction phase. It needs to be constant. The training could also include a whistleblowing system[597] and an explanation of how it works in the company. A whistleblowing system is good because it can make the company's defaults and abuses more known by the management, and it also improves guidance on bribery. The company should also communicate how it takes care of false declarations and how it protects the recipients of such notifications. In any event, the notifier should be known solely for that reason if a criminal investigation subsequently commences.

When the notifications received through the whistleblowing system are documented and reported in a factual way and monitored critically, the correctness of the instruction and the procedure is effective. If the notifications are documented, it is easy to keep track of how quickly things are being responded to. In addition, proper reporting ensures that no financial traffic outside the company results in over-accounting. If the company does not react, some employees may start discussing the matter very quickly on social media. This is not, in turn, in the interests of the company or its managers.[598]

595 Bray, 2007.

596 "Enterprises should ensure that: a) human resources practices, including recruitment, promotion, training, performance evaluation, remuneration, recognition and business ethics in general, reflect these Rules; b) no employee will suffer retaliation or discriminatory or disciplinary action for reporting in good faith violations or soundly suspected violations of the Enterprise's anti-corruption policy or for refusing to engage in corruption, even if such refusal may result in the Enterprise losing business; c) key personnel in areas subject to high corruption risk."

597 In the system, it is possible for employees at different levels to report cases of abuse.

598 Banking risks are dealt with in the Wolfsberg Principles.

In Sweden, the criminality of the inclusion of a bribe has been extended to employees of both private and public employers. A worker is responsible for taking a bribe if he or she "seeks or accepts a bribe or other unfair advantage or approves a pledge in return for his activities".[599] A fine or a maximum of two years imprisonment is the sanction for such an act. If the offence is particularly egregious, the penalty scale ranges from six months to six years of imprisonment. The rules also apply if the worker is involved in bribery before or after the commencement of the employment relationship.

For the private sector, the members of the board, lawyers and auditors are specifically mentioned. Under the Swedish Criminal Code, the authority, judge or foreign arbitrator of a foreign state may also be convicted of bribery. This is, of course, also the case for a foreign worker, working in the private or public sector. Bribe-givers get the same punishment as bribe-takers. Active and passive corruption, which extends to foreign representatives, is forbidden.[600] According to this, a bribery offence may be committed by someone who exercises the authority of a foreign state or foreign arbitration.

18.6. Examples of Buying Influence in France and other parts of the world

Buying influence is not in any way a new phenomenon. In France, the Sun King Louis XIV attempted to get rid of the famous Rothschild family already in the 1700. The family branch had spread throughout the world, and they were wealthy enough to buy influence and decide on issues as a result. The family left the French stock exchange on its knees, leaving the king with no alternative but to tolerate them.[601] Today, digital natives have such power. When digital natives use their power to influence by tweeting and sounding off on social media platforms, their methods may be different to actually buying influence, but the end result is the same.

In France, it is common in a French limited company (SAS) that the chairman of the board of directors also carries out the duties of the executive director, president and CEO. Such a position is called the Président-Directeur Général. The French model of concentrating power in one person has received a lot of criticism. It may be that the managing director of a company is, for

599 Mutbrott; BrB 20:2. Section 20:2 was modified with Act 2012:301 (Lag om ändring i brottsbalken).

600 Swedish Criminal Law (Brottsbalken 1962:700; BrB) Chapter 20. For bribery: mutbrott; BrB 20:2. Hedwall – König, 2014.

601 *Science*, 6 October 2010.

example, also the marketing director. This becomes problematic as it raises the question of who leads and how work is then controlled. In France, the policy is changing and there is also an attempt to differentiate these echelons of power. In addition, the trend is to involve external governments.[602] Influencing purchasing power is criminalised in France.[603]

> In 2021, Kuwait's Sheikh Ahmad, a member of the International Olympic Committee, was convicted to 30 months in jail in Geneva. The case began in 2015 and Ahmad was convicted of forgery in a case where he used a bogus Kuwaiti coup plot to gain an advantage over his political rivals.[604]

***

> In 2015, China was also reported to have had a financial influence on Europe, Africa, and Latin America. Among other things, China invested in a fund under the European Commission because it wanted to be involved in building infrastructure. Similarly, the Chinese state company Cosco has been interested in buying the port of Piraeus in Athens.
>
> Through this activity, China is aiming to establish a "China gate to Europe". Hungary and Poland already agreed with China in June 2015 on land and sea building works. China has also reciprocally wished that European countries would be involved in Asian projects. Finland and Germany have announced their support for the activities of the Asian Investment Bank. The final intentions of China are difficult to assess, though. The achievement of financial interests, such as the autonomous management of raw material reserve areas, may serve as a motive. China may also aim purely for cooperation between continents. It has begun to transfer money to the EU after economic difficulties arose. In early 2015, China also started building close relations with Latin American countries.[605]

---

602 Tiihonen, 2007, 25–31.

603 As we saw previously in the Adidas case, the former French Finance Minister and the current President of the European Central Bank Christine Lagarde was sentenced on 19 December 2016 for failure to act in arbitration. Although Lagarde was sentenced for not having questioned a premium in the course of her role as minister, she did not receive any penalty or fines. The same type of penalty could have been sanctioned under French law as a period of imprisonment.

604 Farge, 2021.

605 Maverick, 9 April 2020. Le Corre, 2018, 161–174. Grier, 2018. *BBC*, 20 April 2019.

18.7. Embezzlement

Embezzlement is a form of fraud where a company (or individual) illegally uses assets for its own benefit. It is also a form of white-collar crime and is referred to directly as "theft". In the case of embezzlement, a person already having access to funds starts to use them as if they were their own. In the case of fraud (see the next chapter) a person convinces a fund owner to give an unauthorised person access to the funds or assets.

Embezzlement could be a misdirection of funds via shadow companies to corrupt employees, skimming foreign aid money, scams or similar. It can also be political, so that a person using political authority seeks personal gain through the illegal use of funds. It can be, for example, redirecting public project money to a private individual's account. This global form of political corruption is known as **graft.**[606]

> One of the largest frauds targeting taxpayer money originally intended for primary education was exposed in 2021. In the US, the founder and CEO of Charter School Network Sean McManus and his colleague Jason Schrock were ordered to pay $37.5 million in fines and sentenced to four years in jail.[607]

***

> In 2017, a South Korean subsidiary of technology company ABB operating on the international market became a party to embezzlement. The company first discovered that its CFO had disappeared, and then the loss of $100 million was also revealed. Prior to that, ABB had to go through allegations of bribery in the UK. In early 2017, ABB announced this embezzlement in South Korea, as the loss of money from the company's accounts affected the company's performance. ABB also had to delay its performance publication as a result of the case.[608]

***

> In 1998, employees of the First National Bank of Chicago stole $70 million by using anonymous dummy accounts in Australia. The embezzlement continued until the bank's customer Merrill Lynch found

606 Chen, 2020 II.
607 *Times of San Diego*, 10 September 2021.
608 Revill, 2017.

$20 million missing from its accounts. Following an FBI investigation, the employees were found guilty. [609]

***

Former Nasdaq executive and one of the most relevant market makers, the penny stock brokerage on Wall Street, Bernard Lawrence "Bernie" Madoff also became known for a massive Ponzi scheme. For almost 20 years, Madoff defrauded thousands of investors out of billions of dollars, making Madoff the largest defrauder of all time. [610]

In late 2008, the former Nasdaq director Madoff was charged with fraud. His own sons made a revelation about him after he had praised himself for his scams. Santander, BNP Paribas, Nomura, and Nordea all suffered greatly from his deception. One of the banks, Medici, went bankrupt as a result. Jewish charities had invested in the network marketing investment idea and also suffered massive losses. Subsequently, the US market supervisor, the SEC, froze the former director's assets. The total estimate of his fraudulent activities was $37 billion, the largest investment scam committed by an individual. The scheme involving securities fraud and investment adviser fraud was exposed in 2008 and probably cost investors $50 billion, including such celebrities as Steven Spielberg and Kevin Bacon. [611]

After a series of dramatic events, he was released in 2009 against bail to live under house arrest in his own luxury apartment. In March 2009, he decided to admit his investment fraud in court. He was sentenced to 150 years in prison. Madoff died in 2021.[612]

18.8. Fraud and Extortion

Fraud is a dishonest white-collar act which intends financial or personal gain and is a crime. The scale of fraud varies. For example, it can be financial statement fraud, identity theft, insurance fraud, securities fraud, wire fraud, bankruptcy fraud, tax evasion, theft of intellectual property rights or treason[613]. In cases of fraud, someone deliberately deceives others for unlawful gain. If a

609 Calcagni, 2017.

610 United States v. Madoff, 2009.

611 Carlsson, 2019.

612 *Wikipedia*: Bernard Madoff.

613 *Thomson Reuters*, 2019 I.

person is convicted of fraud, depending on the gain received, the person can receive either a fine and/or imprisonment. Financial fraud and state frauds are considered among the most serious types of fraud and therefore both fines and imprisonment are used. In 2020, the US Government identified the COVID-19 pandemic as one of the reasons for scams and frauds. Moreover, banking, government and investment scams are still very common. Earlier in this book, pyramid and ponzi schemes were mentioned, which are also examples of fraud.[614] **Extortion** is in question when a person exploits another person's financial or other predicament, dependent position, incomprehension or thoughtlessness. In cases of extortion, someone demands favours or money. In the US especially, many celebrities have been extorted for huge amounts of money. Normally, the extortion relates to revealing secrets to the media. This is a form of blackmail or criminal conspiracy.[615]

> In 2021, JP Morgan Chase & Co settled a long French criminal investigation where the bank was accused of having helped its clients commit tax fraud.[616]

***

> In 2020, Kiev in Ukraine was the centre of a large fraud scheme which cheated citizens in different countries. The fraud involved the sale of fake investments, such as in crypto currencies. The fraud came to light because one of the operation's employees gave information to Swedish magazine *Dagens Nyheter*.[617]

***

> In 2020, the Finnish stock exchange company Cargotec was subject to a large fraud scheme. Between 2002 and 2017, two employees in managerial positions collected a total of €14 million with fraudulent invoices. The money was allocated to foreign bank accounts. The company noticed some misinformation in its internal auditing and requested the Finnish police to intervene.[618]

***

614 *US Government*: Scams and Frauds.
615 *Merriam-Webster*: Definition of fraud.
616 Sebag, 2021.
617 Carlsson, 2020.
618 YLE *News*, 18 February 2020.

In the US, Elizabeth Holmes, the founder of Theranos, lied about the company's achievements. She attracted wealthy investors to back the company. In 2015, it was finally revealed that Holmes had lied to everyone. She stole ideas from other companies and presented them as Theranos' ideas. The SEC threatened Holmes with a fine of over $700 million; however, as she promised to pay $500,000 in fines and give up 19 million Theranos shares, she escaped a prison sentence. She was also banned from leading any public company for 10 years. The case was known as Silicon Valley's biggest fraud.[619]

***

In 2012, healthcare company GlaxoSmithKline pleaded guilty and paid $3 billion in fines. The case involved false reporting, fraud and bribery, in other words, corruption. According to the US Department of Justice, the case was the "largest healthcare fraud settlement in US history with the largest payout ever given by a drug company". "Today's multi-billion-dollar settlement is unprecedented in both size and scope. It underscores the Administration's firm commitment to protecting the American people and holding accountable those who commit healthcare fraud," said James M. Cole, Deputy Attorney General. "At every level, we are determined to stop practices that jeopardize patients' health, harm taxpayers, and violate the public trust – and this historic action is a clear warning to any company that chooses to break the law."[620]

***

One of the biggest healthcare fraud settlements in history was paid in 2009 by Pfizer. The American pharmaceutical giant paid $2.3 billion for fraudulent marketing regarding the misbranding of the anti-inflammatory drug Bextra. Moreover, the healthcare giant agreed to pay $1 billion and resolved allegations regarding antipsychotic drug Geodon, antibiotic Zyvox and epilepsy drug Lyrica. Allegations involved, for example, kickbacks to healthcare providers to prescribe the medicine. The case resulted in the biggest civil fraud settlement in history against pharmaceutical companies. Not only Pfizer but also Johnson & Johnson settled criminal and civil investigations with fines amounting to $2.2 billion in 2013.[621]

619 Michaels, 2018. Kokalitcheva, 2021.

620 *The US Department of Justice*, 2 July 2012.

621 *The US Department of Justice*, 2 September 2009.

In U.S. securities frauds, cases with a smaller "microcap" size are defined as microcap stock frauds. One feature of cases is a market capitalisation under $250 million, while the outcome generates billions of dollars of profit each year. These are mostly used in telemarketing and the internet. Microcap stock frauds do not take place on listed stock exchanges, but rather trading takes place on the OTC Bulletin Board or in the Pink Sheets Electronic Quotation Service. Some may also take place among stocks that are traded on the NASDAQ Small Cap Market. Penny stocks refer to microcap stocks because the security is traded at less than $5 per share.[622]

Microcap fraud[623] can involve, for example, pump and dump schemes, chop stocks and dump and dilute schemes. The first refers to cases where misleading statements are given to hype stocks and dump inflated prices, for example, internet fraud. The second refers to cases where stocks are purchased for pennies and sold for dollars. For stock promoters, this generates big profits. The third example of fraud refers to schemes where shares are issued with only one purpose – to separate investors from their money.[624]

The scam involving a fake CEO is a fairly new angle on fraud. It works like this: during the summer holidays a new person enters the company. At the reception, they get access to the CEO's office by claiming they are substituting for the CEO during the summer. The CEO is usually known to people around the building, but the CEO's substitute is not. Alternatively, fraudsters use AI to mimic a CEO's voice to commit cybercrime. Fraud of this nature, where a CEO requests, for example, the urgent payment of an invoice, could lead to a new social engineering hack where managers are asked to pay a hacker, by a hacker. Although hard to believe, crimes of this nature were on the rise in 2019. In Australia alone, billions of dollars in losses were reported in only 18 months. Some safeguards have been put in place though: the need to verify three times before acting, training your employees and educating them about scams and two-way authentication methods.[625]

> In 2019, a CEO in the United States was led to believe he was having a discussion with his boss and transferred $243,000 of company money to a fraudulent account.[626]

***

622 North American Securities Administrators Association, Micro-cap Fraud. *SEC*, 2013. *Business Week*, 15 December 1997. Loiacono, 2019.

623 Normally, frauds of this nature are made in the US.

624 Dhir, 2021.

625 Sia, 2019.

626 Damiani, 2019.

In 2018, cinema chain Pathé in France lost $21 million in a scheme, which ultimately led to the CEO and CFO losing their jobs.[627]

***

In 2016, German cable manufacturer Leoni AG lost $44 million after the top management was defrauded.[628]

***

In 2016, Austrian aerospace company FACC AG lost $50 million; although it got about one-fifth of the amount back.[629]

***

In 2015, Zoom made a fake internet money transfer which led to the CFO resigning. The lost $30.8 million was never recovered.[630]

In **extortion** and blackmail cases, some sort of threat is always present. It can concern, for example, violence, false imprisonment or the revelation of uncomfortable facts to the media. Keeping secrets beyond public scrutiny usually requires giving money in exchange. One example is influence peddling, which refers to an individual influencing a government worker or those in authority to act according to their preferences or wishes.[631]

In 2017, Anthony Allen and Anthony Conti, trader for Radobank in London, were convicted for conspiracy and wire fraud. Rabobank is a Dutch-owned bank. What makes this case so significant is that this was the first federal criminal appeal in the world known as the Libor case. All in all, the case concerned many companies and individuals who were involved in Libor manipulations.[632]

***

Directors of Barclays Bank were charged in the summer of 2017 for fraud and corruption in connection with agreements with the Qatari state. Barclays was suspected of luring Qatar to support Barclays in the

627 Schwartz, 2018.
628 *Deutsche Welle*, 2016.
629 Nasralla – Croft, 2016.
630 Heller, 2015.
631 *Wikipedia*: Blackmail.
632 *United States v. Conti*, 2017.

post-financial crisis through unclear financial arrangements. As a thank you gift, the bank was suspected of giving Qatar a loan amounting to €3.8 billion.[633]

***

In 2016, five employees who worked for Bernard L. Madoff Investment Securities were convicted of several cases of fraud. These included falsifying SEC filings, tax evasion and bank and securities fraud.[634]

***

In 2014, Finland announced a large extortion case concerning the mobile phone giant Nokia. The company was reported to have paid millions of euros because extorters had the protection key to Nokia's mobile phones.[635] In a report prepared in Europe, extortion rates are skyrocketing. These figures are skewed by Bulgaria's and Romania's over representation in this area.[636]

***

Lawyer Michael Avenatti, famous for making media headlines while representing Stormy Daniels in the case against the former US President Donald Trump, was found guilty of extortion in February 2020. He tried to secure $25 million from the sports apparel giant Nike. "Today, a unanimous jury found Michael Avenatti guilty of misusing his client's information in an effort to extort tens of millions of dollars from the athletic apparel company Nike," US Attorney Geoffrey Berman said. Avenatti was arrested in early 2020 after he and an "uncharged conspirator" threatened Nike. According to court papers, "They said they would make a news event to ruin Nike's reputation, which would also have an effect on Nike's stock price unless Nike agreed to pay Avenatti and his client millions of dollars".[637]

***

633 Liimatainen, 2017.

634 *United States v. Bonventre*, 2016.

635 McGregor, 2014.

636 *CEREU*, 2016, 57.

637 Fieldstadt – Winter – Fitzpatrick, 2020.

> Extortion cases are also rising in Canada. Between 2012 and 2018, cases increased 170%. In 2020, numbers were even higher. One of the cases in 2019 involved a denial of services stunt that threatened to shut down the University of Calgary's computers. The criminals demanded money to reopen the university's system. The university paid $20,000 to get access to its computers.[638]
>
> ***
>
> In 2017, telecommunication company Movistar faced a series of five coordinated IT attacks in Guatemala. Four employees were killed in the attack, and the company was forced to temporarily shut down its activities. Movistar was subject to further criminal attacks in 2020 when it again needed to shut down activities for days.[639]

An ASEAN assessment shows an increased cyber threat in ASEAN countries. Most often, cases of extortion are related to cybercrime. Interpol ASEAN orchestrated two large operations, Goldfish Alpha and Night Fury, which resulted in the arrest of many individuals. Goldfish Alpha ran for six months and reduced crypto jacking in the Southeast Asia region. The operation took place because over 20,000 MikroTik routers were hacked. Operation Night Fury was targeted at taking down the gang and the malware that infected hundreds of e-commerce websites around the world.[640]

Process fraud or **process crime** is a crime that is aimed at misleading an authority. This might happen by misleading a court to make a final judgment incorrectly. It involves interference with the procedure and administration of justice. Process fraud favours one party over another in criminal, civil or administrative proceedings. It causes harm to the public interest and is therefore a prosecutable offence. It might include delaying, losing or destroying evidence or publishing adverse publicity.[641] Process crimes are considered easier to prove when compared to other crimes. Most often, they do not have a statute of limitations problem. Such cases can arise later in the investigation of another crime. Normally, this can be more difficult to prove.[642]

> "A process crime is any crime that is committed through direct or indirect interference with the investigation of another crime. Generally,

---

638 Russell, 2019. Foran, 2021.

639 *Invertalia*, 8 September 2020. Álvarez & Gándara, 2017. C*entral American Extortion Report*, 2019.

640 *INTERPOL*, 17 February 2020.

641 In the US, a process crime is "an offense against the judicial process". This might mean, for example, failure to appear, false statements, obstruction of justice, contempt of court and perjury. USC, 2020. Murphy, 2008. Richman - Stuntz, 2005, 583–640. Weisburd, 2017. *CPS*, 2018.

642 Murphy, 2008, 8.

> process crimes involve some sort of misrepresentation or failure to tell the truth with the intention and effect of hampering a criminal investigation. Common examples of such crimes are obstruction of justice and perjury, both of which entail lying to governmental officials in the process of bringing a criminal to justice. The only defense to a process crime is that the actor honestly believed that he or she was telling the truth when the untrue statements were made."[643]

In the US, the range of process crimes is broad. The country has many federal and state laws. Process crimes are mostly covered by federal criminal law and frequently prosecuted in state courts. There are five typical process charges in the US: "1) failure to appear, 2) false statements, 3) obstruction of justice, 4) contempt of court and 5) perjury." Also, if a citizen does not cooperate with an arrest, process crimes such as resisting arrest, flight to elude arrest or battery on police officers might come into question. A commonality for process crimes is that "prosecutors target defendants based on suspicion of one crime but prosecute them for another".[644] A classic example of this was the prosecution of gangster Al Capone. He was prosecuted for tax evasion in 1931, although he had committed many other crimes.[645]

> One of the most famous cases of process fraud concerned the trial of former US President Bill Clinton in the 1990s. Clinton gave false testimony about Monica Lewinsky. The case is known as a "giant sex trafficking scandal".[646]

***

> In 2017, *Ivey v. Genting Casinos* (2017) UKSC 67 was a significant decision since the UK Supreme Court overruled the test for criminal dishonesty in *R v. Ghosh (1982) QB 1053.* Stacey McEvoy from Allen & Overy wrote in 2017: "This will erode the availability of subjective defences, possibly increasing the frequency of prosecutions for white-collar crime offences against businesses and individuals."[647]

643 Lupica, 2020.

644 Murphy, 2008. Weisburd, 2017. Richman - Stuntz, 2005, 583–640.

645 Murphy, 2008.

646 Flanagan, 2017.

647 McEvoy, 6 November 2017. Dishonesty was governed for 35 years by R v. Ghosh as follows: "A jury must first of all decide whether according to the ordinary standards of reasonable and honest people what was done was dishonest. If it was not dishonest by those standards, that is the end of the matter and the prosecution fails. If it was dishonest by those standards, then the jury must consider whether the defendant himself must have realized that what he was doing was by those standards dishonest." (1982) QB 1053.

19. Fake Food and Business Crime

Fake food and food fraud are concepts that have slightly different meanings. **Fake foods** are products that are modified secretly, such as using cheaper raw materials. **Food fraud** covers a much greater area, and might start already from the use of counterfeit pesticides in cultivation. Both fake food and food fraud aim for greater economic advantages. It is also detrimental to the good faith of consumers, who believe that premium food brands are produced in a premium way.[648]

Fake food is a big concern since it involves tax avoidance, illegal production methods, underpayment and even human trade. But that's not all. Fake food may, in the worst-case scenario, lead to death. This phenomenon is not very new. Over the years, some companies, both big and small, have used deceit. Already in the 18th century, people in England wanted white bread so much that bakeries started to add gypsum to their products. Moreover, companies may add cheaper spices instead of expensive ones, add water to increase the weight or use unwarranted chemicals to give a fresher appearance to their food products.

The number of fake food cases is unknown because cases are not collected inside the EU. Nevertheless, it is estimated to account annually for about $40 billion worth of business. This amount covers only those cases which are exposed, so it is likely there are many more cases not yet exposed. One thing is certain, fake food is a growing phenomenon. One reason to explain this is the impact of climate change on the growth and productivity of crops. Criminal organisations have by now understood that greater profit might be made with fake mozzarella, fake wine, fake olive oil and fake meat than from selling drugs on the street.[649]

> In 2019, Europol revealed a fish scandal worth millions of euros in which tainted tuna was sold onwards as quality tuna.[650]

***

> In 1994, more than 50 people became ill in Hungary from the use of paprika spice. The paprika contained lead. Investigations into lead in

648 *FoodIntegrity Handbook*, 2018. In 1820, Frederick Accum published a book called A *Treatise on Adulterations of Food and Culinary Poisons*. This book is probably the first book discussing food counterfeits. According to Koistinen (2020, 17), the most counterfeited products today are honey, alcohol, meat, coffee and spices.

649 Today, mozzarella and olive oil are considered more profitable than drugs. Meikle - McDonald, 2013 I. *The Daily telegraph*, 8 February 2013. *The Guardian*, 15 February 2013. Koistinen, 2020.

650 Muscat, 2019.

spices have also been conducted in New York between 2008–2017. These investigations showed that over half of the investigated spices contained lead.[651]

***

In 2008, a Chinese milk scandal exposed significant foul play. Some dairy product manufacturers had added the poisonous substance melamine[652] to their milk products. Around 300,000 Chinese consumers had symptoms of some kind, and six babies died as a result of kidney damage due to the presence of melamine in infant formula, while 54,000 babies needed hospital treatment. In 2006, melamine was used in pet food, which led to the deaths of thousands of cats and dogs in the US alone. In China, the scandal was allowed to grow because the Beijing Olympic games were going on and officials chose to keep the issue secret. "Melamine was found in Chinese biscuits and confectionery in the Netherlands and France, and in confectionery in Germany and Belgium. In Austria, melamine was present in Chinese milkshakes and in Hungary in Chinese restaurant food. Melamine was also found in Italy. In Russia, 1.7 tons of milk flour were seized."[653] Every fifth milk product was suspected of melamine contamination. The main responsibility for the scandal was pinned on Tian Wenhua, who received a sentence of life imprisonment in 2009. Other companies publicly apologised and promised to pay compensation to the families. It was claimed the milk products were destroyed, but this was a lie. A year later, in 2010, Chinese milk products were again shown to contain the same melamine. In milk alone, melamine levels over 500 times the normal level.[654]

***

In 1981, the largest Europe-wide food scandal "toxic oil syndrome" came to light in Spain. Almost one thousand people were killed or harmed by poisonous canola oil. The oil was originally produced in France and not meant for human consumption at all. The product was shown to destroy human lung tissue and weaken the body's own

651 Williams, 1994.

652 Melamine is used in formaldehyde by combining mainly melamine resin. It provides a durable plastic. This plastic is used, for example, in kitchen utensils and containers.

653 *WHO*, 29 September 2008.

654 McDonald, 2008. Welford, 2008. *Xinhua News Agency*, 16 September 2008. *The Standard*, 17 October 2008. Note that melamine is not suitable for human food at all.

defences. The Supreme Court of Spain found 13 merchants guilty and much later, in 1997, the Spanish state paid compensation to the victims' families.

***

In 2013, the UK shocked the world when 300 tons of horse meat from a Dutch wholesale dealer, and part of which was not even deemed fit for human consumption, was sold secretly as beef. The case came to light when Irish authorities found a box of beef without adequate packaging labels. They opened the box and investigated the contents further, unaware that this was evidence of a much larger crime.

The scandal took another spectacular turn when Irish investigators discovered among the meat samples ID chips for two Polish horses, Wiktor and Trak, and the ID chip for an Irish horse called Carnesella Lady. Finally, the Dutch businessman was found guilty in 2015. Police in Belgium, Spain, France, Portugal, Italy, Romania, Switzerland and Britain also started their own investigations. In 2017, in Spain alone, 65 suspects were found guilty of forging documents, money laundering and other criminal activities.[655]

***

In 2013, Shanghai authorities confiscated lamb which turned out to be a mixture of rat, mink and fox. In addition, the meat products also included chemicals such as nitrites and gelatin, which preserved the meat for longer. It was suggested that the person behind the scandal had already earned up to €1 million before they were caught.[656]

***

In 2015, in Eastern Europe, quark was changed to mozzarella by using chemicals and waste. This "mozzarella" was, according to a laboratory in Belfast, sold in the US and in EU markets. This was not the first time mozzarella was the subject of a scandal. In 2008, Italy's health authorities found that Mozzarella di Bufala Campana cheese contained hazardous chemicals and a high level of dioxins[657]. In 2015, almost a

655 Lawrence, 2013.

656 Turk – Wong, 2013.

657 Mozzarella di Bufala is known for the location where it is produced in Campania, Italy. McCarthy, 2008.

> third of the fish in Brussels was falsely labelled; for example, pollock was falsely labelled as cod. This was made possible by fishermen removing the head, tail and intestines, and thus rendering the fish unrecognisable to ordinary consumers. According to the Belfast laboratory that investigates fake food issues, Italy, France and Spain lead the world in fake fish cases.[658]

Different countries have different authorities responsible for raising consumer safety awareness. At the EU level, there's the EU Commission and the European Union Food Safety Authority (EFSA), and consumer ombudsmen, national courts and food authorities give guidance and maintain safety. Among the food-related laws which protect consumers in the EU area and internationally, there is the European General Food Law Regulations, the World Intellectual Property Organization (WIPO), European Consumer and Marketing Law, the Unfair Commercial Practices directive and the Consumer Protection Directive.

658 International marine conservation organisation Oceana. About 20–30% of the world's fish sold to consumers is fake. Koistinen, 2020, 53.

20. Money Laundering

Money laundering[659] is almost inevitably connected to organised crime with international features. Money laundering is listed as a crime because it is a way to make large amounts of money generated by criminal activity appear

659 According to the FBI: The term "money laundering" is defined as the act of receiving, using, converting, disposing of, or transferring criminally obtained property in order to conceal or obscure the illicit origin of the proceeds or property. Wikipedia's definition of money laundering is: "The term is thought to have originated in the United States at the time of the Prohibition Act, when the proceeds of the illegal sale of alcohol had to be disguised. One method would have been to use laundries to fade the origin of money. According to the Central Criminal Police's Money Laundering Investigation Center, the value of money laundered assets is considerable when the starting point is the amount of criminal proceeds obtained through economic and drug offenses and other types of financially beneficial crime." There are three steps in the money laundering process: (i) placement, (ii) layering, and (iii) integration. "Placement represents the initial entry of the criminal's proceeds into the financial system. Layering is the most complex step, as it often entails the international movement of funds. Layering separates the criminal's proceeds from their original source and creates a deliberately complex audit trail through a series of financial transactions. Integration occurs when the criminal's proceeds are returned to the criminal from what appear to be legitimate sources". FBI: White Collar Crime; FBI: Money Laundering. Anti-Money laundering rules are the best against corruption. The FBI regularly coordinates money laundering with federal, state, and local law enforcement agencies, along with a host of international partners.

legitimate. It involves covering up assets and often avoiding government action. Money laundering is used as an intermediary for the benefit of private traders. It essentially involves the circulation of money through Micro Finance Institutions (MFIs) by, for example, investing in various types of investments cover up traces. The money received is often used to finance new crimes. One of the most common forms of money laundering is Trade Based Money Laundering (TBML).[660]

Anti-money laundering rules, regulations and other procedures assist governments to minimise money laundering and prevent companies from turning illegally obtained funds into legitimate income.

Money laundering and terrorism can also be tackled internationally.[661] In 1990, the Convention on Laundering, Search, Seizure and Confiscation of the Proceeds from Crime (CETS 141), also known as the Strasbourg Convention, established the confiscation of the proceeds of crime related to money laundering, tracing and confiscation. In 2000, the United Nations Convention against Transnational Organized Crime (UNTOC), also called the Palermo Convention, provided measures against international organised crime, and which are still in use in 2022. At the national level, there are laws that prevent and detect money laundering and terrorist financing. The G7 has also established its own international cooperation network on money laundering and terrorism.

The Financial Action Task Force on Money Laundering (FATF) network exists to provide recommendations to countries on minimum levels of money laundering and terrorist-related legislation. These recommendations form the basis of EU money laundering directives. The situation of non-FATF countries regarding money laundering and terrorism is assessed by experts from the Council of Europe.[662] The fight against money laundering is also being developed by the Egmont Group, a more informal body for cooperation. Europol operates under the auspices of the EU, and its existence is based on the prevention and detection of serious transnational crime, carrying out and developing cooperation between authorities. Interpol is focused on assisting in the investigation of crimes and it is one of the leading police organisation in the world and acts as an information organisation in criminal matters for its 194 member states. An international programme to counter money laundering

660 There are different kinds of TBML schemes, but in normal situations they include misrepresentation of the price, misrepresentation of the quantity or quality of either imports or exports.

661 OECD's *Money Laundering Awareness Handbook for Tax Examiners and Tax Auditors.*

662 *FATF Recommendations.*

has been established under the auspices of the UN's Global Programme against Money Laundering (UNGPML).[663]

Money laundering controls have become stricter.[664] Companies, especially banks, have also noticed this. For example, in 2016, Nordea Bank's Swedish unit was fined the highest possible amount of over €5 million. The Scandinavian bank Handelsbanken also received a fine of €4 million. In addition, Nordea's Swedish unit and Handelsbanken received a warning from the Swedish Financial Supervisory Authority because the banks had not adequately enforced rules and controls on money laundering.

According to the Financial Supervisory Authority, Nordea Bank did not know enough about its customers' backgrounds. The authority noted that Nordea's negligence had enabled individuals to launder money through the Swedish bank. The Swedish Financial Supervisory Authority emphasised that the bank must know its customers. Sweden's share of money laundering is estimated to be over €10 billion and is also estimated to be related to other crimes or terrorist financing.[665]

***

The Panama Papers scandal began when an anonymous source leaked information to German newspapers in 2015. Scandinavian bank giant Nordea was also involved in money laundering allegations in the scandal. The money laundering centre of Panama had been flagged earlier. For example, the International Monetary Fund (IMF) issued one warning because Panama's money laundering laws did not meet the highest standards. Even when the credit rating agency Fitch noticed Panama's negative growth outlook, it did not lower Panama's credit

663 The UK established an economic crime task force with an annual budget of £6 million to target fraud, money laundering and corruption. There has been criticism. One such opinion: "as if to indicate the scale of the problem, about half a million suspicious transaction reports were received by the National Crime Agency in 2018, and it is doubtful that many could be scrutinized properly within the statutory time limit. Moreover, the Bribery Act 2010 came into force in 2011. Since then, there has been a handful of high-profile deferred prosecution agreements by which several businesses have avoided criminal prosecution for bribery and corruption in foreign markets. It is unlikely that the new board will achieve any impact beyond being a talking shop. We have robust laws, but it seems much more needs to be done to strengthen the will to obey and enforce them." Qureshi, 2019.

664 See the OECD's and the ICC's guidelines on money laundering, as well as the guidelines of different bank associations on money laundering. The Bank Secrecy Act and the USA Patriot Act (2001) have a clear message to the banks: "Know your customer."

665 Kervinen, 2015.

rating. Panama did not act promptly when the money laundering was revealed. One possible reason for this may be that the founder of the law firm at the centre of the scandal was at the time also one of the advisors to the President of Panama.[666]

Danske Bank ended its operations in the Baltic countries and Russia as a result of a money laundering scandal in 2018. Its CEO Thomas Borgen resigned earlier because 6,200 customers had initiated suspicious bank transfers. Moreover, Jesper Nielsen, the acting President and CEO of Danske Bank, was fired due to another scandal where 87,000 customers were deliberately misled in a Flexinvest Fri investment product. The Danske Bank scandal was followed by Swedbank and SEB in 2019.

The biggest banking scandal in Sweden's history took place in 2019 and involved Swedbank. Group President and CEO Birgitte Bonnesen was fired and the Chairman of the Board Lars Idemark was forced to leave his position. The scandal resulted in large fines and many years of profit were wiped out and no dividend was paid.[667]

***

In the Azerbaijani Laundromat scheme, money laundering and lobbying was exposed and amounted to $3 billion. It was revealed via the leaked data of thousands of covert payments. The scheme concerned Azerbaijan's elite who, according to investigations, laundered money through British companies in 2012–2014. Some of the money was meant for lobbying of politicians and journalists, such as former members of the Council of Europe's parliamentary assembly. Danske Bank was one of the banks which processed payments via its Estonian branch.[668]

20.1. Money Laundering and Swiss Banks

Switzerland finds itself as one of the world's centres for money laundering activities. This is due to its legislation on taxation in which tax evasion is not defined as a crime, and the fact that it is not a criminal offence to make a deposit in a country with extensive banking secrecy. This becomes a complex issue when the purpose of deposits is to hide funds from the domestic tax authorities, or to launder money.

666 Harding, 2016. Beauchamp, 2016.

667 *Finans*, 24 June 2019. The US authorities might also prosecute the company in the future, which would mean billions of dollars in fines.

668 Harding - Barr - Nagapetyants, 2017. *OCCRP*, 2020.

Following suspicions that British bank HSBC had been assisting its clients evade taxation, a money laundering investigation was launched in early 2016 against its Swiss branch. The case remained secret until investigative journalists set up SwissLeaks, whose allegations were published by the police. The "biggest bank leak case in history", published by SwissLeaks, involved billions of euros that were owed to tax authorities in dozens of countries. A money laundering charge was filed against HSBC Bank, which was extended to those who were involved in the facilitation of money laundering. According to the money laundering charge, the bank helped companies evade taxes in their home countries, concealed customers' property and laundered money. The bank's wealthy customers were also considered suspects. Politicians, gun dealers and celebrities, from top athletes to actors, were all exposed.[669]

The process was further complicated by the fact that this information, published by investigative journalists, was originally stolen by an employee of HSBC's IT department. The employee exported information from his employer to some 30,000 accounts, which amounted to about $100 billion. He also provided material that would have supported the accusation that the bank's management had knowledge of tax evasion. Officially, the bank has never admitted that its management was aware of this. The bank avoided criminal prosecution due to Swiss law, but did pay €38 million as compensation for bringing an end to the money laundering and tax evasion investigation. There was no evidence of deliberate money laundering or that the bank knew about the criminal activity. HSBC also argued that the irregularities had happened so long ago that the practices in question no longer existed. Later, the bank announced it had tightened supervision.[670]

20.2. Money Laundering and UK Banks

At the beginning of 2018, the United Kingdom introduced laws that enable the investigation of unexplained assets.[671] The purpose of these laws is, among other things, to give the authorities better visibility into assets exceeding €57,000. In future, it will be possible to intervene in such a way that if the origin of the

669 Arnold – Barret, 2015. *Financial Times*, 10 December 2019.

670 *Financial Times,* 10 December 2019. Ross, 2019.

671 One of these is the Oversight of Professional Body Anti-Money Laundering and Counter Terrorist Financing Supervision Regulations 2017, No. 1301. These laws can be retrieved from the UK Government's website.

assets is not provided to the bank, the authorities can confiscate all the money in excess of that amount. Britain has long been a safe haven for money laundering, and the country's legislation is set to tighten the grip on financial crimes.[672]

> Russian oligarchs might be at the forefront of British bank investigations. Related revelations by a Russian lawyer explained how money laundering funds end up specifically in the UK.[673]

> In the UK, the activities of the bank giant HSBC have been at such a poor level that it is sometimes referred as a bank that is "specialised" in money laundering for drug cartels. In 2015, the bank paid $1.9 billion in a one-off settlement in the US. Its leaders did not have to resign as the bank never faced a real conviction for money laundering. By comparison, small drug offenses can mean dozens of years in prison in the United States. More than $880 million was laundered through HSBC, money which originated with the Mexican drug cartel Sinaloa and Columbian drug cartel Norte del Valle. The bank giant was close to falling because of this money laundering scheme. As the collapse of the bank would have impacted the global financial system, the benefits of its continued operation were estimated to outweigh the liquidation of the bank. The economic crisis could have particularly hit Europe and Asia. In fact, the allegations were so feared that a British banking regulator specialist sent a request to the US authorities not to prosecute HSBC. To avoid the global crisis, the authorities therefore fined the bankers and the bank itself avoided any charges.[674]

20.3. Money Laundering and Brazil

The Central Bank of Brazil has combatted money laundering and the financing of terrorism for years. In 2020, Brazil updated its money laundering regulations twice, including the enhancement of its anti-money laundering framework. Brazilian law applies only to crimes committed in Brazil. Therefore, there is no

672 Hamilton – O'Neill, 2018.

673 Wallace, 2018.

674 Neate, 2016. BBC, 11 December 2012. White, 2017. Also, one banker can inflict a lot of damage on a bank or even send the bank into bankruptcy. The biggest banking scandals include: Nick Leeson ($1.3 billion loss) at Barings Bank in 1995, Toshihide Iguchi ($1.1 billion loss) at Daiwan Bank in the same year, Yasuo Hamanakan ($2.6 billion loss) at Sumumoto in 1996, John Rusnak ($691 million loss) at Allied Irish Bank in 2002, Jérôme Kerviel ($7.2 billion loss) at Société Générale in 2008, and Kweku Adobol ($2.3 billion loss) at UBS in 2011.

extraterritorial reach. Also, the maximum sentence for money laundering is 16 years.[675]

Operation Car Wash (Operação Lava Jato)[676] in 2016 concerned semi-public multinational petroleum corporation Petróleo Brasileiro S.A. (also known as Petrobras) and privately held Brazilian conglomerate Odebrecht. Both firms and their executives were examined in a case where Odebrecht was suspected of having paid bribes to Petrobras executives. In exchange, Odebrecht gained contracts and influence from Petrobras. The case started with money laundering and soon expanded into one of the greatest corruption scandals of all time. The name "Car Wash" came about as authorities literally found evidence in a car wash in Brazil.

The case was enormous and involved 11 countries and an estimated BRL6.4–42.8 billion (approx. $2–13 billion) of laundered money. The case led to thousands of search and seizure warrants, temporary and preventive detention and plea bargaining involving business figures and politicians from numerous parties.[677] Dozens of politicians were accused, among them Luiz Inácio Lula da Silva (Lula), Brazil's very popular former president. "Three years after the investigation began, Lula was found guilty of the first of five charges against him: that he had been given a beachfront apartment by engineering firm OAS in return for his help in winning contracts with Petrobras. Lula was sentenced to 12 years and one month in prison - and began his sentence on 7 April 2017, with the judges ruling he should not be free during the appeals process."[678]

Along with Lula, the investigators also indicted and jailed other well-known politicians, such as former presidents Fernando Collor de Mello and Michel Temer. The scandal affected the impunity of politicians and business leaders. As well as politics, the scandal also greatly impacted Brazil's economic system.[679] However, the case did not end there. In June 2019, there was a leak of documents that suggested the judge handling the case was partial in his decisions. The documents revealed that the judge violated legal procedure with the aim of preventing Lula's Worker Party winning the 2018 general election. Many authorities and experts considered Lula a political prisoner and demanded his release. Lula was released in November 2019.[680]

675 Roysen - Vianna, 2020.

676 *Wikipedia*: Operation Car Wash.

677 Gilman, 2016. *The New York Times*, 20 June 2015. Fonseca, 2016. *BBC*, 8 March 2016.

678 *BBC*, 8 April 2018. *BBC*, 25 January 2018.

679 Fausto, 2017. Wikipedia: Operation Car Wash.

680 Begins, 2019. *The Intercept*, 17 June 2019. *Carta Capital*, 12 August 2019. Bergamo, 2019. Darlington - Barnes, 2019.

21. Environmental Business Crime

Environmental business crimes mean that nature is impacted through illegal business activities. Here we are talking about a major issue with major consequences. The destruction of nature means increased in skin cancers, a decrease in plant productivity, more natural disasters like erosion and storms. This happens normally through the actions of companies. Environmental business crime occurs when, for example, companies dump waste in rivers, companies mismanage electronic waste or are part in deforestation or animal trafficking. All actions that have an impact on the environment negatively have features of environmental business crime. Worldwide environmental certificates might give the impression that a company is acting according to the laws and guidance given. As people value highly these certificates, the truth might be much harder to accept. Companies might have certificates which have been obtained using money and power.[681] Doing the right thing for nature is not just about telling people what they want to hear but more about telling the truth, even if it is exposes failure of the business, and more importantly shows what could be done to correct such failure. That is when business is at its best. As one Finnish company put it: "Transparency is the new green."[682] Transparency builds honesty and trust.

Environmental business crime is a breach of environmental law. This is important since the damage caused to the environment by white-collar criminals can be enormous, as can the consequences.[683]

Environmental awareness and the active use of corporate governance guidelines should be important factors for any company, even if they do not directly lead to profit. In many ways, they simply back the core business.[684] Having said this, companies cannot forget their original mission and vision—the core product or service that the company is selling. Responsibility should be part and parcel of the agenda of leaders wherever they go and whatever they do. Consumers and customers value those companies that take environmental issues seriously. Shareholders have given even more attention to these issues than purely monetary factors. Today, we talk about social impact. It means that those products which have an advantage for the planet sell. This is one reason why someone like Greta Thunberg receives so much attention. Why is this so?

681 *AlixPartners*, 2019. EIA, 2008.

682 Finnish stock exchange company Luja-talot slogan.

683 *EUROPOL*, 2015. Environmental Crime.

684 The environmental management system often mentions the ISO standard. It applies to industry and services. The idea behind the standard is that companies should define their environmental goals and targets. In addition, a company must either clarify or set the goals to achieve the management system. An enterprise must stick to the requirements set out in all its processes, functions and procedures.

The answer is simple: a responsible company makes more profit in the long run.[685]

> In 2020, there was a lot of debate about microplastics. Micro-waste is hazardous to human health. For developing countries, processing waste is nowadays a business. A lot of waste is transported illegally to countries such as Malaysia. In many countries, the waste crisis is highlighted as China and the Philippines have decided to accept only high-quality waste from developing countries so that they can reuse it. Many countries woke up to the reality that they lack processing plants where waste is burned or handled otherwise.
>
> As of May 2020, the Basel Agreement began to also cover plastic waste. In practice, it will take years before countries are ready to handle their own waste. The US and Haiti are not included in the Basel Agreement, but it still concerns them as well since they export trash to countries which are part of the agreement.[686]

In February 2017, France's parliament accepted the Duty of Vigilance Law (loi sur le devoir de vigilance). According to the law, companies will have vigilance obligations (l'obligation de vigilance) with sanctions if breached. The law intends to stop human rights breaches as well as environmental damage, both inside and outside of France. France's law covers every sector and involves every aspect of human rights. It has some deficiencies, though. It only covers big companies which employ 5,000 in France and over 10,000 worldwide. This, in turn, concerns only 150 companies in the whole world. Why after four years of debate did France enact this law? French scepticism towards multinational companies is possibly one reason, and the attitudes towards state regulation had become more positive. The general public also began to demand more responsibility from companies, especially when thousands of people died and were injured in the collapse of the Rana Plaza textile factory in Bangladesh in 2013.[687]

In Switzerland, the Responsible Business Initiative (Konzernverantwortungs-initiative) was put into action in 2018. The law, if accepted, would concern a duty of care covering the entire company value chain as well as liability for damages. In Switzerland, the parent company is not liable if it demonstrates that it has exercised due diligence. The parent company can also avoid liability for damages if it shows that it was unable to influence the subsidiary's operations.

---

685 Porter – Kramer, 2006. Rangan – Chase – Karim, 2015, 40–49. Greta Thunberg is a Swedish climate and environmental activist.

686 Shrikanth – Palma, 2020.

687 *Conseil Constitutionnel*, 23 March 2017. Brabant – Savourey, 2017.

The law applies to companies that meet two of the following conditions: 1) their balance sheet for the financial year is CHF 40 million (approx. $35 million), 2) their profit is CHF 80 million (approx. $69 million) or they employ at least 500 people. In addition, the law applies to smaller companies operating in high-risk industries.[688]

> In 2020, there was a lot of debate about oil company Shell making a deal with Britain. The deal concerned Shell's intention to leave its oil drilling platforms in the sea and not collect Brent oil drilling steel and concrete parts. Greenpeace was critical of the company of leaving oil and chemicals on the platforms because it would lead to an environmental catastrophe. Germany said it would make an official complaint. Germany's views were backed up by Sweden, Holland, Luxemburg and Belgium. According to EU law, any residual chemicals or oil on drilling platforms are considered problematic waste.[689]

The European Union stated in the summer of 2019 that it had started a project where the EU would create criteria for what are environmentally green and sustainable investments. Also, the European Commission presented "the European Green Deal" programme which aims to establish climate neutrality by 2050 within the EU.[690] The EU has a mission to guide private financing and funding to those investments that are sustainable in terms of nature and the climate. This also meant that, in the future, people who work in the financing field need to state more precisely the environmental risks any investment might possibly have. The EU completed the project before the end of 2020 and gave institute recommendations of how to report pro-environmental acts for companies with over 500 employees.[691]

Environmental fraud is in question if any of the many laws or regulations is intentionally violated. However, detection is, unfortunately, very hard.

21.1. Greenwashing

Greenwashing, a form of marketing tactics, is a method in which a consumer is given a false impression or even misleading environmental information about a company's products. The term is derived from the term whitewash, which means covering up or hiding errors. Normally, the intention of greenwashing is to give products a false, environmentally friendly appearance. This is considered as deceiving or misleading consumers into believing something else or to

688 Due Diligence means steps that are taken in order to avoid civil or criminal wrongdoing. Swiss Coalition for Corporate Justice I and II.

689 Donovan, 5 July 2016.

690 COM, 2019, 640, European Green Deal.

691 *European Commission*, 4 April 2019.

believe in a partial truth, i.e., a company might claim without any proof that its products are "planet-saving", "earth-friendly", "energy-saving" or made from recycled materials.

Greenwashing is an attempt to make a business look more natural, healthier, chemical-free and less wasteful of natural resources than it really is. For example, conventional energy companies have tried to rank themselves as champions of the environment. Greenwashed products might even be rebranded or repackaged.

Not all companies are guilty of greenwashing, though. Some products support their green credentials with evidence and facts. However, the problem is that the original green product manufacturers are often too detailed in the information they give out, so they are not considered green. One example of excessive details is from the website of Allbirds. The company tells consumers that "its sneakers are made from merino wool, with laces made from recycled plastic bottles, and insoles that contain castor bean oil. Even the boxes used in shipping are made from recycled cardboard".[692]

Sometimes it can be hard to understand which part of the product the company means with the labels. On a plastic package that contains, for example, a new shower curtain, there might be a label "recyclable." This kind of marketing is misleading because the consumer does not know which one is recycled: the package or the shower curtain. The labelling is misleading if the package or its contents cannot be recycled. If only minor parts can be recycled, it is considered misleading. [693]

There is little or no regulation around greenwashing in general. In the US, the Federal Trade Commission (FTC) is helping consumers by enforcing laws designed to ensure a competitive and fair marketplace. The FTC gives consumers information on how to differentiate "real green from greenwashed".[694]

Packaging and advertising can relate to greenwashing as follows:

> An area rug has a label that reads "50% more recycled content than before". In reality, the manufacturer increased the recycled content of 1% to 2% or 3%. So while the claims of "50% more recycled content

692 *Investopedia*: Definition of greenwashing.

693 Kenton, 2020.

694 Kenton, 2020. According to its guidelines: "Packaging and advertising should explain the product's green claims in plain language and readable type in close proximity to the claim. An environmental marketing claim should specify whether it refers to the product, the packaging, or just a portion of the product or package. A product's marketing claim should not overstate, directly or by implication, an environmental attribute or benefit. If a product claims a benefit compared to the competition, the claim should be substantiated."

than before" is technically true, it gives a false impression that the rug has a significant amount of recycled fiber.[695]

"A trash bag is labelled 'recyclable'. Trash bags are not ordinarily separated from other trash at the landfill or incinerator, so they are highly unlikely to be used again for any purpose. The claim is deceptive since it asserts an environmental benefit where no meaningful benefit exists." [696]

The reason why this issue is important is because green is a trend. Companies want to be trendy and ahead of their times. They want to get more products sold and attract customers. According to the Zero Waste website, about 95% of eco-friendly products are greenwashed[697]. That is by no means a small amount. Customers, on the other hand, want to do good for nature. They try to make choices that are good for themselves and for the world. A growing number of global consumers really want natural products.

In 2017, black toothpaste was used and marketed for whitening teeth because it contained activated charcoal. It was marketed as a safe and trendy natural product. In fact, the toothpaste destroyed the teeth's natural enamel and made the teeth yellow.[698]

There is a lot debate for and against leather in products. Vegan boots, an alternative to real leather, contain cheap plastics, which turn into microplastics and destroy and kill more life in water than leather ever will.[699]

21.2. Examples of Environmental Business Crime

One of the world's biggest car manufacturers Volkswagen (VW) was involved in a scandal in 2015. The Dieselgate scandal went back to 2009 when cars were first produced with misleading emission data. The company had to pay over $33 billion in fines and settlements. Almost 10 million cars were licensed after faked emission tests in Europe and the US. The company was investigated by both US and German investigators. The company was charged with breach of trust, tax evasion and false certification directly or indirectly (such as aiding in crimes). Even though the Dieselgate 1 ended in 2021 in Germany court as

695 Kenton, 2020

696 Kenton, 2020.

697 *Zero Waste Lifestyle System*, 2020.

698 *Zero Waste Lifestyle System*, 2020.

699 *Zero Waste Lifestyle System*, 2020.

well, Dieselgate 2 is on its way, this time in Korea concerning 210 000 Kia and Hyundai cars.

The company's upper management deceived regulators about VW's diesel exhaust levels. The car manufacturer paid settlement fees of over $14 billion in the US alone. In March 2018, the US Securities and Exchange Commission sued VW, this time accusing the company of defrauding American investors.[700]

Volkswagen's CEO, Martin Winterkorn, was charged on suspicion of fraud, as he was presumed to have been aware of the incorrect emissions data for Volkswagen's cars. The cars polluted more than the company stated in the technical data.

Volkswagen was not the only carmaker in trouble, as one French manufacturer, among others, came under the same suspicion of fraud. In 2017, the case grew even worse, as emission limits were exceeded by many car brands, such as Mitsubishi, Renault, and Audi. [701]

Winterkorn had already stepped down as CEO in 2015 after the scandal went public. At the beginning of 2019, German prosecutors filed further charges against him. By 2015, the case had cost VW tens of billions of dollars, but the deception dates back to 2006 and became a public scandal when VW's senior manager claimed that they had become aware of the false emissions tests only after the US environmental authorities confronted them in 2015.

Winterkorn was criminally indicted over the emissions in Dieselgate 1 in the US in 2018. This involved charges of fraud and conspiracy. In 2019, Winterkorn was criminally indicted in Germany. This involved charges of fraud. At the moment, Winterkorn is fugitive of justice in the US. In 2020, Volkswagen made a settlement agreement with German consumer organisation VZBV. About 400,000 German consumers filed a class action against VW. In April 2020, Volkswagen agreed to settle the case with German consumers for $620 million. In January 2020, a court in Toronto fined VW an additional $135 million. By 2021, the scandal has cost the company at least $30 billion. [702]

***

> Another type of environmental case from 201 involves Burberry. The company incinerated clothes worth €32 million to keep up their exclusive reputation. This obviously caused image issues for the company and its directors. Burberry has claimed it takes environmental issues

700 Hotten, 2015. Atiyeh, 2019. In the US, some companies have been convicted of environmental felony offences. Such companies include, for example, Bankers Trust, Daiwa Bank, F. Hoffman-La Roche, General Electric, Hoechst AG and Samsung. In the example of Volkswagen, the company pleaded guilty to three criminal felonies. *The US Department of Justice*, 11 January 2017.

701 Hotten, 2015. Atiyeh, 2019.

702 Schuetze, 2019. In 2021, the fraud trial case was delayed because Winterkorn had health issues.

seriously; however, burning so many clothes did not, unfortunately, give a positive environmental image of the company.[703]

***

In 2010, one of the largest oil spills in history occurred in the Gulf of Mexico. A massive release of oil into marine waters by British Petroleum (BP) resulted in severe health, economic and environmental consequences. The clean-up of the Deepwater Horizon oil spill used 1.8 million US gallons (43,000 bbl.; 6,800 m^3) of Corexit oil dispersant. This represents the largest clean-up in US history. BP pleaded guilty to 11 counts of felony manslaughter and became the target of massive legal and PR repercussions.[704] In addition, BP pleaded guilty to two misdemeanours and one felony count of lying to the US Congress. BP agreed to pay over $4.5 billion in fines and penalties. This resulted in the largest criminal resolution in US history.[705] In 2015, the company and five states agreed an $18.7 billion settlement. The intention was to use the money for Clean Water Act penalties and various other claims.[706]

***

In late 2019, a huge scandal was exposed in Naples, Italy. A workplace in the immigrant-heavy suburban area of Melito was accused of producing shoes and other leather products for luxury brands such as Armani, St Laurent and Fendi under terrible working conditions. None of the luxury brands admitted to the accusations. The truth will be established in court in the coming years. The lessons learned are nevertheless obvious. Long sourcing chains are beyond the reach of any company, and leaders cannot be expected to know every detail. Normally, companies just enter into agreements with a first provider and, typically, none of these complex chains are revealed.[707]

Companies have (or may have) Supplier Code of Conduct manuals in which applicable laws are stated and an SCM (Supply Chain Management Manual). However, in the case of huge international companies, absolutely no one can really know for sure who is the end producer of their products. International

703 *BBC*, 19 July 2018.

704 Geier, 2014. Roach, 2006. Robertson - Krauss, 2010.

705 Biello, 2010. Goldenberg – Rushe, 2012. Krauss – Schwartz, 2012.

706 Muskal – White, 2012. Geier, 2014.

707 *Reuters*, 18 November 2019.

investigations are underway into brands and how transparent companies are in their sourcing chains. In 2019, brands like Armani, Versace, Dolce & Gabbana were ranked quite low. Fendi did not want to take part in the survey at all. Right now, Italy has about 600,000 immigrants, and most of them are undocumented. The only way for these migrant workers to survive in Europe is to work in such underpaid jobs.[708]

> In 2016, Donald Torriero and Julius DeSimone dumped 400 truckloads of debris into sea – some of the dumped material consisted of asbestos. They appealed against the amended judgement and conviction handed down to them. According to the judgment, Torriero and others used one area of New York illegally and was ordered to pay almost $800,000 for cleaning up of the property. After Torriero pleaded guilty to one count of conspiracy in violation and two counts of wire fraud, he was sentenced to 36 months in prison. DeSimone received a sentence of five years in prison and fined $250,000. Both were guilty of violating the US Clean Water Act.[709]

708 *Clean Clothes*, 2020 investigates responsibility. *The New York Times* found in Italy a middle-aged woman who sewed jackets for Max Mara and got €3.5–4.5 for 4–5 hours of work. The woman worked in a factory which produced Louis Vuitton and Fendi jackets. Italy does not have a minimum salary. As long as buyers of the luxurious brands do not point attention to sourcing chains, there is little that can be done. Over the years, there has been a lot of debate around the clothing industry, so much so that Tuscany's traditional clothing centre is nowadays called "Little China" due to the paperless immigrants from China who work there. Max, 2018.

709 *United States v. Torriero*, 2017.

Part IV Conclusions: White-Collar Business Crime in Practice

In the above, we discussed issues of white-collar business crimes involving employment, computers, competition, taxation, embargoes, IPRs, corruption, money laundering and the environment. As this part was the most intensive one, let us look at the main conclusions.

Competition law aims to establish fair markets. At the heart of competition law is the aim that companies play by the same rules and nothing happens at the expense of consumers. Companies and their officers that operate cartels, fix prices, share markets or limit production are in danger of committing crimes. EU and other competition rules prohibit these kinds of agreements and practices. Companies may not abuse a dominant market position and/or restrict competition. If a company is found to be operating a cartel, the company might find itself facing fines of up to 10 percent of its worldwide turnover. The actual level of the fines handed out to companies do vary as can be seen from the cases. Imprisonment is a possible sanction in some countries (e.g. in the US and the UK).

When it comes to white collar business crimes, the biggest pitfalls for corporations and managers are corporate secrecy violations, accounting crimes, image damage, moral hazard, competition law crimes, tax-legal regulation, money laundering, securities law regulation, bribery, and fraud. Regulations and guidelines for businesses are plentiful, but such regulations are not uniform around the world and so practices are different. Since all companies are different, each should begin its own work by exploring the existing laws and regulations relating to business crime and from there focus on your own company. It is of paramount importance that you write the security instructions for your company and do not copy the security instructions of another company. Ultimately, communication is good but it is not enough; compliance is absolutely the most important factor and it should be constantly monitored.

Computer crimes always cause for companies a risk of losing vast sums of money. Very few people ever stop to think that an everyday device such as a phone charger that is connected to a network is rarely secure.

When it comes to dealing with risk and ensuring compliance, corporate governance needs more attention. The poor handling of risks affects corporate activity, agreements, financing and the owner base. Good corporate governance provides assurance that leaders are on the right track, and it also creates a positive outcome for the company in the future. However, it is not only a company's leaders who impact its success story, as personnel, suppliers, consultants and many other parties working for the company play an important roles in the long run. Stakeholders today expect companies to have a code of conduct on which they base their activities.

Laws and regulations as well as the long-lasting integration of ethical business practices are crucial to companies. Without these in mind it is impossible for companies to deliver value to the community and environment in which the company exists. A company's values are a crucial part of the code of conduct since values explain how ethically and responsively committed the company is and whether it is ready to operate in society. Of course, this is a good start, since a company needs to prove it operates according to the principles of its code of conduct.

A good code of conduct raises an alarm before a company finds itself operating in a grey area or even committing business crimes. However, excellence cannot be reached without training at every level of the organisation, which must be repeated and refreshed over time to remind employees about the company's commitment to honest and fair operations.

A company's reputation rests on the wellbeing of its employees. Employees who are happy and committed to a company are willing to monitor what is happening around the company and are ready to report anything they see as alarming.

Cyber criminals know how to create a backdoor into company systems and how to replicate viruses or other malware, so the first rule of thumb for any company is to make sure its IT programs are up to date. All too often, companies save information in the wrong place. The second rule of thumb is to train employees so well that they understand where the grey areas are. When employees play on the company's side, it becomes almost impossible to manipulate or use employees or for anybody outside company to inflict any harm on the business or brand. Also, companies that consider diversity as an asset and have zero tolerance towards any offensive or discriminatory practices are valued among employees. Such companies are respected and much sought-after as employers.

Business crimes are becoming more common, and there are many reasons for this. One reason is the indifference of attempts at business crimes. Another reason is that there is simply not enough information about business crimes or it is difficult to find information about business crimes. A third reason may be that business crimes are knowingly committed because it is the prevailing practice on the market. A fourth reason for the increase in business crimes may be where subsidiaries and related business are located far from the headquarters or main business, and where no one has the time and does not want to think about business crimes.

Effective tax planning is an opportunity for a company to achieve low-cost taxation by legal means. However, while aggressive tax planning may be morally questionable, it is not illegal.

Intangible rights are an important competitive factor for companies and companies are very protective of their products. However, companies do not defend their rights enough. The importance of intangible rights has been heightened due to business crimes. Intellectual property rights are difficult to enforce because the internet has created a space for the sale of counterfeit products and pirated products: Darknet.

Environmental business crimes are evolving and are acts that harm the environment. This is a major issue with major consequences that affects every single one of us, and in many cases is a catalyst for corruption. Environment business crimes are numerous but include illegal logging and fishing, wildlife crime, dumping hazardous waste and illegal trade of ozone depleting chemicals and ivory. Greenwashing is the attempt to create an environmentally friendly image for products that are in fact far from being environmentally friendly. It is the intentional deception of consumers through misleading communication. Truly green products back up their claims with facts and details not marketing slogans and cherrypicked statistics.

PART V

Closing words: The many Faces of White-Collar Business Crime

The subject of this book, white-collar business crime, has become an all-too-familiar topic in the news. The numerous examples reveal in detail crooked paths and minds of business leaders who thought they could get away with fraud and deception. Environmental fraud, bribery, corporate liability, transborder crime, espionage, employment law crimes, embargo, embezzlement, competition law crimes and money laundering. The list is long and the proverbial barrel is full of rotten apples.

Just as the range of crimes committed is colourful, so too are the perpetrators and their victims. White-collar crimes are typically computer crimes, money laundering, forgery and different types of fraud. The different types of financial fraud are depicted in Image 8 below.

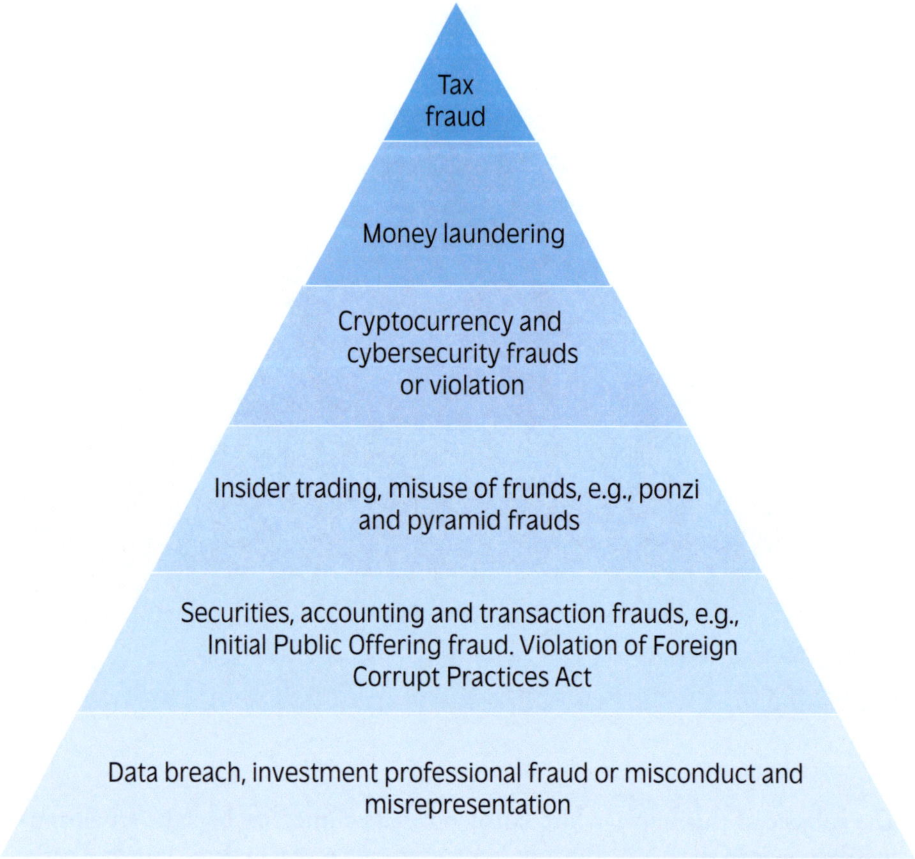

Image 8. Different types of financial fraud. The bottom line means there are a lot of cases but those do not necessarily severely affect a company's existence. The top lines mean the company's existence may be jeopardised.

What lessons can we learn from this? First and foremost, business crime has its roots in the greed of the people who are tempted to commit it. Society's response is to create laws and regulations, while various organisations also create their own guidelines.

The FBI estimates the cost of society compared to street crimes and the difference is enormous: for every street crime committed the cost of white-collar business crime to society is six times more. The total cost of white-collar crimes in the US alone is roughly $450 billion annually. Big companies might survive but small businesses are at risk of going under.

Completely eliminating crime and warding off all scandal is not a realistic aim. Of course, we can and should aim for a fairer and more honest business world, but there will always be those who are tempted by greed. Compliance programmes, personnel training and motivating words in annual reports, for example, play their part in ensuring that people do the right thing. However, decision making in the context of white-collar business crime ultimately boils down to a choice a person makes after evaluating the benefit they will receive from committing a business crime and the likelihood of getting caught: a risk/reward calculation, which is a fundamentally business-oriented thought process. The selfish human impulse to greed appears to be more apparent in these cases that an altruistic calculation of how much damage the crime might cause the company, its employees and other stakeholders.

Over the course of writing this book, the following are the most important takeaways:

"This doesn't involve us/this doesn't happen to me."

At the heart of competition law is the aim that companies play by the same rules and nothing happens at the expense of consumers. Companies and their officers that operate cartels, fix prices, share markets or limit production are in danger of committing crimes. If a company is found to be operating a cartel, the company might find itself facing fines of up to 10 percent of its worldwide turnover. The actual level of the fines handed out to companies do vary as can be seen from the cases. Imprisonment is a possible sanction in some countries (e.g. in the US and the UK).

The biggest pitfalls for companies are corporate secrecy violations, accounting crimes, reputational damage, moral hazard, competition law crimes, tax-legal regulation, money laundering, securities law regulation, bribery and fraud.

There is always resistance to change, but setting the right tone comes from the top. Being in a hurry and rash decision making is not welcomed. Crisis situation is always more difficult to manage without clear instructions. If those instructions start from middle management, the consequences are not good. When it comes to dealing with risk and ensuring compliance, corporate governance needs more attention. The poor handling of risks affects corporate activity, agreements, financing and the owner base. Good corporate governance provides assurance that leaders are on the right track, and it also creates a positive outcome for the company in the future. However, it is not only a company's leaders who impact its success story, as personnel, suppliers, consultants and many other parties working for the company play an important role in the long run.

Build up a culture of openness. Effective managers have the ability to listen but also help employees feel good about themselves and produce good results in the long run. Whistleblowers must be protected. Also, using fear as a management method is fatal for any company. History tells us that people who speak up but are subsequently marginalised, threatened or even punished, never speak up again.

Ensure all employees are aware of the ethical dimensions of their work.[710] In particular, have an overview of the whole organisation and ask if there are any teams or employees whose areas of responsibility are especially open to fraudulent activities, are the company's processes strong enough to deal with threats and is internal control at the level it is supposed to be. Kelly Paxton offers a good rule of thumb: "trust your employees, but always verify information about them and the work they do for you even if they are family members."[711]

"Let's be honest"

The way leaders talk plays an important role in setting the tone from the top – but the way leaders behave, matters even more. If actions contradict words, words mean nothing. Moral decisions are hard – moral decisions include legal, personal, environmental and economic factors. Leaders should realise that it is crucial to create an organisational culture where employees can speak freely and criticise their leaders in a constructive way. Without sensible criticism, leaders have no early warning system or alarm. Important advice from Kelly Paxton is "try to think like a criminal".

As we have seen in so many examples, although excellent risk handling processes might exist, failure to observe good corporate governance or ethics continues. A corrupt company culture, overly distributed organisation models and bad management are fatal. In many of the examples given in this book, one common factor has been aggressive sales targets with high bonuses. Such ambitious targets rapidly evolve into increasingly impossible results, leaving individuals to find increasingly suspect strategies to meet these targets with whatever means are at their disposal.

Even though the leader would have an alarm, the fact is that leaders need to balance with the different shades of grey. Very little attention is paid to the question of why a leader chooses a certain path. There is not only the legal path but also the psychological and economic paths. The risk to information security might increase not just because the coherence of information has changed or because external parties have access to the information without permission but also an error in technical programming.

710 Palazzo, 2019.
711 Paxton, 2020.

Further, if international law is not very familiar, contracts might contain clauses that undermine what has been agreed. Certain risks might not be recognised and other important clauses might be overlooked. As we have seen, IPRs need to be considered in agreements. Otherwise, your whole business might be in jeopardy.

Anti-money laundering measures provide examples of how governments try to minimise money laundering, with laws, regulations and other procedures preventing companies from turning illegally obtained funds into legitimate income.

Corruption, including bribery, embezzlement and other types of fraud, is a serious problem worldwide. Every year bribes are paid in excess of $1 trillion, which relate directly to uncollected taxes. Illicit trade can be tackled with better awareness and education. As information sharing with governments is crucial, so are trends, which should be gathered, monitored and identified constantly. Companies that do business honestly and ethically are respected. Companies should work to maintain their good reputation and adopt a zero-tolerance policy to corruption or to the appearance of corruption. However, this is not enough: companies must demand the same from their partners.[712]

The ICC prohibits kickbacks or emoluments. In the OECD or FCPA, emoluments are not prohibited, but they are not approved of either. Gifts and hospitality are prohibited under ICC rules if they affect the business in question. The FCPA states that moderate payments are accepted as business, sales and marketing. The OECD makes no mention of this.

"Raise your hand – everyone makes mistakes"

We all make mistakes: leaders, stakeholders, company lawyers, employees - everyone. What matters most is the level of the mistake and the intention behind it. If a wrong decision is made on intentionally, this becomes a matter of fraud. Of course, there are grey areas and if you can admit wrongdoing, you can go back. However, if you continue with the fraud, there is no way back and the business is at risk. In this way, leaders can jeopardise everything. Remember, there are always those who have no morals, no regrets, no emotions, no feelings and no conscience. Those people are around us, but our job is to recognise who they are and exclude them from positions of leadership and responsibility in companies and organisations.

Before accepting any form of hospitality or gift, the rule of thumb is to think about what it looks like to an outsider. After that, think twice or sleep on it. White-collar business crimes are not only driven by greed and benefits but more on a feeling – a gut feeling. How many times has a media headline started with "Mr X decided to do something criminal..."? It would be very hard

712 Myint, 2000.

if not impossible to find such a headline. If such a person would have *decided* to commit a crime, they would probably have *understood* the risks and what is at stake. In reality, very little attention is paid to the consequences of the decisions which lead people into the grey area. The feeling that the wrongdoing is not harmful to anybody is the key point.[713]

"You always have an option to choose differently"

When it comes to business ethics, every employee's actions matter – every leader's actions matter. After a breach in behaviour, it is good to see who can look in the mirror and admit there is another way. Apologising is always hard, but it is ultimately cathartic. Choosing the right way, being a role model and not outsourcing responsibility might not only save the company from scandal but also strengthen the company culture.

Information security risks might increase not just because the coherence of information has changed or because an external party has access to the information without permission but also as an error in technical programming. Kelly Paxton said it well: "Passwords are like toothbrushes. Do not share them."

Spoiler alert: "Directors are only humans"

Leading is not hard. Be honest with yourself and set an example, i.e. be transparent. Building a great company culture requires a lot of work. Words which lead to actions and which, in turn, lead to good decisions count for a lot.

Being a visionary, being a human with integrity and kindness – is this too much to ask for?

The late Professor Clayton Christensen said: "...the only metrics that will truly matter to my life are the individuals whom I have been able to help, one by one, to become better people."[714] We cannot stop white-collar business crimes, but understanding and knowing at least a little bit about how white-collar criminals work and act might help you in your daily business. More cases like those presented in this book will certainly happen[715], but at least you now know what to monitor in your organisation.

Most leaders are honest and act with integrity, but there are those who are ready to take power and set themselves above others. There is no perfect leader, but bad leaders erode employee satisfaction and results. A big ego often leads to an abuse of power and disrespectful behaviour. Power can alienate a

713 Soltes, 2016, 1-7.

714 Clayton M. Christensen quote on After Life.

715 In 2021, the Pandora Papers scandal broke. The hidden owners of offshore companies were exposed. See *YouTube*: The Pandora Papers.

leader's values, corrupt behaviour and lead them to make unethical decisions simply because they can. If there is any compensation, it is that most leaders hire people more competent than themselves. The trick is having the humility to listen to them. Leading is about serving others.

Go with your eyes open

As the world grows in complexity, leading and managing different processes and cultures becomes even more challenging. There is no easy path to follow. Constant change means that leaders must be agile in their daily activities, while their companies must be ready to change both service and product lines in step with demand.

Understand what the risks are: even if your business is local, your risks are global. The harm is losing money or harm to the economy. What is acceptable today might not be acceptable tomorrow. Take an appropriate role and act and understand how your business, products or services are connected. Always keep transparency in mind in whatever you do. As we have seen in the 2020s, the world can change in days. Business crime is also changing, and it remains to be seen what has happened in the shadows of the pandemic.

Closing words

Now that you have read this book, I hope you have internalised the message:

The next time you are tempted to act wrongly, think again!

All actions have consequences and victims. A single act of wrongdoing might easily destroy your company or your family and cost investors a lot of money.

Do not rely on just one leader. Surround yourself with good and ethical people. They should all aim for a common goal and base their actions on high moral and ethical principles. Internal competition and bad management can easily alienate real talents. A leader's ambition should NEVER exceed the wellbeing of their employees.

For so many business leaders who like Gordon Gekko in Oliver Stone's film Wall Street believed "greed is good", they ultimately found themselves as convicted criminals serving time in prison. We all have choices to make. In this book, I have shown you there is another way and perhaps a line from another film, The Matrix, is now more appropriate: "Where we go from there is a choice I leave to you."

22. List of Sources

22.1. Books

Aaltonen, T. – Luoma, M. – Rautiainen, R. (2004): *Vastuullinen johtaminen. Inhimillistä päätöksentekoa.* (*English translation: Responsible Management, Humane Decision-Making*). WSOY.

Accum, F. (1820): *A Treatise on adulterations of Food and Culinary Poisons*. Echo Library.

Ahlberg, M. – Romberg, A. (2018): *The Grey Zone.*

Ahokas, N. (2012): *Yrityksen sisäinen valvonta.* (*English translation: Company's internal auditing*). Edita.

Alahuhta, M. (2016): *Johtajuus, kirkas suunta ja ihmisen voima.* (*English translation: Leadership, clear direction and power of humans*). Docendo.

Anderson, H. (2008): *Directors' Personal Liability for Corporate Fault: A Comparative Analysis.* Wolters Kluwer.

Bentham, J. (1921): *An Introduction to the Principles of Morals and Legislation.* Houghton Mifflin Company. The Riverside Press. London.

Benton Foundation (2010): *Encyclopedia Britannica*. British Encyclopaedia. International law. 15th Edition.

Blanchard, K. – Johnson, S. (2015): *The One Minute Manager.* Published originally in 1982. New York. Morrow.

Black's Law Dictionary (2001): Business Judgement Rule.

Blanpain, R. (2010): *Comparative Labour Law and Industrial Relations in Industrialized Market Economies.* Kluwer Law International.

Bowen, W. G. (2008): *The Board Book: An Insider's Guide for Directors and Trustees*, W.W. Norton & Company. New York & London.

Box, S. (1987): *Recession, Crime and Punishment*. Routledge.

Buehler, M. – Socia, K. – McCarthy, K. – Kozak, M. – Walter, E. – Lepkowski, P. – Cator, D. – Lippard, J. – McQuade, S. – Sampat, N. (2009): *Encyclopedia of Cybercrime.* Greenwood Press.

Cernkovich, S.A. – Giordano, P. C. – Rudolph, J.L. (2000): *Race, Crime, and the American Dream.* Journal of Research in Crime and Delinquency 37(2). May 2000.

Clarkson, K. – Miller, R. – Cross, F. (2011): *Business Law, Texts and Cases.* 14th Edition. Cengage Learning.

Currie, J. H. (2008): *Public International law.* 2nd Edition. November 2008. Irwin Law (Canada).

Davies, P. L. – Worthington, S. (2016): *Principles of Modern Company Law*. Sweet & Maxwell.

Degan Đuro, V. (1997): *Sources of International Law*. Martinus Nijhoff Publishers.

Douma, S. – Schreuder, H. (2013): *Economic Approaches to Organizations.* 5th edition. London: Pearson.

Dunleavy, N. (2010): *Competition Law. A Practitioner's Guide*. Legal Books. Ireland.

Durkheim, É. (1895): *Les Règles de la Méthode Sociologique.* (English: The Rules of Sociological Method. Paris.

Enrich, D. (2020): *Dark Towers, Deutsche Bank, Donald Trump, and an Epic Trail of Destruction*. Custom House.

Ezrachi, A (2012): *EU Competition Law*. An Analytical Guide to Leading Cases. Bloomsbury.

Feast, R., (2003): *Kidnap of the Flying Lady: How Germany Captured Both Rolls Royce and Bentley*. Motorbooks.

*Ferrell, C. O. – Fraedrich, J. – Ferrell, L. (2016): Business ethics: ethical decision making and cases. Eleventh ed. Boston, MA.*_

Gilbert, C. (2018): *There's No Right Way To Do The Wrong Thing*. Nobleedge.

Graham, L. (2015): *Internal control audit and compliance*. 1st ed. Hoboken, New Jersey: Wiley.

Grant, J. P. – Barker, C. J. (2009): *Encyclopaedic Dictionary of International Law. Oxford University Press.*

Greig, D. W. (1976): *International Law*. 2nd ed. Butterworths, London.

Greimel, H. – Sposato, W. (2021): *Collision Course: Carlos Ghosn and the Culture Wars That Upended an Auto Empire.* Harvard Business Review Press. 2021.

Goergen, M. (2012): *International Corporate Governance.* Prentice Hall.

Hawthorne, O. E. – Magu, S. (2018): *Corruption Scandals and their Global Impacts.* Routledge. 2018.

Helminen, M. (2012): *EU-vero-oikeus* (*English translation*: *European Union tax law*). Talentum.

Honlet, J-C. – Dufêtre A-S. – Lecompte A. (2016): *The International Arbitration Review*. Chapter 17: France. Seventh Edition. Carter J. H Editor. Law Business Research Ltd.

Hopt, K. J. (1997): *The German Two-Tier Board (Aufsichtsrat), A German View on Corporate Governance*. In Hopt, K. J. – Wymeersch, E. (eds), *Comparative Corporate Governance: Essays and Materials*, de Gruyter, Berlin & New York.

Jones, C. – Parker, M. – ten Bos, R. (2005): *For Business Ethics – A critical approach*. Routledge, Taylor and Francis Group, London and New York. January 2005.

Kazemi, F. (1985): Anglo-Persian Oil Company. In: *Encyclopædia Iranica*, Vol. II. Fasc 1. New York.

Kicenski, K. K. (2017): *The Corporate Prison: The Production of Crime and the Sale of Discipline*. In World Heritage Encyclopedia. Gutenberg Self Publishing Press.

Kinnunen, N. (2015): *Tietoturvaohjeistusten noudattamisen motivaatio ja sen muuttaminen*. (*English translation*: *Motivation for following information security instructions and change therein*). Doctoral Thesis. University of Vaasa.

Koistinen M. (2020): *Syötkö väärennettyä ruokaa* (*English translation*: *Do you eat fake food*). Into kustannus.

Kuoppamäki, P. (2003): *Markkinavoiman sääntely EY:n ja Suomen kilpailuoikeudessa (English translation: Regulation of market power in EC and Finnish competition law)*. Suomalainen Lakimiesyhdistys.

Kuorsalo, A. – Susiluoto, I. – Valkonen, M. (2007): *Venäjä. Kovan linjan energiajätti* (*English translation*: *Russia. Hard energy giant*). Edita.

Kurkela, M. (2003): *Globalisoitunut sopimuskäytäntö ja sopimusoikeudelliset periaatteet*. (*English translation*: Globalized contract practice and contract law principles.) Edita.

Lautjärvi, H. (2018): Business Crime. Edita.

Lawrence, F. (2013): *Not on the Label: What really Goes Into the Food on Your Plate*. Penguin Books.

Leeson, N (2016): *Rogue Trader. The Original Story of the Banker Who Broke the System*. Sphere. Updated ed. edition. 2 August 2016.

Legvold, R. (2009): Corruption, the Criminalized State, and Post-Soviet Transitions. In Robert I. Rotberg (ed.). *Corruption, global security, and world order*. Brookings Institution.

Mallin, C. A. (2011): *Corporate Governance Developments in the UK*. In Mallin, C. A. (ed), *Handbook on International Corporate Governance: Country Analyses*. Second Edition, Edward Elgar Publishing.

Manninen, J. (2016): *Vastuullisuus, Mitä tapahtuu huomenna*. (*English translation: CSR, What happens tomorrow?*). Ellun kanat.

Maier, P. (2010): *Ratification: The People Debate the Constitution,* New York: Simon & Schuster.

Maslow, A. H. (1954): *Motivation and personality*. 2nd ed. New York: Harper & Row.

Mentula, A. – Pokela, H. – Saraste, T. (1998): *Määräävän markkina-aseman väärinkäyttö kilpailuoikeudessa (English translation: Abuse of a dominant position in competition law)*. Lakimiesliiton kustannus.

Merrian-Webster (2020): *Merrian Webster Dictionary*. Merrian Webster US.

Michaela, A. (2015): *Effects doctrine in the European Union Law*. European Encyclopedia of Law. Milligan, J. W. (2016): *Make More Money*. iUniverse.

Milne, A. (2009): *The Fall of the House of Credit: What Went Wrong in Banking and What Can be Done to Repair the Damage?* Cambridge University Press.

Moriarty, J. (2017): *Business Ethics*. The Stanford Encyclopedia of Philosophy. Fall 2017 Edition. Edward N. Zalta (ed.). Stanford.

Nasheri, H. (2005): *Economic Espionage and Industrial Spying*. Cambridge University Press.

Ngwu, F. N. - Osuji, O. K. - Stephen, F. H. (2017): *Corporate Governance in Developing and Emerging Markets*. Frank, S. (eds.). London: Routledge.

O'Grady, W. (2011): *Crime in Canadian Context*. Toronto: Oxford University Press.

Paxton, K. (2020): *Embezzlement. How to Detect, Prevent and Investigate Pink-Collar Crime*. Coppell, TX.

Pearce, F – Snider, L. (1995): *Corporate Crime*. University of Toronto Press.

Pearce, F. – Tombs, S. (1992): *Realism and Corporate Crime. In Issues in Realist Criminology*. (Matthews, R. – Young, J. eds.). London: Sage.

Radcliffe, B. (2009): *The Corporation as a Person: Legal Fact or Fiction?* Osgoode Law School. Canada. 24 September 2009

Rahim, M. – Kuruppu, S. (2016): *Corporate Governance in India: The Potential for Ghandism*. In Ngwu, F. – Osuji, O. – Stephen, F. (eds.). Corporate Governance in Developing and Emerging Markets. London: Routledge.

Roysen, J. – Vianna, V. (2020): Brazil: *Anti-Money Laundering Laws and Regulations 2020*. Joyce Roysen Avogados. 14 May 2020.

Rudanko, M. (1998): *Arvopaperimarkkinat ja siviilioikeus* (*English translation: Securities Markets and Civil Law*). Helsingin yliopiston Kansainvälisen talousoikeuden instituutin julkaisuja 33. Suomen itsenäisyyden juhlarahaston julkaisuja. Kauppakaari Oyj. Lakimiesliiton kustannus.

Salmenniemi, S. – Rotkirch, A. (2008): *Suhteiden Venäjä (English translation: Relations with Russia)*. Gaudeamus.

Salminen A. – Mäntysalo, V. (2013): *Epäeettisestä tuomittavaan: korruptio ja hyvä veli verkostot Suomessa* (English translation: *From unethical to reprehensible: corruption and good brother networks in Finland*). Publication no 182. University of Vaasa.

Schick, N. (2020): Deep Fakes and the Infocalypse – What you Urgently Need to Know.

Schlegel, K. – Weisburd, D. (1992): *White-collar crime reconsidered*. Boston: Northeastern University Press.

Simpson, S. S. (2002): *Corporate Crime, Law, and Social Control*. Cambridge: Cambridge University Press.

Slomanson, W. (2011): *Fundamental Perspectives on International Law*. Boston, USA: Wadsworth.

Snider, L. (1993): *Bad Business*. Scarborough, Ontario. Nelson Canada.

Soltes, E. (2016): *Why They Do it. Inside the Mind of the White Collar Criminal.* Public Affairs. New York.

Strader, K. J. (2017): *Understanding White Collar Crime.* Fourth Edition. Carolina Academic Press.

Strotkamp, E. M. (2019): *The LIBOR Scandal: A Comparison of Banks Involved Concerning the Impact of Disclosure and the Imposition of Fines on Stock Prices.* Wirtschaftswissenschaften, Bachelor of Science.

Suomela, E. (2010): *Hallitus ja Corporate Governance (English translation: Board and Corporate Governance)*. KHTnyt. Otava.

Sutherland, E. (1949): *White collar crime*. New York: Holt, Rinchart and Winston.

Tiihonen, T. (2007): *Hallitus vai toimitusjohtaja – työnjako ja vastuut (English translation: Board or CEO dividing tasks and responsibilities)*. Boardman. Gummerus.

Tricker, A. (2009): *Essentials for Board Directors: An A–Z Guide*, Bloomberg Press, New York.

Vapaavuori, T. (2019): *Liikesalaisuudet ja salassapitosopimukset (English translation: trade secrets and non-disclosure agreements)*. Alma Talent.

Wasastjerna, M. (2019): *Competition, Data and Privacy in the Digital Economy: Testing Conventional Boundaries and Expanding Horizons - Towards A Privacy*

Dimension in Competition Policy? Doctoral thesis. University of Helsinki, Faculty of Law. Unigrafia.

Weisburd, D. (2017). *Quantitative methods in criminology*. Routledge.

Weismann M. (2011): *Parallel Proceedings*. ABA.

Wells, C. (2001): *Corporations and Criminal Responsibility.* (Second Edition). Oxford: Oxford University Press.

Yannaca-Small K. (2008): *Parallel Proceedings.*The Oxford Handbook of International Investment Law. Edited by Muchlinski, P. – Ortino, F. – Schreuer, C. Print Publication Date. June 2008.

Znoj, H. (2009): Deep Corruption in Indonesia: Discourses, Practices, Histories. In *Nuijten, M. – Gerhard A. (ed.). Corruption and the secret of law: a legal anthropological perspective. Ashgate.*

22.2. Articles and Blogs

Aarons, E. (2020): "Football Leaks' Rui Pinto in prison with hard-drive passwords in his head". *The Guardian*. 28 February 2020.

ACCC (2020): "Trivago loses appeal after misleading consumer over hotel ads". *Australian Competition and Consumer Commission, Release*. No 235/20.

Adams T. (2018): "Facebook's week of shame: the Cambridge Analytica fallout". *The Guardian*. 24 March 2018.

Addady, M. (2015): "Toshiba's accounting scandal is much worse than we thought". *The Fortune.* 8 September 2015.

Afterman, A. (2016): "SEC | The Audit Committee Financial Expert". *The CPA Journal.* June 2016 Issue.

Aguado, J. (2019): "Probe into alleged BBVA spying case expands to former CEO: sources". *Reuters.* 2 July 2019.

Alcázar L. – Andrade, R. (2001): "Induced Demand and Absenteeism in Peruvian Hospitals." in Di Tella, R. and Savedoff, W. D. (eds.). *Diagnosis Corruption*. Washington, DC: Inter-American Development Bank.

Al-Hussain, A. H. (2009): "Corporate governance structure efficiency and bank performance in Saudi Arabia.". *UMI Dissertation Services*, 2009.

Al-Hussain, A. H. – Johnson, R. L. (2009): "Relationship between corporate governance efficiency and Saudi banks> performance." *The Business Review*, 14, 111–117.

Alma, M. (2016): "Common Risks that Businesses Face Today". *IFAC org.*

Alt, J. – Lassen, D. (2008): "Political And Judicial Checks on Corruption: Evidence From American State Governments". *Harvard, Economics and Politics.* Volume 20. March 2008. No 1.

Álvarez, C. – Gándara, N. (2017): "Extorsiones a Movistar: Autoridades confirman que ya conocen a la organización criminal que perpetró ataques" *Prensa Libre,* 13 November 2017.

Andrews, S. – Burrough, B. – Ellison, S. (2014): "The Snowden Saga: A Shadowland of Secrets and Light." *Vanity Fair.* May 2014.

Arnold, C. (2016): "Bank of America $1.2 Billion Mortgage "Hustle" Penalty Thrown Out." *NPR News.* 23 May 2016.

Arnold, M. – Barrett, C. (2015): "HSBC in Swiss tax avoidance storm" *Financial Times* 9 February 2015.

Atiyeh, C. (2019): "Everything You Need to Know about the VW Diesel-Emissions Scandal." *Car and Drive.* 4 December 2019.

Australian Broadcasting Corporation (2006): "White collar criminals urged to heed Cooper sentence". *News Online.* 23 June 2006.

Azzali, S. (2016): "The legacies of Sochi 2014 Winter Olympics: an evaluation of the Adler Olympic Park". *Urban Research & Practice.* 10(3), August 2016.

Baltimore Sun (1999): "Sears is fined $60 million; Company pleads guilty to defrauding patrons with credit card debts; Legal matters." *Bloomberg News.* 20 February 1999.

Baltrusaitis, J. (2020). "Top 10 Countries and Cities by Number of CCTV Cameras". *PreciseSecurity* 2020. 20 June 2020.

BBC (2020): "Apple hit with record €1.1bn fine in France". *BBC News* 16 March 2020.

BBC (2020): "The Missing Cryptoqueen. What dreams may come." *BBC News.* Podcast. 6 January 2020.

BBC (2019): "What is Sustainable Palm Oil?" *BBC News.* 3 September 2019.

BBC (2019): "How much of Europe does China Own?" *BBC News.* 20 April 2019.

BBC (2019): "Silvio Berlusconi: Italy's perpetual powerbroker". 29 May 2019.

BBC (2018): "Brazil ex-President Lula loses appeal against corruption conviction". *BBC News.* 25 January 2018.

BBC (2018): "Burberry burns bags, clothes and perfume worth millions". *BBC News* 19 July 2018.

BBC (2018): "Brazil corruption scandals: All you need to know". *BBC News.* 8 April 2018.

BBC (2017): "Tesco fined £129m for overstating profits" *BBC News.* 28 March 2017.

BBC (2016): "Brazil Petrobras scandal: Tycoon Marcelo Odebrecht jailed". *BBC News.* 8 March 2016.

BBC (2014): "Lloyds fined £218m over Libor rate rigging scandal". *BBC News.* 28 July 2014.

BBC (2012): "HSBC money laundering report: Key findings". *BBC News.* 11 December 2012.

BBC (2008):"Italian dairy boss gets 10 years". *BBC News.* 18 December 2008.

BBC (2002): "Murdoch heir defends One.Tel fiasco" *BBC News*. 7 August 2002.

BBC (2001): "One.Tel collapse angers magnates". *BBC News*. 30 May 2001.

BBC (2001, II): "Pressure piles on One.Tel media heirs". *BBC News.* 11 June 2001.

Beattie, A. (2019): "The Copper King: An Empire Built On Manipulation". *Investopedia,* 25 June 2019.

Beauchamp, S. (2016): "Operation Haven, the original Panama Papers, How a 1970s sting could've blown the lid off the tax evasion scandal" 8 April 2016.

Bebchuk L. A. (2004): "The Case for Increasing Shareholder Power". Harvard Law Review.Vol. 118, No. 3, January 2005. *Harvard Law and Economics*. Discussion Paper No. 500.

Begins, V. (2019): "The Dirty Problems With Operation Car Wash: News reports have pointed to serious wrongdoing at the heart of the anti-corruption inquiry that has shaken many Latin American countries". *The Atlantic*. 21 August 2019.

Beltran, L. (2002): "WorldCom files largest bankruptcy ever, Nation's No. 2 long-distance company in Chapter 11 -- largest with $107 billion in assets". *CNN Money*. 22 July 2002.

Beioley, K. (2019): "Libor Scandal. UK Serious Fraud Office closes its 7-year Libor probe". *Financial Times*. 18 October 2019.

Bennett, M. W. – Levinson J. D. – Hioki, K. (2017): "Judging Federal White-Collar Fraud Sentencing: An Empirical Study Revealing the Need for Further Reform". *Iowa Law Review.*

Bergamo, M. (2019): "Juristas estrangeiros se dizem chocados e defendem libertação de Lula" English: Foreign jurists shocked, and call for Lula's release. *Folha de São Paulo.* 11 August 2019.

Berkheimer, J. – Cargile, S. – Richards, G. – Palsson, E. – Shem-Tov, I. (2013): "Issue Guide: Trade Embargoes, Seals, and More". *University of California*, Irvine. 8 April 2013.

Berr, J. (2013): "The Fiscal Times 2013. When Brands Go Bad". *The Fiscal Times*. 21 October 2013.

Bhattacharyya, A. (2015): "Toshiba - a case of internal audit failure." *Businessstandard.com*.

Biello, D. (2010): "Is Using Dispersants on the BP Gulf Oil Spill Fighting Pollution with Pollution?". *Scientific American*. 18 June 2010.

Binnie, I. – Pinedo, E. (2021): "Spanish court to investigate Iberdrola CEO in alleged spying case". *Reuters*. 23 June 2021.

Blanding, M. (2013): "Pulpit Bullies: Why Dominating Leaders Kill Teams". 18 November 2013. *Harvard Business School*.

Bowcott, O. (2018): "Lauri Love ruling 'sets precedent' for trying hacking suspects in UK". *The Guardian*. 5 February 2018.

Buckley, C. (2020): "Ex-President of Interpol Is Sent to Prison for Bribery in China". *The New York Times*. 21 January 2020.

Brabant, S. Savourey, E (2017): "France's Corporate Duty of Vigilance Law – A Closer Look at the Penalties Faced by Companies". *Business-humanrights.org*.

Brand Minds (2018): "Why Did Nokia Fail?" *Multiplier Magazine*. 24 July 2018.

Branton, J. (2008): "Banged up" - imprisonment for breach of competition law in the UK now a reality.*Cobbetts LLP*. 18 September 2008.

Bray, J. (2007): "Facing up to corruption 2007: A practical business guide." Simmons & Simmons.

Brody, R. G. – Kiehl, K.A. (2014): "From white-collar crime to red-collar crime." *Journal of Financial Crime*. 17(3), 18 November 2010.

Brown, K. – Dugan, I. J. (2002): "Arthur Andersen's Fall From Grace Is a Sad Tale of Greed and Miscues". *The Wall Street Journal.* 7 June 2002.

Bungard, M. (2020): "Trivago misled consumers in favour of advertiser dollars, federal court finds". *The Sydney Morning Herald*. 21 January 2020.

Burdick-Will, J. (2016): "Neighborhood Violent Crime and Academic Growth in Chicago: Lasting Effects of Early Exposure". *Social Forces*, Volume 95, Issue 1, September 2016, 11 August 2016.

Burgess, M. (2018): "What is the Internet of Things?" *Wired*. 16 February 2018.

Burton, L. (2019): "Banks facing new wave of cases linked to Libor scandal". *The Telegraph*, 28 April 2019.

Burtsov, P. (2014): "Mafia on Italian suurin yritys – Nykymafioso on käynyt yliopiston". *YLE,* 2 December 2014.

Calcagni, III J. L. (2017): "The Top 7 Embezzlement Cases in US History". *Calcagnilaw.* 7 May 2017.

Carberry, E. J. – Engelen, P-J. - Essen Van, M. (2018): "Which Firms Get Punished for Unethical Behavior? Explaining Variation in Stock Market Reactions to Corporate Misconduct". *Business Ethics Quarterly* 28:2, April 2018.

Carlsen, A. – Salam, M. – Cain Miller, C. – Lu, D. – Ash Ngu, A. – Patel, L.K. – Wichter, J. (2018): "#MeToo Brought Down 201 Powerful Men. Nearly Half of Their Replacements Are Women." *The New York Times*. 29 October 2018.

Carlsson, M. (2020): "Inside the Kiev fraud factory stealing senior citizens' savings". *Dagens Nyheter.* 1 March 2020.

Carlsson, R. (2019): "What Bernie Madoff Did and Who He Defrauded." 3 February 2019.

Carraud, S. – Rosemain. M. (2019). "Google to pay $1 billion in France to settle fiscal fraud probe". *Reuters*, 12 September 2019.

Carroll, R. (2014): "Snowden used simple technology to mine NSA computer networks". *The Guardian*. 9 February 2014.

Carson, V. (2010): "Brad Cooper, last of the HIH three free today". *Sydney Morning Herald.* 30 October 2010.

Carta Capital (2019). "Jurista americana admirada por Dallagnol defende libertação de Lula" English: American lawyer Admired by Dallagnol Advocates for Lula's Release. 12 August 2019.

Chappell, B. (2020). "Bayer To Pay More Than $10 Billion To Resolve Cancer Lawsuits Over Weedkiller Roundup". *NPR*. 24 June 2020.

Chavarria, L. – Walker, Q. – Bahamon, D. (2020): "Illicit Trade in Times of Coronavirus". *Euromonitor International.* August 2020.

Chen, J. (2020 I): Securities and Exchange Commission (SEC). 15 July 2020.

Chen, J. (2020 II): "Embezzlement". *Investopedia*. 30 March 2020.

Chen, J. (2019): "Securities Fraud". *Investopedia*. 16 September 2019.

ChinaDaily (2017): "Huawei wins a victory in Samsung patent dispute" 12 October 2017.

ChinaDaily (2017): "Samsung's heir apparent questioned as suspect over presidential scandal". 12 January 2017.

ChinaDaily (2009): "Watchdog: Rio spying caused 'huge loss'". 10 August 2009.

Clark, A. (2006): "The Real String: how plot to betray Coke fell flat after Pepsi called the FBI". *The Guardian*. 7 July 2006.

CNN (2007): "Two ex-Coke workers sentenced in Pepsi plot deal". 23 May 2007.

CNN (2003): "WorldCom to emerge from collapse". 14 April 2003.

CNN (2001): "Waste Management settles suit". 7 November 2001.

Cole, B (2012): "Volker rule". *TechTarget.* May 2012.

Coleman, M. – McHugh, N. – Irvine, H. – Gascon, D. – Kruse, L. E. (2014): "It's criminal! The criminalization of antitrust continues across the world".*Norton Rose Fulbright*. 20 January 2014.

Comlay, E. – Stempel, J. (2009): "UPDATE 2-BofA to pay Parmalat $100 mln to settle lawsuit". *Reuters*. 28 July 2009.

Computerhope (2021): "Computer Crime". 7 June 2021.

Congressional Research Service (2010): "Constitutional Limits on Punitive Damages Awards: An Analysis of Supreme Court Precedent". 25 January 2010.

Cooper, A. – Valle del, L. (2020): "Harvey Weinstein's sexual assault and rape convictions marked a major #MeToo moment" *CNN.* February 2020.

Copeland, R. (2019): "Google's 'Project Nightingale' Gathers Personal Health Data on Millions of Americans". The Wall Street Journal. 11 November 2019.

Cotterrell, R. (2012): "What Is Transnational Law?". *Law & Social Inquiry*. 1 March 2012. Volume 37 Issue 2. American Bar Foundation.

Cratchley, D. (2009): "One.Tel saga not over for James Packer and Lachlan Murdoch". *The Daily Telegraph*. 20 November 2009.

Curtis, L. – Platts, R. (2020): "HGFAI is Changing How Products are Bought and by Definition Will Change Trade Mark Law". *IPR Help Desk*.

Damiani, J. A. (2019): "Voice Deepfake Was Used to Scam a CEO out of $243,000". *Forbes* 3 September 2019.

Darlington, S. – Barnes, T. (2019): "Brazil's former President Lula released from prison". *CNN*. 9 November 2019.

Datto (2016): "American Small Businesses Lose an Estimated $75 Billion a Year to Ransomware, New Datto Survey Finds." *Datto*. 7 September 2016.

de Brie, C. (2000): "Thick as thieves' Crime the World's biggest enterprise". *Le Monde Diplomatique,* April.

Deng, C. (2021): "China Hands Rare Death Sentence to Former Asset-Management Head". *The Wall Street Journal.* 5 January 2021.

Deutsche Welle (2021): UN calls for arms embargo against Myanmar. 18 June 2021.

Deutsche Welle (2019): "Ericsson fined $1 billion for widespread corruption". 7 December 2019.

Deutsche Welle (2017): "Rolls-Royce agrees to pay massive fines for bribery". 17 January 2017.

Deutsche Welle (2016): "Germany's Leoni 'a victim of massive fraud'". 16 August 2016.

DH Anticounterfeit AB (2021): "Why do we need a ISO standard for brand protection". 20 January 2021.

Dhir, R. (2021): "Pump and Dump." *Investopedia.* 2 June 2021.

Donovan, J. (2016): "Shell plans to leave Brent platform legs in North Sea". 5 July 2016.

Doyle, C. (2013): "Congressional Authority to Enact Criminal Law: An Examination of Selected Recent Cases," *Congressional Research Service.* 27 February 2013.

Duronio, B. (2012): "How 9 Banks Are Exposed to $200 Trillion Worth of Derivatives". *Business Insider*. Finance. 24 April 2012.

Easy GDPR (2019): "DSGVO Strafe für neuen Eigentümer von Delivery Hero" 23 September 2019.

Edwards, S. (2019): "Spain's Watergate: Inside the Corruption Scandal that changed the nation.". *The Guardian*. 1 March 2019.

Ekran (2019): "How to Detect and Prevent Industrial Espionage". *Ekran Systems.* 8 August 2019.

El Mansouri, S. (2021): "Deutsche Bank fined over $130M to Resolve Bribery and Fraud Violations" *The Compliance Lady.* 9 January 2021.

Elbalti, B. (2021): "The Supreme Court on Punitive Damages". *Conflict of Laws Net.* 4 June 2021.

Ellery, B.- Ford, R. – Thomson, A. (2020): "Ryanair boss Michael O'Leary wants extra checks on Muslim men". *The Times*. 22 February 2020.

Ellman-Golan, E. – Sandick, H. (2019): "Circuit Upholds Rajaratnam SEC Civil Penalty". *Patterson Belknap Webb & Tyler LLP*. 7 March 2019.

Erickson, J. M. (2008): “Corporate Misconduct and the Perfect Storm of Shareholder Litigation.” *University of Richmond*.

Evans, R. – Watt, H. – Pegg, D. (2016): “Rolls-Royce middlemen may have used bribes to land major contracts.” *The Guardian*. 31 October 2016.

Faggella, D. (2019): “AI for Crime Prevention and Detection – 5 Current Applications”. 2 February 2019.

Farge, E. (2021): “Kuwait’s Sheikh Ahmad convicted of forgery in Geneva trial”. Reuters. 10 September 2021.

Fausto, S. (2017). The Lengthy Brazilian Crisis Is Not Yet Over. Issue Brief, 2.

FC Barcelona. (2020): Barcelona to take legal action against ex-vice president Rousaud. 13 April 2020.

Fernando, J. (2020): “Bre-X Minerals Ltd”. *Investopedia*. 12 October 2020.

Fibre2Fashion (2008): “Marimekko, Dolce & Gabbana settle unikko trademark dispute”. 15 October 2008.

Fieldstadt E. – Winter, T. – Fitzpatrick, S. (2020): “Michael Avenatti guilty on all counts in Nike extortion case.” *NBC News* 15 February 2020.

Financial Times (2019): “HSBC to pay $192m penalty in US tax evasion case”. *Financial Times*. 10 December 2019.

Financial Times (2017): “LuxLeaks: Luxembourg’s response to an international tax scandal”. *Financial Times* 23 June 2017.

Financial Times (2012): “Banks’ Libor costs may hit USD22bn.” 12 July 2012.

Financial Times (2010): “Rio sacks staff jailed by China for bribery”. 30 March 2010.

Finans.dk (2019): ”Bankdirektør Jesper Nielsen fyret i Danske Bank”. 24 June 2019.

Flanagan, C. (2017): “Bill Clinton: A Reckoning”. *The Atlantic.* 13 November 2017.

Fonseca, P. (2016): “Former Odebrecht CEO sentenced in Brazil kickback case”. *Reuters*. 8 March 2016.

Foran, P. (2021): “Extortion scams are on the rise. Here are some tips to avoid them”. *Toronto News*. 2 March 2021.

Forgues-Puccio, G.F. (2013): “Corruption and the Private sector: a review of issues, Economic and Private Sector, Professional Evidence and Applied Knowledge services”. February 2013.

Fox News (2015): “WorldCom Timeline”. *Associated Press*. 8 August 2002. Updated 13 January 2015.

Freeland, J. (2017): "Could Trump go the way of Nixon? The Watergate parallels are uncanny". *The Guardian,* 17 May 2017.

Freifelt, K. - Schuetze, A. (2017): "Deutsche fined $630 million for failures over Russian money-laundering." *Reuters,* 31 January 2017.

Freudenheim, M. (2004): "HealthSouth Audit Finds as Much as $4.6 Billion in Fraud." *New York Times*, 21 January 2004.

Frosio, G. (2019): "Artificial Intelligence and Intellectual Property: Mapping Legal Challenges for the European Digital Single Market." *University of Strasbourg.*

Fruhlinger, J. (2018): "The Mirai botnet explained: How teen scammers and CCTV cameras almost brought down the internet". *CSO Online.* 9 March 2018.

Gallas, D. (2019): "Brazil's Odebrecht corruption scandal explained". *BBC.* 17 April 2019.

Gandel, S. (2020): "Facebook lawsuit wants Mark Zuckerberg to give up control of social network". *CSB News*.17 January 2020.

Gardiner, H. (2011): "Johnson & Johnson settles Bribery Complaint for $70Million in Fines". *The New York Times,* 8 April 2011.

Garside, J. - Watt, H. - Pegg, D. (2016): "The Panama Papers: how the world's rich and famous hide their money offshore". *The Guardian*. 3 April 2016.

Gastorn, K. (2017): "Defining the Imprecise Contours of Jus Cogens in International Law". *Chinese Journal of International Law*, Volume 16, Issue 4, December 2017.

Geier, B. (2014): "Could GM be charged with murder?" *Fortune.* 5 June 2014.

Gellene, D. (1992): "Sears to Repair Image With $46 Million in Coupons: Retailing: It may be the largest such consumer fraud settlement ever. California auto centers will be on probation for 3 years". *Los Angeles Times*. 3 September 1992.

Gelter, M. (2012): "Why do Shareholder Derivative Suits Remain Rare in Continental Europe?" *Brooklyn Journal of International Law*. 37/2012.

Gendron, R. – Husted, C. (2012): "Economic Cycles Predicting Corporate Misconduct?" *American Association of Behavioral and Social Sciences*, Las Vegas, Nevada. February 16–17.

Gendron, R. – Husted, C. (2011, I): "Socialization of Individuals into Deviant Corporate Culture". *American Association of Behavioral and Social Sciences*, Las Vegas, Nevada. Perspectives 14.

Gendron, R. – Husted, C. (2011, II): "Using Gang and Cult Typologies to Understand Corporate Crimes". 2011 paper. *Academy of Criminal Justice Sciences' Annual General meeting*, Toronto, Canada.

Gendron, R. – Husted, C. (2010): "Organi-cultural Deviance". *Administrative Sciences Association of Canada*, Regina, Saskatchewan.

Gerson M. J. (2020): "DSM-5 Diagnoses and Defense Mechanisms." Blog. *Psychological Studies. Diagnostic and Statistical Manual of Mental Disorders* (DSM-5) was published originally in 1952 by American Psychiatric Association.

Gerstein, M. – Connelly, B. – Lightdale, S. – Rowen, Z. (2015): "Delaware Courts' Recent Decisions on Appraisal may Discourage Opportunistic Appraisal Arbitrageurs". *Latham & Watkins LLP*. 20 February 2015.

Gilioli, E. L. (1981): "Defining Jurisdictional Limits in International Antitrust: Should EEC Adopt the Timberlane Approach?" *Fordham International Law Journal*. Vol. 5, Issue 2, Article 9.

Gilman, E. (2016): "Petrobas" *Fortune*. 20 July 2016.

Goldenberg, S. – Rushe, D. (2012): "BP to pay $4.5bn penalty over Deepwater Horizon disaster". *The Guardian*. 15 November 2012.

Gonçalves, A. (2019): "The Top 100 Companies with the best CSR (Corporate Social Responsibility) Reputation". *YouMatter*.

Gonzalez Ribeiro, A. (2021): "Financial Villains: Where Are They Now?". *Investopedia*. 8 June 2021.

Goodwin, B. (2020): "Maze Ransomware Attack will Cost Cognizant at Least $50m to $70m". *Computer Weekly*. 12 May 2020.

Grabianowski, E. (2020): "How Mafia Works." *HowStuffWorks*.

Grechenig, K. – Sekyra, M. (2011): "No derivative shareholder suits in Europe: A model of percentage limits and collusion". *International Review of Law and Economics* (IRLE) 2011, vol. 31. Revised 12 March 2014.

Green, N. (2007): "Gazprom wrests control of Sakhalin-2 gas project from Shell." *WSWS,* 9 January 2007.

Greenwald, G. – MacAskill, E – Poitras, L. (2013): "Edward Snowden: the whistleblower behind the NSA surveillance revelations". *The Guardian*. 10 June 2013.

Greenwood, C. (2010): "Blockade as Act of War". *Crimes of War*. 21 November 2010.

Grieger, G. (2018): "Briefing China, the 16+1 format and the EU". *European Parliament.* September 2018.

Gumbel, P. (2004): "How It All Went So Sour". *Time*. 21 November 2004.

Hakala, P. (2016): "Kenraali pidätettiin Sotšissa epäiltynä olympiakorruptiosta – asunnosta löytyi miljardi ruplaa käteisenä." *Helsingin Sanomat,* 26 November 2016.

Hall, M. (2019): "What is Insider Trading and Is It Illegal?" Top 3 Most Scandalous Insider Trading Debacles. 31 July 2019.

Hamilton, F. – O'Neill, S. (2018): "Unexplained wealth orders are new weapon in war on illicit assets". *The Times*, 3 February 2018.

Harding, L. (2019): "Deutsche Bank faces action over $20bn Russian money-laundering scheme" *The Guardian*. 17 April 2019.

Harding, L. (2016): "What are the Panama Papers? A guide to history's biggest data leak." *The Guardian*. 5 April 2016.

Harding, L. – Barr, C. – Nagapetyants, D. (2017): "UK at centre of secret $3bn Azerbaijani money laundering and lobbying scheme". *The Guardian* 4 September 2017.

Harper, J. (2020): "Mother and daughters told 'too big' for business class". *BBC*, 7 February 2020.

Harris, D. (2006): "Haggard Admits Buying Meth". *ABC News*. 3 November 2006.

Hawkes, A. (2017): "Top bank bosses 'knew Libor rate was being rigged, says former UBS broker". *This is Money*. 10 December 2017.

Heal, P. - Serafeim, G. (2019): "White-collar Crime". *Harvard Business Review* July-August 2019 Issue.

Hedwall, M. – König, O. (2014): Global Compliance News. Anti-Corruption in Sweden. *Baker & McKenzie*.

Heller, M. (2015): "Xoom CFO Resigns As Firm Discloses $30M Fraud". *CFO*. 7 January 2015.

Hellmann, T. F.- Murdock, K. C. - Stiglitz, J. E. (2000): "Liberalization, Moral Hazard in Banking, and Prudential Regulation: Are Capital Requirements Enough?" *The American Economic Review*. March 2000.

Herold, T. (2020): "What was the Tyco International Scandal?" *Herold Financial Dictionary*.

Hill, M. – Swinhoe, D. (2021): "The 15 biggest data breaches of the 21st century." *CSO*. 16 July 2021.

Hindustan Times (2015): "Satyam scam: All you need to know about India's biggest accounting fraud". 9 April 2015.

Hossain, K. (2005): "The Concept of Jus Cogens and the Obligation Under the U.N. Charter". *Santa Clara Journal of International Law.* Volume 3, Issue 1, Article 3.

Hotten, R. (2015): "Volkswagen: The scandal explained". *BBC*, 10 December 2015.

Hurmelinna, P. (2001): "Immateriaalioikeuden lähtökohtia" (English Translation: *The basics of IP Law*). Telecom Business Research Center Lappeenranta. Working Papers 8. *Lappeenranta University of Technology.*

Husted, C. (2008): "Systematic Differentiation Between Dark and Light Leaders: Is a Corporate Criminal Profile Possible". *Capella University.*

Ignatius, A. – McGinn, D. (2015): "Novo Nordisk CEO Lars Sorensen What Propelled him to the Top." *Harvard Business Review.* November 2015.

Inman, J. (2005): "Atlanta attorney gets 30 years for real estate fraud. Woman masterminded multimillion-dollar scheme." *Inman.* 26 August 2005

Interpol (2020): "Interpol report highlights key cyberthreats in Southeast Asia." 17 February 2020.

Invertalia (2020): "Macroeconomy – Guatemala. Movistar Guatemala will close its offices until Tuesday, after criminal attacks". 8 September 2020.

Isaac, M. (2020): "Star Engineer who Crossed Google is Ordered to pay $179". *The New York Times.* 4 March 2020.

Jaeger, J. (2019): "Microsoft to pay $25M in FCPA case". *ComplianceWeek.* 23 July 2019.

Javers, E. (2021): "Hackers steal $600 million in major crypto theft" CNBC. 11 August 2021.

Jibilian, I. – Canales, K. (2021): "The US is readying sanctions against Russia over the SolarWinds cyber attack. Here's a simple explanation of how the massive hack happened and why it's such a big deal". *Business Insider.* 15 April 2021.

Jones, H. (2021): "UK watchdog alleges three traders manipulated futures market". *Reuters.* 10 September 2021.

Jowit, J. (2011): "Howlers and omissions exposed in world of corporate social responsibility". *The Guardian.* 24 November 2011.

JP Morgan (2012): "Year in Review".

Jäppinen, S. (2019): "Suomi kulkee nyt kohti yritysvastuulakia – mitä tapahtuu muualla Euroopassa" (English: Finland is on its way to CSR law – what happens in the other parts of the world). *Fingo.* 10 June 2019.

Kagan, J. (2020): National Association of Securities Dealers (NASD). Investopedia. 10 May 2020.

Kanninen, J. (2015): "Kuubalaisia sikareita Yhdysvaltoihin ja puhelimien osia Kuubaan – tätä ja muuta merkitsee vihamiesten lähentyminen". *YLE.* 21 January 2015.

Kapersky (2021): "Secure IoT Devices on your home network." 2021.

Kaplan, S. N. (2012): "Executive Compensation and Corporate Governance in the US: Perceptions, Facts and Challenges". Chicago Booth Paper No. 12-42, *Fama-Miller Center for Research in Finance*, Chicago. July 2012.

Keller, M. (2019): "The UAW didn't learn from General Motors Bankruptcy". *Forbes*. 19 September 2019.

Kenton, W. (2020): "What is Greenwashing". *Investopedia*. 30 January 2020.

Kervinen, E. (2015): "Pankeille isot maksut heikosta rahanpesun valvonnasta Ruotsissa". *Helsingin Sanomat*. 20 May 2015.

Kippenberg, J. (2019): "Netherlands Takes Big Step Toward Tackling Child Labor". *HRW*. 4 June 2019.

Kleinman, Z. (2020): "Therapy patients blackmailed for cash after clinic data breach". *BBC*. 26 October 2020.

Kokalitcheva, K. (2021): "Silicon Valley's biggest fraud, Elizabeth Holmes, is on trial" *Yahoo News*. 28 August 2021.

Kolcak, H. (2014): "The Sovereignty of the European Court of Justice and the EU's Supranational Legal System". *Inquiriesjournal.com*. Vol 6, No 4.

Korosec, K. (2020): "Self-driving car engineer Anthony Levadowski files motion to force Uber into arbitration". *TechCrunch*. 1 April 2020.

Korosec, K. (2019): "Anthony Levandowski, former Google engineer at center of Waymo-Uber case, charged with stealing trade secrets." *Techcrunch*. 27 August 2019.

Kostov, N. – McLain, S. (2020): "Carlos Ghosn's New Life in Exile". *The Wall Street Journal*. 22 February 2020.

Kozyreva, T. – Leopold, J. (2017): "Here's How Ukraine's Ousted Government Got Away With $40 Billion". *BuzzFeed. News*. 12 July 2018.

Kramer, D. J. (2018): "Red-Collar Crime: The Darkness Behind White-Collar Crime". *Novilaw*.1 February 2018.

Krauss, C. - Schwartz, J. (2012) "BP Will Plead Guilty and Pay Over $4 Billion". *The New York Times*. 15 November 2012.

Kuckreja, A. (2005): "The Disney Decision of 2005 and the precedent it sets for corporate governance and fiduciary responsibility" 23 August 2005. Corporate Governance Alert. *Akin Gump Strauss Hauer & Feld LLP.*

Kurkela, M. – Mettälä, K. (2018): "Case Bernard Tapie, year 2015 Bernard Tapie -tapaus ja fraus omnia corrumpit välitystuomion kumoamisperusteena" (English translation: Bernard Tapie case and fraus omnia corrumpit as grounds for annulment of arbitration). *Defensor Legis*, 6 June 2018.

Lai, K. (2020): "BIP Asia: AI-related IP policies need more work globally". *Managing IP*. 13 January 2020.

Lam, B. (2016): Why is Utah the First State to Have a White-Collar Crime Registry? *The Atlantic*. 29 March 2016.

Lambert, L. (2017): "Citigroup fined $28.8 million for harm to home borrowers". *Reuters*. 23 January 2017.

Lambsdorff, G. (2006): "Transparency International – The Global Anti-Corruption Coalition". *Transparency International. www.transparency.org.* "Corruption Perceptions Index 2006". *Transparency International.*

Landon, T (2016): "Deutsche Bank Singled Out in I.M.F. Stability Warning". *New York Times*, 5 October 2016.

Landon, T. - Andelman, L. – Breeden, A. (2016): "I.M.F. Stands by Christine Lagarde, Convicted of Negligence" *The New York Times*. 19 December 2016.

Lawson, K. (2011): "Scareware: How a Fake Internet 'Security' Company Conned Millions Around the World". 24 October 2011.

Le Corre, P. (2018): "Chinese Investments in European Countries: Experiences and Lessons for the "Belt and Road" Initiative" Chapter 10 in Rethinking the Silky Road, Mayer (ed).

Lee, J. - Shailer, G. (2008): "The Effect of Board-Related Reforms on Investors Confidence." *Australian Accounting Review*, 18(45) 2008.

Levin, A., (2017): "6 Things About the "Darknet" All Businesses Should Know". *Inc. com*. 3 April 2017.

Lichtblau, E. - Dougherty, C. (2008): "The bribery scandal of Siemens hitted Siemens paying more than 1.6 billion dollars in fines in 2008. Siemens to pay $1.34 billion in Fines". *The New York Times*. 15 December 2008.

Liimatainen, K. (2017): "Pankkijätti Barclaysin finanssikriisin aikaiset johtajat saivat syytteet petoksesta – epäillään miljardisopimusten suhmuroinnista Qatarin kanssa." (English Translation: Barclays financial crisis-time executives facing charges of fraud — suspected of grieving billions of deals with Qatar) *Helsingin Sanomat* 21 June 2017.

Lin T. C. W. (2012): "The Corporate Governance of Iconic Executives" *Notre Dame Law Review* 351 (2011). 16 April 2012.

Loftus, P. (2020): "Missouri Court Cuts Talc-Powder Verdict Against J&J to $2.1 Billion". *Wall Street Journal*. 23 June 2020.

Loiacono, S. (2019): "How to identify a microcap scam." *Investopedia*. 25 June 2019.

Loomis, D. C. (2016): "In the courts: Court confirms legal status of Happy Birthday to You!" *WIPO Magazine.* February 2016.

Lupica, M. (2020): "What is Process Crime". *Wisegeek.* 2 September 2020.

Lynch, I. J. (2021): "Off the Hook: Acquittals of Swedish Telecom Officials Linked to Uzbek Bribery Scandal Upheld". *The Diplomat.* 10 February 2021.

Lyngaas, S. (2020): "Czech Republic's second-biggest hospital is hit by cyberattack". *Cyberscoop.* 13 March 2020.

MacAskill, E. (2011): "Barack Obama acts to ease US embargo on Cuba". *The Guardian.* 15 January 2011.

Mach, P. (2020): "How Can AI and Machine Learning Take Fraud Detection To The Next Level?" *Ideamotive.* 27 July 2020.

Mae Koo, A. (2021): "China's New Civil Code: Punitive Damages from IP Infringements Claims". *INTA.* 14 April 2021.

Magee, T. (2019): "Huawei controversies timeline: everything you need to know". *Computerworld.* 10 September 2019.

Mandis, S. G. (2013): "What Happened to Goldman Sachs: An Insider's Story of Organizational Drift and Its Unintended Consequences". Harvard Business Review. 1 October 2013.

Manoukian, J. (2016): "What's the Difference Between Internal Audit & Internal Control?" *Enablon. WoltersKluwer.* 5 May 2016.

Manson, M. (2019): "The 3 Paradoxes of Life". Mark Manson web pages. 8 December 2019.

Mathews, L. (2021 I): "Nearly 600 Arrested In Massive Cybercrime Bust". *Forbes.* 31 May 2021.

Mathews, L. (2021 II): "A Mysterious Cyberattack Is Completely Erasing Western Digital MyBook Live Drives". *Forbes.* 27 June 2021.

Mattera, P. (2017): "Deutsche Bank: Corporate Rap Sheet". 1 June 2017.

Maverick, J.B. (2020): "The 3 Reasons Why Chinese Invest in Africa". *Investopedia.* 9 April 2020.

Max, D.T. (2018): "The Chinese Workers Who Assemble Designer Bags in Tuscany". *The New Yorker.* 9 April 2018.

McCarthy, M. (2008): "Italy's toxic waste crisis, the Mafia – and the scandal of Europe's mozzarella". *Independent.* 22 March 2008.

McCausland, R. - Vivian, A. (2010): "Why Do Some Aboriginal Communities Have Lower Crime Rates Than Others?" A Pilot Study. Australian and New Zealand Journal of Criminology, The, Vol. 43, No. 2. August 2010.

McCormick, J. (1999): "The Sorry Side of Sears". *Newsweek*. 2 February 1999.

McCoy, K. – Johnson, K. (2014): "Bank of America pays record $16.65B penalty". *USA Today*. 21 August 2014.

McDonald, S. (2008): "Nearly 53,000 Chinese children sick from milk". *Associated Press*. 22 September 2008.

McEvoy, S. (2017): "Re-defining criminal dishonesty: why does it matter?" *Allen & Overy*. Global News. 6 November 2017.

McGhee, A. (2018): "The Cabinet Files". *Media company ABC*. 10 February 2018.

McGrath, M. (2015): "Millennials: The Money – Conscious Generation?" *Forbes*. 22 June 2015.

McGregor, J. (2014): Nokia was Blackmailed Out of Millions By Hackers Six Years Ago". *Forbes*. 17 June 2014.

McNair Chambers (2020 I): "UK Bribery Act 2010, Ten Years on". 23 January 2020.

McNair Chambers (2020 II): "English court approves deferred prosecution agreement between serious fraud office and airbus, Director of the Serious Fraud Office and Airbus". 6 February 2020.

Meikle, J. – McDonald, H. (2013 I): "Findus beef lasagna contained up to 100% horsemeat, FSA says". *BBC News*. 16 January 2013.

Meikle, J. – McDonald, H. (2013): "Cameron tells supermarkets: horsemeat burger scandal unacceptable." *The Guardian*. 16 January 2013.

Merton, R. (1938): "Social structure and anomie". *American Sociological Review*.

Meyersohn, N. (2019): "Walmart settles with US government over international bribery investigation". *CNN Business* 20. June 2019.

Michaels, M. (2018): "The most memorable and expensive financial fraud cases of all time." *Business Insider*. 24 April 2018.

Mikolajczyk, S. J. (1995): "Sears Slapped with Tire Service Fraud Suit". *Tire Business*. 21 August 1995.

Milne, R. (2018): "Swedish Oil Bosses Set to be Charged over South Sudan Deaths". *Financial Times*. 18 October 2018.

MIP (2020): The 50 Most Influential People in IP. Managing IP.

Miyoung, K. (2012): "Samsung shares drop $12 billion after Apple's court victory". *Reuters*. 27 August 2012.

Mojeed, M. (2015): "INVESTIGATION: Files Open New Window on $182-Million Halliburton Bribery Scandal in Nigeria". *Premium Times*. 10 February 2015.

Monaghan, A. (2017): "Massive cyber-attack could cost Nurofen and Durex maker £100m." *The Guardian*. 6 July 2017.

Monash University (2003): "Final report: The Failure of HIH: a critical assessment." Royal Commission. 2003.

Moné, L. (2019): "Which Governments Are Using Blockchain Right Now?" *Consensys*. 18 November 2019.

Murphy, E. (2008): "Manufacturing Crime: Process, Pretext, and Criminal Justice". *Georgetown Law Journal*, 97. 7 October 2008.

Muskal, M. – White, R. D. (2012): "BP fined, charged in oil spill that showed 'profit over prudence'". *Los Angeles Times*. 15 November 2012.

Muscat, C. (2019): "Malta exposed: A hub for the 'laundering' of prized Bluefin tuna worth millions". *The Shift News*. 12 February 2019.

Myint, U. (2000): "Corruption: Causes, Consequences and Cures". *Asia-Pacific Development Journal*. Vol. 7, No. 2. December 2000

Narula, R. – Pandey, S. (2019): "India: Challenges faced in the protection and enforcement of patent rights". *Managing IP*. 18 September 2019.

Nasralla, S. – Croft, A. (2016): "Austria's FACC, hit by cyber fraud, fires CEO". *Reuters*. 25 May 2016.

Neate, R. (2016): "HSBC escaped US money-laundering charges after Osborne's intervention". *The Guardian*. 11 July 2016.

Neate, R. – Kollewe, J. (2019): "Credit Suisse chief operating officer fired over spying scandal". *The Guardian*. 1 October 2019.

Nichols, M. - Charbonneau, L. (2012): "U.N. chief says sanctions on Iran affecting its people". *Reuters*. 5 October 2012.

Oinonen, M (2011): "Pienten markkinoiden yritysten syrjintä EU:n yrityskauppavalvonnassa tutkimuskohteena: kokemuksia, haasteita ja kehityssuuntia" (English Translation: Discrimination against small market enterprises in the EU's M&A surveillance area: experience, challenges and developments). *Lakimies* 1/2011.

Palazzo, G. (2019): "Ethical Blindness Explains Why Good People Do Bad Things". Joanna Sinclair. Aalto University Executive Education.

Pandey, A. (2015): "A timeline of IAAF doping scandal". *Deutsche Welle*. 9 November 2015.

Paulsen, D. J. (2002): “Wrong Side of the Tracks: Exploring the Role of Newspaper Coverage of Homicide in Socially Constructing Dangerous Places”. *Journal of Criminal Justice and Popular Culture*, 9(3).

Papachristou, L. (2019): “Swedish Telecom Boss Acquitted in Uzbekistan Bribery Probe. *OCCRP* 2019. 19 February 2019.

Perlroth, N. (2014): “Russian Hackers Targeting Oil and Gas Companies”. *New York Times*. 30 June 2014.

Petsche, M. (2010): “Jus Cogens as a Vision of the International Legal Order.” *Penn State International Law Review*. Volume 29, Article 2, Number 2. 9 January 2010.

Pierpoint, G. (2019): “Is white-collar crime treated more leniently in the US?” *BBC*. 11 March 2019.

Pietruszewska, A. (2020): “Mutual Agreement”. *CEOpedia*.

Piskora, B. (2002): “Citi Agrees to $240M in fines for fleecing customers”. *New York Post*. 20 September 2002.

Porter, M. - Kramer, M. R. (2006): ”Strategy and Society: The Link Between Competitive Advantage and Corporate Social Responsibility”. *Harvard Business Review*. December 2006.

Poster, M. S. – Samios, E. (2019): “Weinstein Clauses. Best Practices for Negotiating, Drafting and Responding”. *Law.com*. 1 October 2019.

Press Trust of India (2013): ”Address Legal-Cultural disconnects in international laws: VP”. 14 November 2013.

PWC (2020): “The fight against tax avoidance and other financial crimes vs the right of data protection. A regulatory tug-of-war for financial services?” *PWC*. April 2020.

PWC (2017): Leveraging the upcoming disruptions from AI and IoT. How Artificial Intelligence will enable the full promise of the Internet-of-Things.

Quigley, J. (2019): “Suicide, Corruption Probe Rattle Peru’s Political Class”. *Bloomberg*. 9 May 2019.

Qureshi, K. (2019): “Economic crime task force will be no more than a talking shop”. Law Comment, *The Times*. 24 January 2019.

Radiocor (2019): “Parmalat: sindacati, ad Bernier ha confermato centralita’ attivita’ in Italia”. 8 February 2019.

Rangan, K. – Chase, L. – Karim, S. (2015): “Truth about CSR”. *Harvard Business Review* 93, nos. 1/2. January–February 2015.

Raymond, N. – Stempel, J. (2013): Apple colluded on e-book prices, judge finds. *Reuters*. 10 July 2013.

Reed, G. E. – Yeager, P. C. (1996): "Organizational offending and neoclassical criminology: Challenging the reach of a general theory of crime". *Criminology*, 34.

Reuters (2020): "US prosecutors seek 27 months imprisonment for former Uber self-driving head." 29 July 2020.

Reuters (2019): "Italian police uncover Naples sweatshop linked to luxury groups". Reuters. 18 November 2019.

Reuters (2019): Google shifted $23 billion to tax heaven Bermuda in 2017: filing. 3 January 2019.

Reuters (2018):"Bayer CEO says Monsanto's reputation is a 'major challenge'". April 28, 2018.

Reuters (2008): "EU fines Microsoft record 899 million euros". *Reuters*. 27 February 2008.

Revill, J. (2017): "Switzerland's ABB hit by $100 million South Korean fraud". *Reuters*. 22 February 2017.

Richman, D. C. – Stuntz, W. J. (2005): "Al Capone's Revenge: An Essay on the Political Economy of Pretextual Prosecution". *Columbia Law Review*. 105 (2).

Rijkers, B. – Freund, C. – Nucifora, A. (2014 I): "Tunisia's golden age of crony capitalism". *The Washington Post*. 27 March 2014.

Rijkers, B. – Freund, C. – Nucifora, A. (2014 II): "All in the family, State Capture in Tunisia". *The World bank*. Middle East and Northern Africa Region. March 2014.

Roach, J. (2006): "Alaska Oil Spill Fuels Concerns Over Arctic Wildlife, Future Drilling". *National Geographic*. 20 March 2006.

Roberts, P. (2020): "What's the Difference between white collar versus blue collar crime?" Roberts Law Group PLLC.

Roberts, P. (2016): "Botnet of 140,000 Cameras, DVRs Behind Biggest DoS Ever". The Security Ledger. 27 September 2016.

Robertson, C. – Diyab, A. – Al-Kahtani, A. (2013): "A cross-national analysis of perceptions of corporate governance principles". *International Business Review*. 22 (1).

Robertson, C. – Krauss, C. (2010): "Gulf Spill Is the Largest of Its Kind, Scientists Say". *The New York Times*. 2 August 2010.

Robinson, P. (2019): "Former Boeing Engineers Say Relentless Cost-Cutting Sacrificed Safety". *Bloomberg Businessweek*. 9 May 2019.

Rojas, C. (2017): "Eclipse of the Public Corporation Revisited: Concentrated Equity Ownership Theory". *The University of Oxford*. 22 June 2017.

Rosencrance, L. (2020): "Dodd-Frank Act". *TechTarget.* June 2019.

Rosendahl, N. (2021): "The 7 Sins of "Wellbeing Washing" – When Talk and Actions Don't Match". *Hintsa Newsletter.* 9 June 2021.

Ross, M. (2019): "HSBC's Money Laundering" *Investopedia.* 25 June 2019.

Rosten, M. - Bowler, A. (2018): "Five Things to Know about Red Collar Crime". *CCBA.*

Russell, A. (2019): "Extortion cases increased 170% from 2012 to 2018 in Canada: StatCan". *Global News.* 23 July 2019.

Russia Monitor (2010): "IKEA Scandal – Furniture Giant's Corruption Troubles Far from Over". 4 April 2010.

Safjanski, Tomasz (2017): "The Impact of the European Union Agency for Law Enforcement Cooperation (Europol) on Combating Cross-Border Crime – Legal and Practical Aspects". Law and Forensic Science. *Modern, International Academic Journal.* 30 December 2017.

Saint-Amans, P. (2016): "Global tax and transparency: We have the tools, now we must make them work". OECD

Samia, A. (2018): "Starbucks Success Story". *Start up Stories.* 12 August 2018.

Sanger, D. – Krauss, C. – Perlroth, N. (2021): "Cyberattack Forces a Shutdown of a Top U.S. Pipeline". *The New York Times.* 8 May 2021.

Saudelli, G. (2018): "Deutsche Bank's 5 biggest scandals". *Deutsche Welle.* 29 November 2018.

Schmidt, C. (2016): "Toshiba Accounting Scandal." *YouTube video.*

Schreer, S. (2019): "Workers at Israeli surveillance firm NSO sue Facebook for blocking private accounts". Reuters. 26 November 2019.

Schuetze, C. F. (2019): "Former VW C.E.O. Martin Winterkorn Is Charged by Germany in Diesel Scheme." *The New York Times.* 15 April 2019.

Schulte-Bockholt, A. (2001): "A Neo-Marxist Explanation of Organized Crime". *Critical Criminology*, 10.

Schwartz, M. (2018): "French Cinema Chain Fires Dutch Executives Over 'CEO Fraud'". *Bank of Security.* Blog. 13 November 2018.

Schwartz, M. - Sandick, H. (2018): "Takeaways from 2nd Circ. Reversal of Litvak Conviction". *Patterson Belknap Webb & Tyler LLP.* 7 May 2018.

Schultheis, E. (2019): "*Der Spiegel* Made Up Stories. How Can It Regain Readers' Trust? Germany's top news magazine reckons with a star reporter's brazen lies in the age of fake news." The Atlantic. 10 January 2019.

Science (2010): "Juutalaisten pankki-imperiumit, finanssikriisit ja keinottelu". 6 October 2010.

Sebag, G. (2021): "JPMorgan Settles French Tax-Fraud Case for $30 Million". *Bloomberg.* 2 September 2021.

SEC (2010): "Goldman Sachs to Pay Record $550 Million to Settle SEC Charges Related to Subprime Mortgage CDO."

SEC I (2009): "SEC Charges Attorney in Insider Trading Scheme". 10 December 2009.

SEC II (2009): "SEC Charges Wall Street Lawyers and Traders in $20 million Insider Trading Scheme". 5 November 2009.

Segall, L. – Pagliery, J. – Wattles, J. (2016): "FBI says it has cracked terrorist's iPhone without Apple's hel" . *CNN Money*. 28 March 2016.

Seidenberg, S. (2016): "US Perspectives: US High Court Restores Treble Damages For Patent Infringement". *Intellectual Property Watch.*26 July 2016

Sen, M. (2020): "Bernie Ebbers, ex-CEO convicted in WorldCom scandal, dies." *CNBC.* 3 February 2020.

Serrano, A (2006): "Evangelist: I Bought Meth From Gay Escort". CBS News. 2 November 2006.

Seth, S. (2020): "Racketeering". Investopedia. 10 April 2020.

Shah, A (2009): IBM, Intel Executives Face Insider Trading Charges. *PC World*. 16 October 2009.

Sherwood, H. (2021): "Cardinal denies financial crimes in biggest ever Vatican trial". *The Guardian*. 27 July 2021.

Shiff, B. (2019): "13 CEOs who didn't make it to 2020.". Business Leaders. *Fox Business.*31 December 2019.

Shrikanth, S. – Palma, S. (2020): "Malaysia to return 3,000 tonnes of contaminated plastic waste." *Financial Times*. 28 May 2020.

Sia, D. (2019): "Fake CEO Fraud: Don't fall for the con." *Techware Australia*. 5 March 2019.

Sial, S. – Shrivastava, D. K. – Mishra, P. N. (2018): "Advantages of Corporate Governance for Indian Enterprises" *2018.*

Siewert, R. (2020): "New Threat Intelligence Report, 100 Days of Coronavirus". *Mimecast*. 5 May 2020.

Sifuna, A. P. (2012): "Disclose or Abstain: The Prohibition of Insider Trading on Trial". *Journal of International Banking Law and Regulation*. 27 (9).

Simona, A. (2016): "The legacies of Sochi 2014 Winter Olympics: an evaluation of the Adler Olympic Park." August 2016.

Slashdot (2014): "Ex-Microsoft Employee Arrested For Leaking Windows 8"._20 March 2014.

Smith, G. (2017): The Volcker Rule: What Is It, and Why Does It Need Changing? Fortune 6 April 2017.

Smith, M. (2013). "Should the USA follow the UK's lead and split the dual CEO/ chairperson's role?". *www.academia.edu*. 15 April 2013. Student paper.

Sokala, H. (2015): "Tämä on kaikkien aikojen ryöstö" (English Translation: This Is all Time Robbery). *YLE News*. 13 January 2015.

Stauffer, B. (2019): "Ghosts in the Clouds: Inside China's Major Corporate Hack". *Wall Street Journal*. 30 December 2019.

Stead, W. E. – Worrell, D. L. - Stead, J. G. (1990): "An integrative model for understanding and managing ethical behavior in business organizations". *Journal of Business Ethics*, 9(3).

Stenzel, R. (2017): "Brazil Supreme Court judge handling graft probe killed in plane crash". *Reuters. 20 January 2017.*

Strebel, P. Blanding, M. (2013): "Why Dominating Leaders Kill Teams". Harvard Business review 18 November 2013.

Sun, M. (2019): "More U.S. Companies Separating Chief Executive and Chairman Roles" *The Wall Street Journal.* 23 January 2019.

Sylt, C. (2017): "Liberty Media Boarsts of Formula One's "Brilliant" Tax Scheme". *Forbes*. 30 March 2017.

Taylor, A. (2017): "5 signs Your Organization might be headed for an ethics scandal". *Harvard Business Review*. 18 December 2017.

Teather, D. (2005): "Nike lists abuses at Asian factories". *The Guardian*. 14 April 2005.

Teather, D. (2004): "Halliburton suspends bill for army meals". *The Guardian*. 18 February 2004.

Tessian (2021): "20 Biggest GDPR Fines of 2019, 2020, and 2021 (So Far)". Blog. 6 September 2021.

The Daily Telegraph (2013): "Horse meat scandal: timeline." 8 February 2013.

The Daily Telegraph (2010): "Pennies earned for life after jail for HIH conman Brad Cooper." *Daily Telegraph*. 30 October 2010.

The Economist (2013): "The Origins of the financial crisis. Crash Course." 7 September 2013.

The Guardian (2020): "Apple fined record €1.1bn by French competition regulator". 16 March 2020.

The Guardian (2017): "Formula One pulled a fast one on the UStaxman – and it's all perfectly legal." 21 January 2017.

The Guardian (2013): "How the horsemeat scandal unfolded – timeline". *The Guardian*. London. Press Association. 15 February 2013.

The Guardian (2003): *"Parmalat files for bankruptcy". The Guardian. 24 December 2003.*

The Intercept (2019). "Judge Sergio Moro Directed Car Wash Prosecutors on Lula Case". 17 June 2019.

TheLocal.Se (2017): "Swedish telecom firm Telia to settle bribery case involving billions in payments to Uzbek official". 22 September 2017.

The New York Times (2015): "Brazil Arrests Head of Odebrecht in Petrobras Scandal". 20 June 2015.

The New York Times (2010): "50-year Term for Minnesota Man in $3.7 Billion Ponzi Fraud." 8 April 2010.

The Standard (2008): "More kidney stone cases found". *The Standard*. Hong Kong. 17 October 2008.

The Telegraph (2016): "Russia's anti-corruption boss arrested with $120 million in cash." 13 September 2016.

The United Stated Department of Justice (2017): Deutsche Bank Agrees to Pay $7.2 Billion for Misleading Investors in its Sale of Residential Mortgage-Backed Securities. 17 January 2017.

The United States Department of Justice (2012): "GlaxoSmithKline Plead Guilty and Pay 3 billion resolve Fraud Allegations and Failure Report". 2 July 2012.

The United States Department of Justice (2009): "Justice Department Announces Largest Health Care Fraud Settlement in Its History." 2 September 2009.

The Week (2018): "Cambridge Analytica scandal: Mark Zuckerberg refuses to appear before MPs." 27 March 2018.

Thielman, S. (2016): "Apple v FBI: what's the beef, how did we get here and what's at stake." *The Guardian*. 20 February 2016.

Thomas, W. C. (2002): "The Rise and Fall of Enron". *The Journal of Accountancy*. 1 April 2002.

Thomson Reuters (2019 I): "Everything You Need to Know About Fraud Crimes and Fraud Law."

Thomson Reuters (2019 II): "Today in 2002: California jury awards $28 billion in damages against Phillip Morris". 4 October 2019.

Thorburn, M. (2008): "Justifications, Powers, and Authority". *Yale Law Journal*. 117 (6). April 2008.

Times of San Diego (2021): "Founder, CEO Must Pay $37.5 Million in Fines, Face Prison Terms, in Charter School Fraud Case". 10 September 2021.

TMC Asser Instituut (2019): "Towards Criminal liability of corporation for HR violations. The Lundin case in Sweden". 23 May 2019.

Tozzi, L. M. (2011): "The US and Japan Differ in Court Analyses of Gray Market Goods, But Yields Same Results." *The Journal of Business & Intellectual Property Law*. 21 February 2011.

Tran, M. (2002): "WorldCom accounting scandal". *The Guardian*. 9 August 2002.

Tribbett, C. A. (2012): "Splitting the CEO and Chairman Roles – Yes or No?" *Russell Reynolds Associates*.

Turk, G. – Wong, S. (2013): "Rat-meat ring busted in China for selling rodents, fox and mink as mutton". *Bloomberg*. 3 May 2013.

UK Finance (2021): "Fraud – The Facts 2021. The Definitive Overview of Payment Industry Fraud." *UK Finance*.

UNCTAD (2019): Trade war leaves both US and China worse off. 6 November 2019.

United Nations Office on Drugs and Crime (2016):"Material on Grand corruption". 19 August 2016.

Valladares Rodríguez, M. (2014): "Where Is the Outrage Over Foreign Exchange Manipulation?" *The New York Times*. 20 November 2014.

Valleala, A. ja Letto-Vanamo, P. (2015): "Suomen lainsäädäntö, kansainvälinen liiketoiminta ja ihmisoikeudet" (English Translation: Finnish law, international business and human rights). Työ- ja elinkeinoministeriön julkaisuja. 14/2015.

Varonis (2020): 110 Must-Know Cybersecurity Statistics for 2020. Data Security.

Varottil, U. (2012): "The rarity of derivative actions in India: Reasons and consequences." *National University of Singapore*.

Vaughan, L. (2017): "Broken Benchmarks, Fighting Financial Fiddling". *Bloomberg*. 8 August 2017.

Waelbroeck, D. – Slater, D. – Even-Shoshan, G. (2004): "Study on the conditions of claims for damages in case of infringement of EC competition rules". *Ashurst.* 31 August 2004.

Wagner, S. – Dittmar, L. (2006): "The Unexpected Benefits of Sarbanes-Oxley". *Harvard Business Review*. April 2006.

Wallace, B. (2018): "Russian Oligarchs in UK Told to Explain Luxury Lifestyle". *BBC News*. 3 February 2018.

Wallius, A. (2015): "Rolex-skandaali johti ministerieroon Italiassa" (English translation: Rolex scandal led to ministerial resignation in Italy). *YLE News*. 19 March 2015.

Walsh, A. (2020): "German military laptop with classified data sold on eBay". *Deutsche Welle*. 16 March 2020.

Walsh, F. (2007): "BA fined £270m for price fixing". *The Guardian*. 1 August 2007.

Weaver, M. (2010): "Naomi Campbell's 'blood diamond' testimony at war crimes trial: live updates". *The Guardian*. 5 August 2010.

Weiner, B. (2008): "Reflections on the History of Attribution Theory and Research: People, Personalities, Publications, Problems". *Social Psychology* 39(3):151-156. September 2008.

Weiss, G. (1997): "Investors Beware: Chop Stocks Are on the Rise". Business Week, 15 December 1997.

Welch, C. (2012): "Sony hacker gets year in prison for involvement in 2011 data breach". *The Verge*. 18 April 2012.

Welford, R. (2008): "The Chinese milk crisis: Lessons for CSR". CSR Asia. 3 November 2008.

Whelan, T. - Kronthal-Sacco, R. (2019): "Research: Actually Consumers Do Buy Sustainable Products". *Harvard Business Review*. 19 June 2019.

White, L. (2017): "HSBC draws line under Mexican cartel case after five-years on probation". *Reuters*. 11 December 2017.

Wickman, F. (2012): "Working Man's Blues: why do we call manual laborers blue collar". *Slate*. 1 May 2012.

Williams, C. J. (1994): "Market Focus: Tainted Paprika Poisons Hungary's Culinary Pride: Fifty-nine people are arrested in the scandal, which sent 46 to the hospital. The health of the industry is also at stake." *Los Angeles Times.* 11 October 1994.

Williams, Y. (2020): "Blue-Collar Crime: Definition, Statistics & Examples" Video & Lesson Transcript. *Study.com.*

Wilson, A. (2008): "Former British Airways executive to be jailed over cargo price-fixing". *The Telegraph*. 1 October 2008.

Wong Joon, I. (2016): "First Google, now Facebook: tech giants are caving in and paying millions more in UK tax". *Quartz*. 4 March 2016.

Wyatt, E. (2011): "Citigroup to Pay Millions to Close Fraud Complaint." *The New York Times*. 19 October 2011.

Xinhua News Agency (2008): China seizes 22 companies with contaminated baby milk powder". 16 September 2008.

YLE News (2020): "Four suspects in 14m euro Cargotec fraud". 18 February 2020.

Yun Chee, F. (2019): "EU demands scrutiny of 5G risks but no blockwide Huawei ban." *Reuters*. 26 March 2019.

Zacharek, S. – Dockterman, E. – Sweetland Edwards, H. (2017): "The Silence Breakers. The voices that Launched a Movement." *Time Magazine*. 10 December 2017.

22.3. Court Cases

Airtrust (Hong Kong) Ltd v. PH Hydraulics & Engineering Pte Ltd (2015). Singapore High Court 307.

Arthur Andersen LLP v. United States (2005). 544 US 696, 125 S. Ct. 2129.

Aronson v. Lewis (1984). 473 A.2d 805, 812.

Bernard Crehan v. Courage Ltd and Others (2001). Court of Appeal (England and Wales) (Civil Division) - United Kingdom. Case C-453/99, ECLI:EU:C:2001:465 (right to full compensation). European Court Reports 2001 I-06297.

Bhasin *v.* Hrynew, (2014). SCC 71, 3 S.C.R. 494. Supreme Court of Canada, 13 November 2014. SCC Case 35380.

Bristol & West Building Society v. Mothew (1998). Ch. 1, EWCA Civ 533.

Confédération européenne des associations d'horlogers-réparateurs (CEAHR), v. European Commission, acting as Agents, defendant, supported by LVMH Moët Hennessy-Louis Vuitton SA, Rolex, SA, The Swatch Group SA, (2017). Judgement of General Court (Second Chamber), Case T-712/14, 23 October 2017

Cede & Co. v. Technicolor, Inc. (1993). 634 A.2d 345, 361. Delaware.

Courage Ltd v. Bernard Crehan (2001). 20 September 2001. C-453/99.

Crocs Inc v. Holey Soles Holdings Ltd (2010). Case R 9/2008-3. 26 March 2010.

CSU L.L.C v. Zerox Corporation (2000). 203 F.3d 1322, WL190351 (Fed. Cir. 17 February 2000.

Democratic Republic of the Congo v. Belgium (2000). ICJ 1 Press Release 2000/32. 17 October 2000.

Dodge v. Ford Motor Co. (1919). 204 Mich. 459, 170 N.W. 668.

DuPont – Dow merger (2017). Case M.7932. 27 March 2017.

Eisenberg v. Flying Tiger Line, Inc (1971). 451 F.2d 267.

European Court of Justice (2020). Judgment of the Court (Grand Chamber), 16 July 2020. ECLI:EU:C:2020:559. Case C311/18.

Foss v. Harbottle (1843). 2 Hare 461, 67 ER 189.

Gencor Ltd v. Commission (1999). ECR II-753. T-102/96.

Grobow v. Perot (1988). 539 A. 2d. 180 Delaware.

Guth v. Loft (1939). 5 A.2d 503.

Halo Electronics, Inc. v. Pulse Electronics, Inc. et al. (2016). No. 14–1513. Argued 23 February 2016. Decided 13 June 2016.

Harris v. Balk (1905). 198 U.S. 21. U.S. Supreme Court

HealthSouth Corp. (2003). Shareholders Litigation., 845 A.2d 1096, Delaware Ch. 2003.

Intel Corp. v. VIA Technologies, Inc. (2002). EWCA Civ 1905, 20 December 2002.

International Court of Justice (2019). Certain Iranian Assets (Islamic Republic of Iran v. United States of America). Press Release. 51/2019. 26 November 2019.

Irish Sugar plc v. Commission of the European Communities (2001). Case C-497/99 P, ECR p. I-05333

Islamic Republic of Iran v. United States of America (2003). Oil Platforms - Judgment of 6 November 2003 - Judgments ICJ 4; ICJ Reports 2003, (2003) ICJ Rep 161. 6 November 2003.

Kaplan v. Centex Corp. (1971). Del. Ch., 284 A.2d 119, 124.

K Mart Corp. v. Cartier, Inc. (1988). 486 US 281. US Supreme Court.

MCI Inc (2003). SC 13D/A – LCC International Inc. US Securities and Exchange Commission. 14 March 2003.

N. MC. Co. v. Schulyro Trading Co. (1970). 27 February 1970, Osaka Dist. Ct., 234, Hanrei Taimuzu. Parker Pen cases.

North Carolina State Board of Dental Examiners v. Federal Trade Commission (2015). 574 U.S. 494. US Supreme Court.

NOSA Corporation v. AXO Sport spa (2017). Corte de Cassazione, Italy, Italian Supreme Court judgment no. 16601/2017. 5 July 2017.

Oracle America Inc v. Google Inc. (2016). No. C 10-03561 WHA. United States District Court. Document 1988. 16 June 2016.

Puma v. Marriott (1971). Del. Ch., 283 A.2d 693, 695.

Regina v. Ghosh (Deb Baran) (1982). EWCA Crim 2. QB 1053; 1982, 3 WLR 110.

Regina v. Skansen Interiors Ltd. (2018). Southwark Crown Court, Case Number: T20170224, 21 February 2018.

Roberts (FC) v. Gill & Co Solicitors and others (2010). UK Supreme Court 22. On appeal from: 2008, EWCA Civ 803.

Robinson v. Pittsburgh Oil Refinery Corp. (1926). Del. Ch., 14 Del. Ch. 193, 126 A. 46.

Salomon v. A Salomon & Co Ltd (1897). AC 22.

Securities and Exchange Commission v. Raj Rajaratnam (2019). 918 F.3d 36. 2d Cir. 2019.

SFO v. Rolls-Royce (2017). Deferred Prosecution Agreement Serious Fraud Office v (1) Rolls-Royce plc; (2) Rolls-Royce Energy Systems Inc, Case No: U20170036.

Shaffer v. Heitner (1977). 433 US 186.

Silhouette International Schmied GmbH & Co. KG v Hartlauer Handelsgesellschaft mbH. Preliminary ruling: Oberster Gerichtshof - Austria. Judgment of the Court of 16 July 1998.

Sinclair Oil Corp. v. Levien (1971). 280 A.2d 717, 720, Delaware.

Stichting Brein v. Ziggo BV and XS4ALL Internet BV (2017). C-610/15. ECLI:EU:C:2017:456. 14 June 2017.

The United Kingdom v. Iran (1952). ICJ 2 *(also known as the Anglo-Iranian Oil Co. case). 22 July 1952.*

The United States Department of Justice (2017). Justice Department Challenges AT&T/DirecTV's Acquisition of Time Warner. Press release, 20 November 2017.

The United States Department of Justice (2012). Press release, 14 June 2012. Allen Stanford. Updated 15 September 2014.

The United States Department of Justice (2010). BAE Systems PLC Pleads Guilty and Ordered to Pay $400 Million Criminal Fine. Office of Public Affairs. 1 March 2010.

The United States District Court, Southern District of New York (2013). L*IBOR-Based Financial Instruments*, 935 F. Supp. 2d 666. S.D.N.Y., 29 March 2013.

United States v. Anderson (1946). 328 US 699.

United States v. Bonventre (2016). 646 F. App'x 73. 2d Cir. 2016.

United States v. Conti (2017). 864 F.3d 63. 2d Cir. 2017.

United States of America v. Iran (1980). United States Diplomatic and Consular Staff in Tehran. Judgment of 24 May 1980 – Judgments. ICJ 1; ICJ Reports 3 (24 May 1980). French version: Consultatifs et Ordonnances Affaire Relative au Personnel Diplomatique et Consulaire des *États*-Unis à Téhéran.

United States v. Litvak (2018). 889 F.3d 56. 2d Cir. 2018.

United States v. Madoff, (2009). US Dist. S.D.N.Y. 26 June 2009.

United States v. Rigas (2009). 583 F.3d 108. 2d Cir. 2009.

United States v. Torriero (2017). 712 F. App'x 33. 2d Cir. 2017.

United States of America v. Joya Williams (2010). United States Court of Appeals, Eleventh Circuit. 610 F.3d 271. 5th Cir. 2010.

United States of America, Plaintiff-Appellee, v. Ibrahim Dimson, a.k.a. Dirk, Defendant-Appellant. Nos. 07-12525 and 07-12653. 20 March 2008.

United States v. Scrushy (2013). 11th U.S. Circuit Court of Appeals, No. 12-10694. 11th Cir. 2013.

United States v. Stanford (2015). 805 F.3d 557. 5th Cir. 2015.

United States v. Watchmakers of Switzerland Info. Center, Inc. (1960). Trade Reg. Rep. CCH. 69,655. S.D.N.Y. 9 March 1960.

The United States Supreme Court, Santa Clara County v. Southern Pacific Railroad (1886). 118 US 394.

The Walt Disney Co. Derivative Litigation (2006). 906 A.2d 27. Del. 8 June 2006.

The Walt Disney Co. Derivative Litigation (2005). C.A. No. 15452. 9 August 2005.

Wigand v. Bachmann-Bechtel Brewing Co (1918). 222 NY 272. New York Court of Appeal. 8 January 1918.

WorldCom, Inc. ERISA Litigation (2004). No 2. Civ. 4816. DLC. S.D.N.Y. 2004.

WorldCom, Inc. Sec. Litigation (2005). No. 02 Civ. 3288. DLC. S.D.N.Y. 21 March 2005.

Yam Seng Pte Ltd v. International Trade Corp Ltd. (2013). EWHC 111.

22.4. Acts and Principles

Africa

African Union (2020): African Union Convention on Preventing and Combating Corruption. Date of Adoption: 1 July 2003. Date of last signature 10 February 2020. Date entry into force: 5 August 2006 In different languages: https://

au.int/en/treaties/african-union-convention-preventing-and-combating-corruption, In English: https://au.int/sites/default/files/treaties/36382-treaty-0028_-_african_union_convention_on_preventing_and_combating_corruption_e.pdf

European Union

CESR (2009): Market Abuse Directive, Level 3 – Third set of CESR guidance and information on the common operation of the Directive to the market. CESR/08-717. The Committee of European Securities Regulations.

COM (2019): European Green Deal, 640. https://ec.europa.eu/info/strategy/priorities-2019-2024/europeangreen-deal_en.

Council of Europe (2003): Council of Europe, ETS No 174 Civil Law Convention on Corruption 1 November 2003. https://www.coe.int/en/web/conventions/full-list/-/conventions/treaty/174.

Council of Europe (2002): ETS No 173 Criminal Law Convention on Corruption. 1 July 2002. https://www.coe.int/en/web/conventions/full-list/-/conventions/treaty/173.

Council Directive (2011): 2011/96/EU of 30 November 2011 on the common system of taxation applicable in the case of parent companies and subsidiaries of different Member States. Document 32011L0096, https://eur-lex.europa.eu/legal-content/en/TXT/?uri=CELEX:32011L0096.

Council Directive (2009): 2009/133/EC of 19 October 2009 on the common system of taxation applicable to mergers, divisions, partial divisions, transfers of assets and exchanges of shares concerning companies of different Member States and to the transfer of the registered office of an SE or SCE between Member States. Document 32009L0133.

Council Directive (2003): 2003/49/EC of 3 June 2003 on a common system of taxation applicable to interest and royalty payments made between associated companies of different Member States. Document 32003L0049. https://eur-lex.europa.eu/legal-content/EN/TXT/?uri=CELEX%3A32003L0049.

Directive (EU) 2016/943 on the protection of undisclosed know-how and business information.

Directive 89/104/EEC - Exhaustion of trade mark - Goods put on the market in the Community or in a non-member country. Case C-355/96, Silhouette.

European Commission, Trade Secrets. https://ec.europa.eu/growth/industry/policy/intellectual-property/trade-secrets_en.

European Commission Green Paper on Merger Regulation. https://ec.europa.eu/competition/publications/cpn/2002_1_65.pdf.

European Community (2001): European Community (EC) regulation no 44/2001.

European Data Protection Board (2020): Guidance. 24 July 2020.

European Parliament (2019): Directive (EU) 2019/1937 of the European Parliament and of the Council of 23 October 2019 on the protection of persons who report breaches of Union law. https://eur-lex.europa.eu/legal-content/EN/TXT/PDF/?uri=CELEX:32019L1937&rid=4. 26 November 2019. L305/17.

European Parliament (2019): Regulation (EU) 2019/518 of the European Parliament and of the Council of 19 March 2019 amending Regulation (EC) No 924/2009.

European Parliament (2015): 2015/849 of the European Parliament and of the Council of 20 May 2015 on the prevention of the use of the financial system for the purposes of money laundering or terrorist financing, amending Regulation (EU) No 648/2012 of the European Parliament and of the Council, and repealing Directive 2005/60/EC of the European Parliament and of the Council and Commission Directive 2006/70/EC (Text with EEA relevance). Document 32015L0849. https://eur-lex.europa.eu/legal-content/EN/TXT/?uri=CELEX%3A32015L0849.

European Parliament (2014): The non-financial reporting Directive (2014/95/EU)

European Parliament (2014): Directive 2014/95/EU of the European Parliament and of the Council, of 22 October 2014 amending Directive 2013/34/EU as regards disclosure of non-financial and diversity information by certain large undertakings and groups.

European Parliament (2013): Directive 2013/34/EU of the European Parliament and of the Council of 26 June 2013 on the annual financial statements, consolidated financial statements and related reports of certain types of undertakings, amending Directive 2006/43/EC of the European Parliament and of the Council and repealing Council Directives 78/660/EEC and 83/349/EEC Text with EEA relevancehttps://eur-lex.europa.eu/legal-content/EN/TXT/?uri=CELEX:32013L0034. Directive 2013/34/EU on the annual financial statements, consolidated financial statements and related reports of certain types of businesses.

European Parliament (2007): European Parliament resolution on SWIFT, B6-0042/2007. https://www.europarl.europa.eu/doceo/document/B-6-2007-0042_EN.html.

General Data Protection Regulation (GDPR) legislation https://eur-lex.europa.eu/legal-content/EN/TXT/PDF/?uri=CELEX:32016R0679.

Palermo Convention also known as Palermo Protocol. United Nations Convention against Transnational Organized Crime and the Protocols Thereto. Adopted by the UN General Assembly: 15 November 2000, by resolution 55/25. Entry into force: 29 September 2003, in accordance with article 38.

Regulation (EC) No 864/2007 of the European Parliament and of the Council of 11 July 2007 on the law applicable to non-contractual obligations (Rome II).

France

Code du commerce, Article L. 225-102-5.

Conseil Constitutionnel 23 March 2017. https://www.conseil-constitutionnel.fr/decision/2017/2017750DC.htm. Décision n° 2017-750 DC du 23 mars 2017 Conseil constitutionnel.

CSR, France: https://www.legifrance.gouv.fr/affichTexte.do?cidTexte=JORFTEXT000034290626&categorieLien=id.

JORF no 0074, 28 March 2017 *www.legifrance.gouv.fr*.

Loi Sapin2. Economie : transparence, lutte contre la corruption et modernisation (loi SAPIN2). Assemblée Nationale. Loi n° 2016-1691 du 9 décembre 2016 relative à la transparence, à la lutte contre la corruption et à la modernisation de la vie économique publiée au Journal Officiel du 10 décembre 2016 http://www.assemblee-nationale.fr/14/dossiers/transparence_lutte_corruption_economie.asp

Netherlands

CRS Netherlands: https://www.eerstekamer.nl/behandeling/20170207/gewijzigd_voorstel_van_wet

Dutch Child Labour Due Diligence: https://www.government.nl/binaries/government/documents/reports/2020/10/16/management-summary-new-rbc-policy/management-summary-new-rbc-policy.pdf

UK

The Bribery Act 2010. UK Public General Acts. 2010 c. 23 https://www.legislation.gov.uk/ukpga/2010/23/contents

The Oversight of Professional Body Anti-Money Laundering and Counter Terrorist Financing Supervision Regulations 2017, No. 1301. These laws can be retrieved from www.Gov.uk, Money Laundering Regulations.

UK Bribery Act (2010): http://www.justice.gov.uk/downloads/legislation/bribery-act-2010-quick-start-guide.pdf

UK Companies Act (2016): https://www.legislation.gov.uk/ukpga/2006/46/contents

UK Updated guidance on international transfers: https://ico.org.uk/for-organisations/guide-to-data-protection/guide-to-the-general-data-protection-regulation-gdpr/international-transfers/

USA

Bank Secrecy Act (1970): 31 USC 5311 et seq. Also known as the Currency and Foreign Transaction Reporting Act. US 26 October 1970.

Corporate Law Economic Reform Program (Audit Reform & Corporate Disclosure) Act 2004, CLERP 9

Delaware General Corporation Law (1953): https://delcode.delaware.gov/title8/c001/

Dodd-Frank Act. Known also as: Dodd-Frank Wall Street Reform and Consumer Protection Act. Pub.L. 111-203, H.R. 4173. 21 July 2010.

FCPA (1977): Public Law 95-213 – 19 December 1977. 15 USC. § 78dd-1, et seq.

FCPA (2021): Foreign Corrupt Practices Act Guide. Second Edition. https://www.justice.gov/criminal-fraud/file/1292051/download

Model Business Corporation Act (2003): MBCA 2000/01/02. Also referred as United States corporate law in this book. http://www.lexisnexis.com/documents/pdf/20080618091347_large.pdf

Patent Act. 35 US Code 284 https://www.law.cornell.edu/uscode/text/35/284

Privacy Shield. International Trade Association. 12 June 2016. Designated by US Department of Commerce, Swiss Administration and European Commission.

Restatement Second 549 F.2d 615 (9th Cir. 1976).

Sarbanes-Oxley Act (2002). (SOX) also known as Public Accounting Reform and Investor. 24 July 2002. The Sarbanes–Oxley Act of 2002 (Pub.L. 107–204, 116 Stat. 745, enacted 30 July 2002.)

Securities Exchange Act of 1934. SEC Rule 10b-5, C.F.R. §240.

Sherman Antitrust Act (1890), 2 July 1890, ch. 647, 26 Stat 209, 15 USC. §1–7.

The Clayton Antitrust Act (1914). Pub.L. 63-212, 38 Stat. 730, enacted 15 October 1914, codified at 15 USC. § §12-27, 29 USC. § § 52-53.

The Public Health and Welfare. USA Patriot Act (2001): H.R. 3162. 26 October 2001. https://epic.org/privacy/terrorism/hr3162.html

Wolfsberg Principles. https://www.wolfsberg-principles.com/wolfsberg-group-standards

United Nations

UNCITRAL (1980): CIGS, United Nations Convention on International Sale of Goods (1980). The UN-certified English text is published in 52 Federal Register 6262, 6264-6280 (March 2, 1987). http://cisgw3.law.pace.edu/cisg/text/treaty.html.

Other countries

Corporate Act Australia

FATF (2016): FATF Recommendations. Financial Action Task Force on Money Laundering. International standards on Combating Money Laundering and the Financing of Terrorism and Proliferation. http://www.fatf-gafi.org/media/fatf/documents/recommendations/pdfs/FATF_Recommendations.pdf

Fighting Bribery - a corporate practices manual

Finnish Ministry of Foreign Affairs (International Embargo)

German Ministry of Labour and Social Affairs 2020. Business and Human Rights. https://www.csr-in-deutschland.de/EN/Business-Human-Rights/business-human-rights.html

ICC Guidelines for money laundering.

ICC Guidelines for managing corruption.

ICC (2012): ICC anti-corruption clause. https://icc.tobb.org.tr/docs/ICCAnti-corruptionClauseebook.pdf

ICC (2011): ICC Rules on Combating Corruption. https://iccwbo.org/content/uploads/sites/3/2011/10/ICC-Rules-on-Combating-Corruption-2011.pdf

ICC (2017): ICC Guidelines on Agents, Intermediaries and other Third Parties. https://iccwbo.org/content/uploads/sites/3/2017/02/ICC-Guidelines-on-Agents-and-Third-paries-ENGLISH-2010.pdf

ICC (2008): ICC Guidelines on Whistleblowing. https://iccwbo.org/content/uploads/sites/3/2008/06/ICC-Whistleblowing-Guidelines.pdf

ICC (2016): Resisting Extortion and Solicitation in International Transactions. RESIST. https://iccwbo.org/content/uploads/sites/3/2016/11/RESIST-English.pdf

ICC (2014): Guidelines on Gifts and Hospitality. Prepared by the ICC Commission on Corporate Responsibility and Anti-Corruption.

ICN (2008): International Competition Network Cartel Working Group Subgroup 1 – General Legal Framework Cartel Settlements 2008, Appendix A.

ILO the declaration. https://www.ilo.org/declaration/thedeclaration/textdeclaration/lang--en/index.htm. ILO: the Declaration on Fundamental Principles and Rights at Work.

ILO (2018 I): Rana Plaza Accident and its aftermath.

ILO (2018 II): Bangladesh Move towards Employment injury Insurance: The Legacy of Rana Plaza, Fact Sheet, 13 June 2018.

Kamerstuk (2017): Eerste Kamer der Staten-Generaal. 34506 nr. A. Voorstel van wet van het lid Van Laar houdende de invoering van een zorgplicht ter voorkoming van de levering van goederen en diensten die met behulp van kinderarbeid tot stand zijn gekomen (Wet zorgplicht kinderarbeid). https://zoek.officielebekendmakingen.nl/kst-34506-A.html. The Netherlands. 8 February 2017.

Ministry of Economic Affairs and Employment of Finland (2020): Judicial Analysis on the Corporate Social Responsibility Act. 2020:44. Analysis in English here: http://julkaisut.valtioneuvosto.fi/handle/10024/162411

Nachhaltige Wertschöpfungskettengesetz – NaWKG). English unofficial translation here: https://die-korrespondenten.de/fileadmin/user_upload/die-korrespondenten.de/DueDiligenceLawGermany.pdf

OECD (2015): OECD Guidelines on Corporate Governance of State-Owned Enterprises. oecd.org.

OECD (2009): Money Laundering Awareness Handbook for Tax Examiners and Tax Auditors. https://www.oecd.org/ctp/crime/43841099.pdf

OECD (2004): Principles of Corporate Governance. https://www.oecd.org/daf/ca/Corporate-Governance-Principles-ENG.pdf

OECD (2003): Guidelines for Money Laundering.

Tax Crime Academy (2020): OECD International Academy for Tax Crime Investigation. http://www.oecd.org/ctp/crime/tax-crime-academy.htm

OECD Watch Parallel Proceedings. https://www.oecdwatch.org/how-to-file-a-complaint/other-filing-considerations/parallel-proceedings/

Public Company Accounting Reform and Investor Protection Act 2002. An Act to protect investors by improving the accuracy and reliability of corporate disclosures made pursuant to the securities laws, and for other purposes. No. 107-204, 116 Stat. 745. https://www.congress.gov/bill/107th-congress/senate-bill/2673/text

Securities and Exchange Board of India (2003): "Report of the SEBI Committee on Corporate Governance, February 2003". Committee on Corporate Governance.

UNDOC (2004): September 2004. United Nations Office on Drugs and Crime Vienna. United Nations Convention against Corruption. United Nations New York 2004. http://www.unodc.org/documents/treaties/UNCAC/Publications/Convention/08-50026_E.pdf

UNICEF (2014): United Nations Children's Fund (UNICEF), May 2014. Child Labour and UNICEF in Action: Children at the Centre.

Uniform Commercial Code (1952): U.C.C. The American Law Institute.

United Nations (1945): The Charter of the United Nations (also known as the UN Charter) of 1945. Treaty of the United Nations.

United Nations (2020): UN Guiding Principles on Business and Human Rights. "Protect, Respect and Remedy" Framework.

United Nations (1931): UN Convention. United Nations Treaty Collection 1931.

United Nations Convention against Transnational Organized Crime 2003. Adopted by General Assembly resolution 55/25 of 15 November 2000.

United Nations, Universal Declaration of Human Rights https://www.un.org/en/universal-declaration-human-rights/index.html.

United Nations (2020). Principles for Responsible Investment (PRI). https://www.unpri.org/.

United Nations (2006): Guidance on Good Practices in Corporate Governance Disclosure. United Nations Intergovernmental Working Group of Experts on International Standards of Accounting and Reporting (ISAR).

United Nations (2006): "International Standards of Accounting and Reporting, Corporate Governance Disclosure". United Nations Conference on Trade and Development. TD/B/COM.2/ISAR/31".

Vienna Convention on the Law of Treaties, 1969.

WTO Trips. https://www.wto.org/english/docs_e/legal_e/27-trips_04d_e.htmPart II — Standards concerning the availability, scope and use of Intellectual Property Rights. Section 7: protection of undisclosed information. https://www.wto.org/english/docs_e/legal_e/27-trips.pdf

Sweden

Swedish Criminal Law (1962): Mutbrott; BrB 20:2.

Swedisch Criminal Law (1962): Brottsbalk 1962:700; BrB

22.5. Other sources

Agence francaise anticorruption (2020): Les Apports du Guide Pratique de l'agence Francaise Anticorruption sur les "verifications anticorruption dans le cadre des fusions acquisitions"17 January 2020. Alerte Client. GIDE Loyrette Nouel A.A.R.P.I., Conformité & Investigations internes.

Airbus (2020): Press Release. Airbus reaches agreements with French, UK and US authorities.

Albuquerque, F. - Wallin. N. (2019): IRRI Survey – Nordic Sneak Peek. the online research network for sustainable investment and corporate governance.

AlixPartners (2019): Global Anticorruption Survey 2019.

Alliuris (2019), Corporate Criminal Liability in Europe. 17 October 2019. Homepage News.

Alliuris (2018): Board Structures. June 2018.

Anti-Corruption Resource Centre U4, (2020): Glossary. Chr. Michelsen Institute. Norway.

BAFA (2020): Embargos. BAFA's web page. file:///C:/Users/HMM/Downloads/afk_embargo_uebersicht_laenderbezogene_embargos.pdf

Bank for International Settlements (2011): Basel Committee on Banking Supervision. Progress report on Basel III implementation.

Cambridge Dictionary (2020): Moral Hazard

Central American Extortion Report (2019): The Global Initiative Against Transnational Organized Crime. An InSight Crime-Global Initiative Report. A Criminal Culture Extortion in Central America. May 2019.

CEPOL (2020): Darknet. Webinar. 12 May 2020. https://www.cepol.europa.eu/tags/darknet.

CEREU (2016): Extortion Racketeering in the EU vulnerability factors. Center for the Study of Democracy.

CFO (2017): "Two CFOs Tell a Tale of Fraud at HeathSouth". *CFO Magazine*. 27 March 2017.

CFTC (2014): CFTC Orders Five Banks to Pay over $1.4 Billion in Penalties for Attempted Manipulation of Foreign Exchange Benchmark Rates. CFTC 12 November 2014

CISG Contracting states: http://www.cisg.law.pace.edu/cisg/cisgintro.html

Clean clothes (2020). Webpage. https://cleanclothes.org/

Clifford Chance (2019): A Guide to Anticorruption in Asia Pacific. 6th Edition. April 2019.

CNBC (2017): "New EU sanctions over Siemens turbines violate international law, Russian energy minister says". 5 August 2017.

CNBC (2010): American Greed, Episode 30, Sholam Weiss. 19 March 2010.

Consultancy Europe (2019): Growing number of CEOs fired for ethical lapses and misconduct.

Cornell Law School 17 CFR § 240.10b-5 - Employment of manipulative and deceptive devices.

CourtListener (2003): HealthSouth Corp. Shareholders Lit., 845 A.2d 1096 (Del. Ch. 2003). Court of Chancery of Delaware, New Castle County. Submitted: November 20, 2003. Decided: November 24, 2003.

CourtListener (1995): Wheelabrator Tech. Shareholders Lit., 663 A.2d 1194 (Del. Ch. 1995) Court of Chancery of Delaware. Filed: May 18th, 1995. Precedential Status: Precedential. Citations: 663 A.2d 1194. Docket Number: Civ. A. No. 11495. CourtListener.

CPS September (2018): Legal guidance. Abuse of Process.

Delaware (2020): About the Division of Corporations. Delaware Division of Corporations.

Department of Justice (2012): Yazaki Corp., Denso Corp. and Four Yazaki Executives Agree to Plead Guilty to Automobile Parts Price-Fixing and Bid-Rigging Conspiracies. Washington, Justice News. 31 January 2012.

Economic Times (2020): Moral Hazard.

EIA (2008): Environmental Crime. A Threat to the Future. Environmental Investigation Agency. October 2008.

EMCDDA (2020): European Monitoring Centre for Drugs and Drug Addiction, 2020. Increase in darknet market activity for cannabis as users stock up for lockdown. 5 May 2020.

Ernst & Young (2018): UK Bribery Digest. Ernst & Young. Edition 12 March 2018.

EUIPO (2021): Global Trade in Fakes: A worrying Threat. 2021.

EUIPO (2020): Trends in Trade in Counterfeit and Pirated goods/trends in Trade in Counterfeit and Pirated goods.

Euromonitor (2019): Understanding the Five Drivers Shaping Megatrends. Euromonitor International. Market Research Blog. 5 January 2019.

European Commission (2021): Antitrust: Commission fines USB, Barclays, RBS, HSBC and Credit Suisse €344 million for participating in a Foreign Exchange spot trading cartel. Press Release. 2 December 2021.

European Commission (2020): White Paper on Artificial Intelligence: a European approach to excellence and trust. 19 February 2020.

European Commission (2019) The Environmental Implementation Review 2019. Country Report Malta. 4 April 2019.

European Commission (2017): CSR. The regulations can be found here: UK: http://www.legislation.gov.uk/ukpga/2015/30/contents/enacted.

European Commission (2017): Questions and Answers on new tax transparency rules for intermediaries. 21 June 2017.

European Commission (2016): Press release, 30 August 2016.

European Commission (2016): EU sanctions against Russia over Ukraine crisis. European Commission Newsweek, 26 July 2016.

European Commission (2016): Antitrust: Commission fines Crédit Agricole, HSBC and JPMorgan Chase € 485 million for euro interest rate derivatives cartel, European Commission Press release, 7 December 2016.

European Commission (2014): Antitrust: Commission settles RBS-JPMorgan cartel in derivatives based on Swiss franc LIBOR; imposes € 61.6 million fine on JPMorgan. 21 October 2014. https://ec.europa.eu/commission/presscorner/detail/en/IP_14_1189

European Commission (2013): Antitrust: Commission fines banks € 1.71 billion for participating in cartels in the interest rate derivatives industry. 4 December 2013.

European Commission (2009): Antitrust: Commission imposes fine of €1.06 bn on Intel for abuse of dominant position; orders Intel to cease illegal practices. 13 May 2009. Press release. https://ec.europa.eu/commission/presscorner/detail/en/IP_09_745

European Council (2009): Communication from the Commission to the European Parliament, The Council, the European Economic and Social Committee of the Regions. 28 April 2009.

European Council, Council of the European Union (2016): Taxation: EU list of non-cooperative jurisdictions

European Parliament (2020): Artificial intelligence: EU must ensure a fair and safe use for consumers. 23 January 2020. Press Release.

European Parliament (2019): Transparent Taxation. News. 17 December 2019.

European Parliament (2018): List of Tax Heavens by the EU.

European Parliament (2018): Tax avoidance: multinationals to pay taxes where profits are made, News 13 March 2018.

European Union Newsroom. 10 March 2016.

Europol (2020): Intellectual property crime.

Europol (2020): €7,9 million of illegal products seized in a hit against medicine traffickers. Europol, press release, 6 March 2020.

Europol (2020): Metal thieves arrested in France and Romania for Great Train Robbery, Europol News article 13 February 2020.

Europol (2019 I): Global Law Enforcement Action Against Vendors And Buyers On The Dark Web. 26 March 2019.

Europol (2019 II): No Crime Goes Unpunished On The Darknet: 11 Arrested for Buying Counterfeit Euros. Europol Press Release.

Europol (2017 I): Intellectual property crime on the darknet. Europol brochure. 20 September 2017.

Europol (2017 II): Massive blow to criminal dark web activities after globally coordinated operation. Europol Press Release. 20 July 2017.

Europol (2015): Environmental Crime.

Farlex Dictionary (2020): International Law.

FBI (2020): Money Laundering.

FBI (2020): White Collar Crime.

FBI (2014): Former Rabobank LIBOR Submitter Pleads Guilty in Scheme to Manipulate Yen LIBOR. 18 August 2014.

FBI (2001): FBI's ANSIR Program Testimony.

Finland Chamber of Commerce (2019): "Yritysten kybervarautumisen tilanne ei juurikaan ole muuttunut, uhat ovat yleistyneet" Yrityksiin kohdistuvat kyberuhat 2019. https://helsinki.chamber.fi/yritysten-kybervarautumisen-tilanne-ei-juurikaan-ole-muuttunut-uhat-ovat-yleistyneet/

Fondia (2020): Convention on International Sale of Goods CIGS. Fondia Virtual Lawyer.

Food integrity Handbook (2018): A Guide to Food Authenticity Issues and Analytical Solutions.https://virtuallawyer.fondiatools.com/Sivut/Kansainv%C3%A4linen%20kauppalaki%20(CISG).aspx

FSA (2012): Barclays fined £59.5 million for significant failings in relation to LIBOR and EURIBOR. 27 June 2012.

FSB (2014): Financial Stability Board. Final Report on Foreign Exchange Benchmarks. 30 September 2014.

FSC (2016): IKEA Creating a Sustainable World. IKEA's Sustainable Strategy for 2020. Forest Stewardship Council.

Global Financial Stability Report Press Conference (2016): IMF Annual Meetings, 5 October 2016.

Global Times (2020): "New US rules Huawei draw backlash". 18 August 2020.

Gov.uk (2014): Chancellor confirms manipulation of key FOREX benchmark to be made a criminal offence. 22 December 2014.

GPO (2010): https://www.govinfo.gov/content/pkg/CFR-2010-title26-vol2/pdf/CFR-2010-title26-vol2-sec1-162-22.pdf

GRI Sustainable Reporting Standards

Harris Poll (2016): IBM Survey Reveals Consumers Want Businesses To Do More To Actively Protect Their Data.

History (2015): Watergate info. 16 July 2015.

HSGAC David Viniar's testimony: https://www.hsgac.senate.gov/imo/media/doc/STMTVINIARDavid.pdf.

IKEA (2020): IKEA Sustainability Report 2020. https://www.ikea.com/se/sv/files/pdf/c3/e2/c3e2b54b/ikea_sustainability_report_fy20.pdf

Infosecurity Magazine (2014): LightOut is Latest Cyber Threat to target Energy Sector. 15 March 2014.

INTERPOL (2020): "Interpol report highlights key cyberthreats in Southeast Asia". 17 February 2020.

Investopedia (2021): Embargo.

Investopedia (2021): Greenwashing definition.

Investopedia (2020): Allen Stanford.

Investopedia (2020 and 2019): Nick Leeson.

Investopedia (2020): White Collar Crime.

Investopedia (2020): The differences between bribery and lobbying.

Investopedia (2020): Ponzi scheme, 10 February 2020.

Investopedia: Watergate.

Investor.gov. (2021): Pump and dump schemes. The US Securities and Exchange Commission's website.

IRM (2017): Information Risk Management. UK's first cyber crime intervention workshop. 26 July 2017.

ISO standards. ISO 26000 standards.

ITV (2014): Five famous French sex and politics scandals. 13 January 2014.

JonesDay (2020): 2020 Cross-Border Corporate Criminal Liability Survey.

Leskinen, K. (2021): Webinar Presentation for Entrepreneurs, IPs and IPRs. 15 September 2021.

Luja Talot (2020): Finnish stock exchange company Luja-talot slogan.

Merriam-Webster (2020): Definition of Fraud.

Merriam-Webster (2020): Definition of due diligence.

Milton Keynes UK (2020): Extraterritoriality – protective jurisdiction and the 'effects doctrine' Open University. Open Learn. Walton Hall.

Nasdaq (2019): The technology trends that are driving the world markets forward.

National Security Agency Data Collection Programs (2013): National Security Agency Data Collection Programs "Quotations from NSA Director in reply to question asked in open hearing of the House Intelligence Committee by Representative Lynn Westmoreland (R-GA) beginning at 02:14:00 on video counter."

NCJRS (National Criminal Justice Reference Service). "Abstracts Database - National Criminal Justice Reference Service". www.ncjrs.gov.

Neste corporate web page (2019): Neste Releases and News. https://www.neste.com/releases-and-news/investors/us-blenders-tax-credit-decision-support-nestes-2019-result

Nielsen, M. (2019): AI Possibilities for Protection. Michael Nielsen's (2019) presentation 11 September 2019.

North American Securities Administrators Associations (2005) Micro-cap Fraud," North American Securities Administrators Association".

NPR (2018): Grumpy Cat Awarded $710,000 In Copyright Infringement Suit. 25 January 2018.

OAS (2009): Private International Law. Oas.org. August 2009.

OCCRP (2020): Laundromat. Oas.org.

Oceana. International marine conservation organization.

Office of the Director of National Intelligence, The National Counterintelligence and Security Center, Economic Espionage.

OECD (2011): Guidelines for Multinational Enterprises.

Palm Oil Innovation Group, POIG Charter.

PCAOB (2020): AS 2605: Consideration of the Internal Audit Function. Amendments: Amending releases and related SEC approval orders. Guidance on AS 2605: Staff Audit Practice Alerts No. 11 and No. 12.

RFERL (2019): "Three Ex-Telia Executives Acquitted In Uzbek Bribery Case". Radio Free Europe Radio Liberty. 15 February 2019.

Rigas, J. (2020): Website.

Scandal (1989): Movie. Michael Caton-Jones. 3 March 1989.

Schultz, Howard (2020): My Story. Web page.

SEC (2020): Sarbanes Oxley Act.

SEC (2020): "Penny Stock Rules".

SEC (2013): The US Securities and Exchange Commission (2013): Pump-and-Dumps and Market Manipulations. 25 June 2013.

Securityweek (2014): Cryptowall Ransomware Cost Victims More Than $18 Million Since April 2014. FBI. 24 June 2014.

State of Cyber Resilience (2020).

Swift (2017). US Payment market infrastructures agree to support SWIFT gpi tracking of cross-border payments. 13 March 2017.

Swiss Coalition for Corporate Justice I Coalition – Swiss Coalition for Corporate Justice Swiss Coalition for Corporate Justice. Compromise remains open – Swiss Coalition for Corporate Justice Swiss Coalition for Corporate Justice.

Swiss Coalition for Corporate Justice II Swiss Coalition for Corporate Justice: How does the parliamentary counter-proposal differ from the popular initiative (RBI)? corporatejustice.ch.

Swiss Reinsurance Company, 2012. http://www.biztositasiszemle.hu/files/201206/punitive_damage_in_europe.pdf

TAdviser (2020): Cybercrime in the World. 20 July 2020.

Technology and IP Law Glossary (2013): Effects Doctrine. 14 June 2013.

TransLex (2020): Good Faith as an international principle of law.

Transparency International (2019): 25 Corruption Scandals that Shook the World. 5 July 2019.

Transparency International (2016): Global Corruption report: Sport. 22 February 2016.

The State of Sustainable Markets (2015), XVI.OECD (): Guidelines for Multinational Enterprises.

United Nations (2016): Combating transnational crime. International Organization for Migration (IOM). Issue Brief. July 2016.

United Nations (2011): Guiding Principle Interpretative Guide.

United Nations (2011): Organized crime, organized responses – countering cross-border crime. 9 June 2011.

United Nations (2000): Global Compact.

United Nations, FAQ. http://yk.fi/node/219

United Nations, Consolidated United Nations Security Council Sanctions List.

United Nations (2015): Note by the UNCTAD Secretariat: The role of competition policy in promoting sustainable and inclusive growth, 2015.

United States Ministry of Justice (2021): Indonesian Company Admits To Deceiving U.S. Banks In Order To Trade With North Korea, Agrees To Pay A Fine Of More Than $1.5 Million. Press release number 21-67. 17 January 2021.

United States Ministry of Justice (2012): Barclays Bank PLC Admits Misconduct Related to Submissions for the London Interbank Offered Rate and the Euro Interbank Offered Rate and Agreed to Pay $160 Million Penalty. 27 June 2012.

United States Senate (2014): Wall Street Bank Involvement With Physical Commodities. 20 November 2014.

UNRIC library: Research guides.

The United States Department of Justice (2017): Volkswagen AG Agrees to Plead Guilty and Pay $4.3 Billion in Criminal and Civil Penalties; Six Volkswagen Executives and Employees are Indicted in Connection with Conspiracy to Cheat US Emissions Tests. 11 January 2017.

The United States Government: Scams and Frauds.

USC (2020): Fraud and Corruption Control Procedures.

YouTube (2020 I): Causes and effects of the 2008 Financial Crisis.

YouTube (2020 II): Vatican crimes, 10 January 2020.

YouTube (2019, I): Ivan Boesky. YouTube video.

YouTube (2019, II): The Spectacular Rise and Fall of WeWork. 7 November 2019.

WHO (2008): Melamine-contaminated powdered infant formula in China - update 2. 29 September 2008.

Wikimili (2019). Derivative Suit, 24.3.2019.

Wikipedia (2020): Andean Community.

Wikipedia (2020): Bernard Madoff.

Wikipedia (2020): Blackmail.

Wikipedia (2020): Casare Beccaria.

Wikipedia (2020): Pirate Bay. Countries blocking access to the pirate Bay.

Wikipedia (2020): Corruption.

Wikipedia (2020): Derivative Suit.

Wikipedia (2020): East African Community.

Wikipedia (2015) FIFA Corruption case.

Wikipedia (2019): Government Pension Fund of Norway.

Wikipedia (2019): Industrial Espionage

Wikipedia (2019): International Criminal Tribunal for the former Yugoslavia.

Wikipedia (2019): International Law.

Wikipedia (2019): List of Data Breaches.

Wikipedia (2019): Max Schrems.

Wikipedia (2019): Money Laundering.

Wikipedia (2020): Operation Car Wash.

Wikipedia (2021): Paradise Papers.

Wikipedia (2021): European Union Tax haven blacklist.

Wikipedia (2020): Predatory Pricing.

Wikipedia (2019): Pump and Dump Schemes.

Wikipedia (2019): Re-engineering.

Wikipedia (2020): Tangentopoli. Written by Onorato, L.

Wikipedia (2021): Union of South American Nations.

WIPO (2020): "What is Intellectual Property?" World Intellectual Property Organizations.

Worksafe (2017): Preventing and Responding to bullying at work. Good Practice Guidelines. New Zealand Government. March 2017.

Zero Waste Lifestyle System (2020): Top 9 Worst Greenwashed Products.